University of Plymouth Library

Subject to status this item may be renewed
via your Voyager account

http://voyager.plymouth.ac.uk

Exeter tel: (01392) 475049
Exmouth tel: (01395) 255331
Plymouth tel: (01752) 232323

THE NEW POLITICAL ECONOMY OF
UNITED STATES-CARIBBEAN RELATIONS

The International Political Economy of New Regionalisms Series

The International Political Economy of New Regionalisms Series presents innovative analyses of a range of novel regional relations and institutions. Going beyond established, formal, interstate economic organizations, this essential series provides informed interdisciplinary and international research and debate about myriad heterogeneous intermediate level interactions.

Reflective of its cosmopolitan and creative orientation, this series is developed by an international editorial team of established and emerging scholars in both the South and North. It reinforces ongoing networks of analysts in both academia and think-tanks as well as international agencies concerned with micro-, meso- and macro-level regionalisms.

Recent Titles in the Series

The Nordic Regions and the European Union
Edited by Søren Dosenrode and Henrik Halkier

Transnational Democracy in Critical and Comparative Perspective
Edited by Bruce Morrison

Globalization and Antiglobalization
Edited by Henry Veltmeyer

The Political Economy of Interregional Relations
Alfredo C. Robles, Jr.

Reconfigured Sovereignty
Edited by Thomas L. Ilgen

The New Political Economy of United States-Caribbean Relations

The Apparel Industry and the Politics of NAFTA Parity

TONY HERON
University of Sheffield, UK

ASHGATE

Published by
Ashgate Publishing Limited
Gower House
Croft Road
Aldershot
Hampshire GU11 3HR
England

Ashgate Publishing Company
Suite 420
101 Cherry Street
Burlington, VT 05401-4405
USA

Ashgate website: http://www.ashgate.com

British Library Cataloguing in Publication Data
Heron, Tony
    The new political economy of United States-Caribbean
    relations : the apparel industry and the politics of NAFTA
    parity. - (The international political economy of new
    regionalisms series)
    1.NAFTA 2.Clothing trade - United States 3.Clothing trade -
    Caribbean Area 4.Free trade - United States 5.Free trade -
    Caribbean Area 6.United States - Foreign economic relations
    - Caribbean Area 7.Caribbean Area - Foreign economic
    relations - United States 8.Caribbean Area - Economic
    conditions - 1945-
    I.Title
    337.7'29'073

Library of Congress Cataloging-in-Publication Data
Heron, Tony, 1971-
    The new political economy of United States-Caribbean relations : the apparel industry
    and the politics of NAFTA parity / Tony Heron.
        p. cm. -- (The international political economy of new regionalisms series)
    Includes bibliographical references and index.
    ISBN 0-7546-3922-3
        1. Clothing trade--United States. 2. Clothing trade--Caribbean Area. 3. United
    States--Foreign economic relations--Caribbean Area. 4. Caribbean Area--Foreign
    economic relations--United States. I. Title. II. Series.

HD9940.U42H47 2003
382.4'5687'0973--dc22

                                                                                    2003062888

ISBN 0 7546 3922 3

Printed and bound in Great Britain by
Athenaeum Press Ltd., Gateshead, Tyne & Wear

Contents

List of Tables

Acknowledgements

Even though the following work bears my name and the responsibility for its contents is mine alone, it reflects the work of many others who have contributed to it. I would therefore like to take this opportunity to acknowledge the support of a number of people in the writing of this book. First, many thanks to Tim Shaw and everyone at Ashgate for their advice and support over the last six months; particular thanks go to an anonymous reviewer, whose comments contributed significantly to the improvement of the manuscript. Second, I would like to acknowledge the UK Economic and Social Research Council (ESRC), whose generous financial assistance enabled me to conduct the research on which the book is based. Third, I would like to thank my friends and colleagues within the Department of Politics at Sheffield who have assisted me in the research and writing of the book - especially, Rob Collins, Sarah Cooke, Jean Grugel, Petr Kopecký, Tony Payne, Georgina Waylen and Christine Whittaker. Finally, and most importantly, a special mention for Clare Jones - to whom I owe everything. In the last four years Clare has made many sacrifices in order to enable me to pursue my chosen career. So, thank you, Clare - for the love, patience and support.

Tony Heron
Sheffield
August 2003

List of Abbreviations

AAFA	American Apparel and Footwear Association
AAMA	American Apparel Manufacturers Association
ACS	Association of Caribbean States
AFL-CLO	American Federation of Labor-Congress of Industrial Organization
AGOA	Africa Growth and Opportunity Act
APEC	Asia-Pacific Economic Cooperation
ASEAN	Association of South East Asian Nations
ATC	Agreement on Textiles and Clothing
ATMI	American Textile Manufacturers Institute
CAD	Computer-Assisted Design
CARICOM	Caribbean Community and Common Market
CARIFTA	Caribbean Free Trade Association
CBERA	The Caribbean Basin Economic Recovery Act
CBI	Caribbean Basin Initiative
CBTEA	Caribbean Basin Trade Enhancement Act
CBTPA	Caribbean Basin Trade Partnership Act
CITA	Committee for the Implementation of Textile Agreements
EAI	Enterprise for the Americas Initiative
ECLAC	Economic Commission for Latin America and the Caribbean
EEC	European Economic Community
EIEA	Export Industry Encouragement Act
EIU	Economist Intelligence Unit
EPZ	Export Processing Zone
EU	European Union
FDI	Foreign Direct Investment
FLA	Fair Labor Association
FTAA	Free Trade Area of the Americas
GATT	General Agreement on Tariffs and Trade
GDP	Gross Domestic Product
GSP	General System of Preferences
HTS	Harmonized Tariff Schedule
IDB	Inter-American Development Bank
IMF	International Monetary Fund
ISA	International Studies Association
LDC	Less Developed Country
LTA	Long Term Arrangement Regarding International Trade in Cotton Textiles
MFA	Multi-Fibre Arrangement
MFN	Most-Favoured Nation
NAFTA	North American Free Trade Agreement

NGO	Non-Governmental Organization
NIC	Newly Industrializing Country
NIDL	New International Division of Labour
NJM	New Jewel Movement
OBM	Original Brand Name Manufacturing
OECD	Organization for Economic Cooperation and Development
OEM	Original Equipment Manufacturing
OPEC	Organization of Petroleum Exporting Nations
SAP	Special Access Program
STA	Short Term Arrangement Regarding International Trade in Cotton Textiles
SYE	Standard Yard Equivalent
TNC	Transnational Corporation
TPA	Trade Promotion Authority
TPL	Tariff Preference Level
TRIM	Trade-Related Investment Measure
TRIP	Trade-Related Intellectual Property
UNCTAD	United Nations Conference on Trade and Development
UNIDO	United Nations Industrial Development Organization
UNITE	Union of Needle Trades and Industrial and Textile Employees
USAID	United States Agency for International Development
USDA	United States Department of Agriculture
USGOA	United States General Accounting Office
USITC	United States International Trade Commission
USTR	United States Trade Representative
VER	Voluntary Export Restraint
WTO	World Trade Organization

For Clare and George

Introduction

In 1998, Tony Payne published an article in the British journal *Millennium* entitled 'The New Political Economy of Area Studies'. In this, Payne identified two sets of inter-related problems associated with conventional approaches to area studies. First, he argued, area studies have generally not connected well with wider theoretical debates within the social sciences as a whole; and, second, they have tended to operate on the basis of fixed definitions, which have usually been colonial in origin, of the areas to be studied. According to Payne, these two set of problems combined have resulted in the failure of area studies - typically understood as meaning 'developing area studies' (e.g. Africa, Asia, Latin America and the Caribbean) - to engage fully with the more traditional theoretical and empirical research agendas developed by a broader range of scholars operating within the discipline of international studies. In addressing this problem, Payne proposed his own eclectic framework - drawn from a synthesis of 'new' international political economy (IPE), the political economy of development (PED) and state theory - which was expressly designed to enable area specialists to investigate their own particular research concerns in a manner that was also of relevance and interest to those in the wider field. In short, the purpose of this framework was to reformulate area studies and to situate it more firmly within the general parameters of international studies (Payne, 1998).

By way of an illustrative example, Payne went on in a subsequent part of the article to outline a research agenda drawn from the Caribbean. Rather than operationalize this in accordance with established practice, however, he preferred to draw attention to the creation of a new regional political economy operating across the Caribbean *and* the United States. Payne (1998: 270-3) defined this as 'Caribbean America', which he described as a new 'structural context' linking the political economies of the US and the Caribbean across a range of issues, e.g. production, trade, migration and narcotics. In redefining the Caribbean in this way, Payne argued that regional specialists could avoid the problems of traditional area studies identified above in two ways. First, because 'Caribbean American' was a political economy as opposed to a geographical expression, the concept went some way towards redefining the region in a manner that reflected the degree of integration between what were previously taken to be two distinct geographical areas. Second, in articulating the idea of a 'structural context' linking the political economies of the US and the Caribbean, Payne was self-consciously attempting to advance a reformulated areas studies research programme which paid due attention to issues - specifically, globalization and regionalization - of particular concern to those scholars working in the wider field of international studies.

This book constitutes an attempt to develop further this research agenda by utilising a similar framework. Rather than adopting the term 'Caribbean America', it prefers (for reasons to be outlined shortly) to call this the new political economy of US-Caribbean relations. It starts from the premise that most studies of this relationship have, irrespective of other merits, generally failed to connect in sufficient depth with the wider theoretical and substantive concerns that have come to preoccupy scholars within the discipline of international studies and the sub-discipline of IPE more specifically. The book begins with a review of this literature and identifies the main areas of debate therein; it then seeks to investigate these particular issues further through an examination of US-Caribbean political economy both historically and contemporaneously via an industry-specific case study drawn from the global apparel industry. Overall, the central aim of the book is to demonstrate the utility of an empirically grounded research programme closely tied to the generic concerns of the wider discipline of IPE, and in turn to show how this research programme can itself contribute to the further delineation and advancement of these generic concerns.

This short introductory chapter presents an overview of the book as a whole. The first section begins by placing the present study within the particular context of US-Caribbean area studies and then identifies the general research questions that will be subsequently addressed. The second section introduces the particular case study to be used and also draws attention to a set of more specific research questions that will be asked in relation to this. Finally, a third section sets out briefly the overall structure of the book and describes how the remainder of it will proceed.

The 'New' Political Economy of US-Caribbean Relations

In the following investigation the term 'new' political economy is used in two different - though complementary - ways. First, 'new' political economy refers to the body of theoretical literature that will be used to enframe the study. As already indicated, one of our primary tasks is to draw upon a body of theory that will enable us to examine the empirical aspects of the case study in a manner that is also of relevance and interest to a range of scholars working within the wider discipline of international studies/IPE. For this purpose, the book begins by reviewing the theoretical literature as a whole and then proceeds via 'new' IPE to establish the specific theoretical and conceptual framework which will be subsequently applied to our particular research concerns. Hence, in this first sense of the term, 'new' political economy refers to the mode of analysis and the theoretical framework underpinning the empirical aspects of the book.

A second sense in which the term 'new' political economy is deployed refers to the actual empirical aspects of contemporary US-Caribbean relations that are being investigated. From this perspective, the term 'new' political economy represents no more than a means of describing the most recent phase of US-Caribbean relations. To put it another way, the term 'new' political economy captures the essence of a newly emerging 'structural context', presaged by the ending of the Cold War and the onset of globalization and regionalization within the wider world order, which now arguably links the political economies of the US and the Caribbean in a qualitatively different way than in the past.

According to these two usages of the term 'new' political economy, our general research questions can thus be identified as follows. What has been the historical nature of US-Caribbean political economy? How have structural changes within the wider global political economy impacted upon this relationship? What have been the major economic and political manifestations of these structural changes?

Defining the Caribbean

In most conventional accounts of US-Caribbean relations, the latter region is usually understood in geographical and historical terms. That is to say, the Caribbean is defined as those islands in the Caribbean Sea, stretching 'some 2,500 miles from the southern tip of Florida in the north to the coast Venezuela in the south, facing Central America to the west and the Atlantic Ocean to the east' (Payne and Sutton, 1993: 1). A more complex historical dimension is usually added to this conventional definition which emphasizes the shared history in respect of slave-based European imperialism between these islands and the former European enclaves on the Central and South American coast: Belize, Guyana, Suriname and French Guiana. Understood in this way, the Caribbean region - which is often referred to as the 'insular' Caribbean - is said to possess an intellectual coherence that makes it possible to analyse its political economy within a single analytical framework (Payne, 1994: 154).

More recently, some analysts have extended this definition of the Caribbean to include *all* of those territories whose shores are washed by the Caribbean Sea. This definition is usually referred to as the Caribbean Basin and is made up of the insular Caribbean alongside the so-called 'group of three' (Columbia, Mexico and Venezuela) and the six Central American nations (Costa Rica, El Salvador, Guatemala, Honduras, Nicaragua and Panama), even though one of them, El Salvador, does not actually touch the Caribbean Sea (Pastor, 1984). Although the popularity of concept of the Caribbean Basin has increased noticeably in the last several decades - especially among US policy makers who have used it in order to deal with the separate problems of the insular Caribbean and Central America within a single policy framework (see Chapter Two) - it is far less historically and intellectually coherent than the definition of the insular Caribbean previously offered. Two main points support this observation. First, even though the concept of the Caribbean Basin has served effectively to enframe US economic and security policy since the early 1980s, it has not been internalized with any degree of success by political elites within the region (Payne, 1994). Second, while the concept of the Caribbean Basin does capture important aspects of the predicament shared by the insular Caribbean and Central America with regard to their peripheral position within the global political economy, it also masks important differences between the two regions in terms of history, culture, political organization and economic structure (Payne and Sutton, 1993; Payne, 1994).

For our specific purposes, then, the more limited definition of the region as the insular Caribbean is preferred. However, rather than focusing on the entirety of the insular Caribbean the book deals mainly with just three countries: Haiti, the Dominican Republic and Jamaica. Although there is an obvious practical reason for this decision (i.e. the difficulty of examining so many countries within a single work), it is also justified on more important intellectual grounds. This relates to the underlying premise of the book: namely, it is Haiti, the Dominican Republic and Jamaica - hereafter referred to collectively as the 'northern' Caribbean - which stand in closest geographical proximity to the US and which have experienced the most significant level of *de facto* integration with the US. The remainder of the insular Caribbean, which we might refer to as the 'southern' Caribbean, still remains more closely tied economically to its former colonial powers in Europe and is thus of less relevance to our particular study (this argument is developed at greater length in Chapter Two).

The omission of the other two notable northern Caribbean territories from our study - Puerto Rico and Cuba - also requires some explanation. Unlike the majority of the insular Caribbean, which gained formal independence between the late nineteenth century and the mid twentieth century, Puerto Rico remained a colony after the Spanish-American War (1898) when it was ceded to the US by Spain as part of the 'spoils of war' and has since operated as a 'free associated state'. As a result, Puerto Rico has generally lacked political autonomy from the US and as such has related to it in a qualitatively different way than the formally independent territories of the insular Caribbean.[1] It is for this reason that Puerto Rico is omitted from our study, although it is retained as an important historical reference point.

Cuba, on the other hand, is omitted for different reasons. In many ways, Cuba can be regarded - at least from a traditional international relations (IR) standpoint - as the pivotal case study in any investigation of contemporary US-Caribbean relations, given the decisive way that its chosen revolutionary course has shaped US policy towards the region as a whole. Equally, this argument could be applied in the contemporary period to political economy as well, in the sense that US-Cuban relations are now increasingly defined by a range of transnational linkages (e.g. narcotics and migration) of a type similar to those which this work is seeking to investigate.[2] Despite all of this, however, for the purpose of the specific issue on which we have chosen to focus in this book - apparel - the case of Cuba is less useful. This is due to the fact that, even though Cuba continues to play a central role in the political and security aspects of US-Caribbean relations, it does not, as yet at least, perform a significant function in US-Caribbean economic affairs because of the maintenance of the forty-year-old US trade embargo.[3] Hence, for this reason, Cuba is omitted from our study, although, like Puerto Rico, it is mentioned occasionally as an important historical reference point.

The Global Apparel Industry as a Case Study

In many ways, the apparel sector can be seen as the archetypal industry on which to base a study of the changing political economy of North-South relations in general and the political economy of US-Caribbean relations more specifically. In general terms, the industry is among the most geographically dispersed of all forms of manufacturing activity and has historically played a key role in the initial stages of economic development for both developed and developing countries. At the same time, because the apparel industry is still generally characterized by low levels of technological sophistication and low-cost barriers to entry, it has come to represent an important reference point in the theory of a new international division of labour (Fröbel *et al.*, 1981) and in related trade disputes between developed and developing countries. There is thus much that can be learned about the political economy of North-South relations from a study of the global apparel industry.

Applied specifically to the United States and the Caribbean, there are a number of additional reasons why the global apparel industry represents an appropriate case study. The apparel industry - along with agriculture - is among the most highly protected sectors of the US economy and at the same time is the industry to suffer most from the intensification of global competition. Since 1974, the Multi-Fibre Arrangement (MFA) has governed the international trade in textiles and apparel and has served to protect the US and other developed countries from low-wage competition, particularly from East Asia. In addition to this, the US apparel industry is and has historically been shielded from the forces of global competition by the implementation of punitive import quotas which act to discourage foreign imports. Despite all of this, however, US industry continues to suffer adversely from low-wage competition: foreign imports currently account for more than one half of all apparel consumed by American citizens while domestic industry has experienced more than half a million job losses since 1970 and today is responsible for nearly one tenth of all business failures in the US. The case of the US apparel industry thus raises a number of questions regarding the position of 'mature' industries in developed countries in the light of the emergence of new sources of competition. Why has trade protectionism failed to protect adequately US industry from global competition? What are the consequences of this failure? In what ways has US industry sought to respond to the onset of global competition?

The global apparel industry has been no less significant in respect of the Caribbean. Largely because of the structural characteristics outlined above, the apparel industry has come to be regarded in the Caribbean, and in other developing countries, as the 'ideal' manufacturing sector by which to establish industrialization via foreign direct investment and export-orientated growth. Because apparel manufacturing requires relatively little in the way of capital equipment, and since it is reliant disproportionately on low-skilled labour, it is seen as a key 'start up' industry in terms of facilitating industrial upgrading and the transition towards the manufacture of higher value added goods. Accordingly, as early as the 1950s Caribbean policy makers have sought to lure foreign investors to the region by promoting it as an 'offshore' platform for the assembly and export of apparel and other 'light' manufactured items. The importance of the global apparel industry in respect of the Caribbean thus raises a further set of questions. In what ways have Caribbean economic planners sought to encourage offshore investment in the apparel sector? What have been the various economic consequences of these policies? What contribution has apparel assembly in the Caribbean made to the long-term industrial development of the region?

At the interface of the two sets of questions identified above lies the particular issue which this book seeks to investigate further. Specifically, what role is the global apparel industry now playing in integrating the political economies of the US and the Caribbean? To put it another way, the book is concerned with the process by which US apparel firms have responded to low-wage competition by turning increasingly to offshore assembly sites in Mexico and the Caribbean Basin in order to reduce production costs and thereby remain price-competitive in their own domestic market. Describing this process as the regionalization of the North American apparel commodity chain (this notion is defined more fully in Chapter Five), this book seeks to examine it in specific relation to the northern insular Caribbean. In so doing, it aims to understand both the emerging structural context of US-Caribbean relations and the various political consequences that this has had for this relationship more generally. The specific research questions that will be addressed in respect of this case study can thus be put as follows. What are the major structural forces behind the restructuring of the North American apparel industry? In what ways has the regionalization of the North American apparel commodity chain impacted upon the northern Caribbean? What have been the political consequences of this process for the wider political economy of US-Caribbean relations?

The Outline of the Book

The remainder of the book has been organized in the following order. Chapter One serves to introduce and review critically the IPE literature and to establish the key theoretical and conceptual terrain on which the empirical aspects of the book will be investigated. It begins by tracing the origins of mainstream IPE and presents a historical and theoretical critique of this literature and introduces via 'new' IPE a framework more suited to our particular research concerns. For this purpose, the chapter advances the work of Robert Cox and his method of 'historical structures' as way of an introduction to three key debates - production, development and governance - dealing with various aspects of economic globalization that are of direct relevance to our case study. Accordingly, these debates will serve to enframe the subsequent parts of the investigation.

Chapter Two provides an examination of the historical development of US-Caribbean political economy since 1945 and sets up the specific research questions that will be addressed in the remaining parts of the book. It starts by looking at the various historical dimensions of US power in the Caribbean and at the particular purpose served by the region in terms of the wider material and ideological manifestations of US hegemony in the post-1945 period. The chapter then introduces and evaluates critically President Reagan's Caribbean Basin Initiative (CBI), both in terms of its basic economic provisions and its wider political role in facilitating the agenda that subsequently emerged in the late 1980s and early 1990s. Describing this agenda as the 'new' political economy of US-Caribbean relations, the chapter ends by setting up the specific research issues to be addressed in the remaining chapters.

The first of these specific research issues is addressed in Chapter Three. This relates to the particular role played by Caribbean industrial policy in terms of the new political economy of US-Caribbean relations, especially in relation to the promotion of export processing zones (EPZs). In more specific terms, the chapter investigates the origins of these EPZs and then assesses their contribution to economic development in the region in terms of four key areas: (1) the costs and benefits associated with offering preferential treatment to export-orientated investment; (2) the issue of backward linkages fostered between assembly operations and the domestic economy; (3) the extent of technology transfer; and (4) the wider social and economic effects of using EPZ as the basis of a long-term development strategy.

In Chapter Four, the new political economy of US-Caribbean relations is analysed in terms of the restructuring of the United States textile and apparel industry. The chapter addresses the restructuring of the US industry against the backdrop of the failure of the MFA to protect it from low-wage competition. Specifically, it asks why the MFA was unable to shield US industry from low-wage competition, despite the implementation of increasingly restrictive import quotas. The chapter then turns to analyse the impact of this failure and the ways in which specific parts of the industry have responded to it. Finally, the introduction and subsequent growth of the practice of offshore production in the US textile and apparel industry is examined.

In Chapter Five, this practice is investigated further via an analysis of the regionalization of the North American apparel commodity chain. The chapter begins by establishing an appropriate definition of the term regionalization and then proceeds to examine the case of North American apparel in respect of three inter-related causes - the role of government policy in the US and the Caribbean respectively, and the competitive strategies adopted by US apparel firms in response to these policies. It then analyses the consequences of the regionalization of the North American apparel commodity chain in terms of the creation and consolidation of a sourcing hierarchy across the US, Mexico and the Caribbean Basin and also draws attention to the impact of NAFTA on this trade and production network.

In Chapter Six, we deal with the wider political manifestations of these structural changes by examining the issue of NAFTA parity for the Caribbean garment sector, which culminated in the enactment by the United States Congress of the Caribbean Basin Trade Partnership Act (CBTPA) in May 2000. In focusing on this issue the chapter attempts to address three inter-related aspects of US-Caribbean political economy. First, in focusing on the issue of NAFTA parity for the Caribbean, it is anticipated that the chapter will allow us to gauge some of the wider political implications of the process of *de facto* integration that has taken place in the North American apparel industry. Second, the chapter seeks to untangle the relationship between this political process and apparel production in the Caribbean through an examination of the specific entitlements offered to the region by the CBTPA. Third, it is hoped that these findings should provide us with a broader measure of the new political economy of US-Caribbean relations.

Notes

1 The peculiar relationship between Puerto Rico and the rest of the Caribbean in respect of the US is explored in Heine and García-Passalacqua (1993).

2 A brilliant account of Cuba's role in the US-Caribbean narcotics trade is provided by Oppenheimer (1992).

3 The US embargo has not, however, prevented Cuba from fostering closer political and economic ties with the rest of the Caribbean. For more details, see Erisman (1998).

Chapter One

Theories of International Political Economy

Introduction

This chapter serves to introduce and critically review theories of international political economy (IPE). It aims, in the process, to highlight the limitations of conventional approaches, particularly those associated with variants of neo-realism and neo-liberal institutionalism. Principally, it is suggested that mainstream IPE has largely abandoned the ideas of transnationalism and interdependence, which originally enframed the discipline, in favour of a more statist form of political economy, focused on the problems of state co-operation within the structural confines of international anarchy. While this in itself may not seem sufficient cause for rejection, it is argued, however, that such a narrow theoretical focus provides an inadequate basis for addressing the research questions in hand. Instead, we turn to the ideas associated with what has been termed 'new' IPE (Murphy and Tooze, 1991). The work of Robert Cox, as the main exemplar of this movement, is considered. In the ensuing discussion Cox's ideas and concepts are engaged with critically as a means of moving towards an eclectic and open-ended approach to international political economy, suited to our particular research concerns. This, in more specific terms, will involve using Cox's method of 'historical structures' as way of an introduction to three key debates - production, development and governance - dealing with various aspects of economic globalization that are of direct relevance to the study of the new political economy of US-Caribbean relations.

The chapter is accordingly divided into three sections. The first deals with mainstream theories of IPE, with particular focus being directed towards the key debates that have occupied these scholars over the last several decades, including the ideas of transnationalism and interdependence, hegemonic stability and co-operation under anarchy. Here, it will be suggested that the ideas of transnationalism and interdependence - which, in many ways, served as the original critique of the parent discipline of IR - have steadily been replaced with concerns over the extent to which state co-operation can be fostered in conditions of international anarchy. These concerns, it will be observed, have allowed for a coalescence of neo-liberal institutionalist and neo-realist ideas, which have been underpinned by a commitment to a methodological orthodoxy derived from microeconomics and game theory. In the process this coalescence has served to narrow the theoretical parameters of the discipline, leading to the marginalization of those perspectives which fail to embrace the methodological orthodoxy. Evidence of this can be found in the extent to which more eclectic forms of IPE have largely been ignored by the mainstream (Krasner, 1994; Katzenstein *et al.*, 1998).

The second section is directed towards 'new' IPE. Taking the work of Cox as the exemplar of this movement it introduces his method of 'historical structures' as the basis of an alternative form of IPE. Within this ambit it also considers Cox's treatment of the notion of hegemony, which is seen as resulting from a particular form of dominance, consisting of both coercive and consensual elements of power, and suggests that this offers several advantages over mainstream usage. Beyond the specific development of a neo-Gramscian school of IPE, it is emphasized that Cox's thinking has been important in opening up the discipline to more critical and eclectic modes of enquiry. Upon this basis the third section uses Cox's method of 'historical structures' as an introduction to the key debates within 'new' IPE broadly concerned with the causes and consequences of economic globalization. These debates are designed to raise a number of themes and issues salient to the study of the new political economy of US-Caribbean relations, which will subsequently be used to guide and inform the remaining parts of the book. Ultimately, then, this chapter serves as both a critique of much of the existing IPE orthodoxy, and as a means of introducing via 'new' IPE the key theoretical and conceptual terrain upon which a study of the new political economy of US-Caribbean relations can proceed.

Mainstream Theories of International Political Economy

As is well known, the emergence of IPE as a critique of the methods and assumptions of IR scholarship was triggered by a series of economic crises in the early 1970s, which seemed to undermine many of the features of world order that the parent discipline had taken for granted. In particular, the 'triple crisis' in terms of monetary, energy and trade regimes - brought about, respectively, by the Nixon administration's decision unilaterally to devalue the dollar in August 1971, effectively ending the Bretton Woods system of fixed exchange rates between the major currencies, the first OPEC 'oil shock' in 1973 and the general rise in so-called 'new protectionism' in the midst of global recession - pointed to the unravelling of the political and economic framework that had underpinned the post-1945 international order. In response to this a number of theoretical innovations were advanced to account for these changes, the most notable of which were the twin concepts of transnationalism and interdependence. Although initially derivative of functionalist and neo-functionalist ideas associated with the first wave of post-war European integration (Haas, 1964), the ideas of transnationalism and interdependence were quickly adopted by a broader group of scholars who sought to question the efficacy of the state in its ability to regulate what were increasingly internationalising socio-economic processes. Central to this intellectual movement was the collaborative work of Robert Keohane and Joseph Nye (1971: 317), who put forward the notion of transnational relations, defined as 'the movement of tangible or intangible items across state boundaries when at least one actor is not an agent of a government or international organization'. Notwithstanding the voluminous writings that followed Keohane and Nye's intervention, however, most mainstream scholars at the time did not regard the notions of transnationalism and interdependence as worthy of serious theoretical reflection (for a notable exception, see Mansbach and Vasquez, 1981). In fact, Keohane and Nye's own work was largely interpreted as 'a pointing exercise that made clear how much interesting activity had escaped the attention of analysts imprisoned in the "state-centric" paradigm' (Katzenstein *et al.*, 1998: 565).

Despite this, the literature on transnational relations set in motion by Keohane and Nye's work did - at least implicitly - promote one important theoretical point: the preference for a 'society-dominated' perspective over the existing 'state-centred' paradigms (Risse-Kappen, 1995: 14). Although this characteristic did not by any means cover the entirety of the transnational relations literature of the 1970s, much of this work did carry within its remit an, often implicit, anti-statist bias (Leaver, 1994). This bias had a number of consequences for the transnational relations literature, the most important of which was that it exposed its vulnerability to realist accusations of political naiveté. Central to this realist counterattack was Stephen Krasner (1976: 317), who argued that, 'in recent years, students of international relations have multinationalized, transnationalized, bureaucratized, and transgovernmentalized the state until it has virtually ceased to exist as an analytical construct'. The lessons from this were clear, at least to him. In attempting to map out an IPE approach that could transcend the limits of mainstream theories of IR, the concept of transnational relations had underestimated the importance of state power. Moreover, this literature also encouraged a bifurcation process within the discipline of IPE between society-centred and state-centred approaches, without providing much in the way of further theoretical insight into the actual nature of the international political economy. Ultimately, the bifurcation process initiated by the transnational relations literature acted to confirm - at least in the short term - the realist, state-centred worldview (Risse-Kappen, 1995).

In their subsequent work even Keohane and Nye took on board this state-centred worldview, as well as the more general critique of the transnational relations literature, by seeking a rapprochement with realism. *Power and Interdependence*, published in 1977 six years after the aforementioned article in *International Organization*, thus sought to reconcile the notions of transnationalism and interdependence with an emphasis on power politics. In this work Keohane and Nye also introduced the idea of 'complex interdependence' in order to account for the increasing inter-societal linkages and mutual economic vulnerabilities that were changing the strategic setting in which international politics took place. They described this as a 'world in which actors other than states participate directly in world politics, in which a clear hierarchy of issues does not exist, and in which force is an ineffective instrument of policy' (Keohane and Nye, 1977: 24). Nevertheless, the idea of 'complex interdependence' was never fully explored by Keohane and Nye, and, as they later conceded (1987: 733), 'remained a relatively underdeveloped and undervalued concept'. Instead, Keohane and Nye turned to explore what they later came to refer to as 'strategic interdependence' - defined as bargaining situations where outcome is 'determined by the intersection of decisions arrived at independently by the participants' (Little, 1996: 81) - as a means of examining the dynamics of inter-state bargaining, governed by asymmetrical power relations. The major achievement of this, according to their own subsequent self-analysis, was to 'broaden neo-realism and provide it with new concepts rather than to articulate a coherent alternative theoretical framework for the study of world politics' (Keohane and Nye, 1987: 733). In short, they confirmed their own compromise with realist orthodoxy.

In this sense, the idea of 'strategic interdependence' shared much in common with the notion of 'hegemonic stability', which was independently developed in the same period. Initially based on Charles Kindleberger's (1973) seminal analysis of the Great Depression, the notion of hegemonic stability later became synonymous with the work of Robert Gilpin (1975) and Stephen Krasner (1976). In essence, what these theorists argued was that the smooth operation of a liberal international economic order required the provision of 'public goods', such as international monetary arrangements and multilateral trading rules. However, given the anarchical character of the international system, such goods were unlikely to be forthcoming unless a leader, or hegemon, was willing to impose them and accept a disproportionate share of the cost of their provision (for an excellent summary, see Gilpin, 1987: 72-80). The essence of the argument underpinning the hegemonic stability thesis as a whole was well summarized by Keohane (1980: 132):

> Hegemonic structures of power, dominated by a single country, are conducive to the development of strong international regimes whose rules are relatively precise and well obeyed. According to the theory, the decline of hegemonic structures of power can be expected to presage a decline in the strength of corresponding international economic regimes.

The theory of hegemonic stability has been tremendously important in the development of mainstream theories of IPE, not least because it has also set up a number of more specific debates in the field (Payne, 1998). The first of these relates to the normative purpose of hegemonic power in respect of the manner in which it is exercised. Duncan Snidal (1985) has helpfully distinguished between 'benign' hegemony that operates either through persuasion or coercion, and 'exploitative' hegemony, which merely serves to meet the hegemon's own narrowly defined objectives. More broadly, this debate has centred on the suitability of the public goods analogy for understanding the exercise of hegemonic power in the international political economy. For liberals, such as Kindleberger, international economic regimes are understood as genuine 'public goods', in so far as the hegemon has an independent interest in supplying them that outweighs any individual benefit it may receive from the system. From this perspective, paradoxically, it is not the self-serving actions of the hegemon that pose the biggest threat to the maintenance of international economic rules, but the actions of 'free-riders' who have an incentive not to contribute to the system, ultimately leading to its downfall. This assertion has been questioned on a number of grounds. First, as Haggard and Simmons (1987) suggest, most regimes do not constitute 'public goods' - which are characterized by both jointness of supply and non-excludability - in the sense that compliance *can* be enforced through, for example, the threat of exclusion. Second, a number of critics have pointed to the inappropriateness of applying the theory of collective action to the context of hegemony stability. Both Keohane (1984) and Snidal (1985) have argued that there is nothing in the theory of collective action to suggest that a single hegemon is necessary for the provision of public goods.

A second debate to emanate from the hegemonic stability literature has been concerned specifically with American power, and the extent to which it has, or has not, been in decline since the early 1970s. The notion of American decline is now most famously associated with Paul Kennedy's 1988 work, *The Rise and Fall of the Great Powers*, in which the notion of imperial 'over-stretch' was introduced in order to account for the seemingly intractable difficulties that the American state faced in the 1970s and 1980s. In terms of the more specific IPE literature, also, the notion of American decline was widely accepted in this period.[1] Indeed, such a presumption was an integral component of the hegemonic stability literature and the subsequent work that this generated. It was Robert Keohane (1984: 43) who best captured this mood with the core question of his influential work, *After Hegemony*; namely, 'how can international co-operation be maintained among advanced capitalist states in the absence of American hegemony?' With the benefit of hindsight, it is easy to argue that Keohane and others could not have been more wrong on this point. As Bruce Cumings (1999: 271-2) has somewhat polemically expressed the obvious criticism, 'it is disconcerting to recall the towering influence of the work of "declinists"…and it is positively embarrassing to read recent accounts…that still seem to assume an America on the road to ruin'. Nevertheless, as will be argued, the central problem that mainstream IPE has faced in relation to the question of US hegemony has not, primarily, been related to its failure to appreciate the enduring nature of American power, but rather to its failure to address a more fundamental theoretical weakness.

A third debate generated by the hegemonic stability literature has centred specifically on evaluating the substantive claims of the theory itself, namely, the extent to which a decline in American power has led to a corresponding weakening in international economic regimes. Krasner (1982: 186) has defined a regime as 'a set of implicit or explicit principles, norms, rules, and decision making procedures around which [state] actors' expectations converge in a given area of international relations'. This understanding of regimes has been particularly influential in mainstream IPE (for dissenting voices, though, see Strange, 1982; and Kratochwil and Ruggie, 1986), underpinning much of the substantive debate over the link between American hegemony and the viability of the various economic regimes associated with the Bretton Woods system. This relationship has been subject to numerous empirical studies. Keohane (1980) authored one of the most important, which sought to test the theory of hegemonic stability against changes in monetary, trade and energy regimes between 1967 and 1977. In this study he concluded that a strong causal link between regime change and shifts in the international structure of power lacked compelling evidence, particularly in terms of trade (Keohane, 1980; 1984: Ch. 9). In his subsequent work, Keohane (1984) himself attempted to shift the focus of hegemonic stability theory away from 'testing' the theory and towards the next logical step: examining the viability of regimes once the hegemonic conditions which led to their creation had dissipated. For this purpose Keohane employed game theoretical approaches, including Prisoner's Dilemma, to demonstrate how institutions could in fact mitigate the absence of hegemonic forms of international economic governance. In his view, international institutions could enhance co-operation by providing information, monitoring compliance and facilitating issue linkages. Thus, from this perspective, states could gain from international co-operation even in the absence of hegemonic leadership, given the appropriate institutional setting and the necessary learning.

In summary, the theory of hegemonic stability has provided the theoretical underpinnings of three separate - though closely related - debates in IPE. These very underpinnings are, nevertheless, themselves open to criticism on a number of grounds. As previously noted, many of the problems that mainstream IPE faces with regard to the question of hegemony can be related, in one way or another, to its failure to grasp the deeper meaning of the concept. In fact, as Robert Cox (1989: 45) suggests, hegemony is 'probably the single most important issue underlying the adequacy of conventional [IPE] theory'. There is thus much at stake in seeking to determine how satisfactory or otherwise are mainstream conceptions of hegemony. The most often cited definition from this perspective is provided, again, by Keohane (1984: 32), who describes hegemony as a 'preponderance of material resources', in terms of raw materials, sources of capital, market dominance and advantages in the production of highly valued goods. For Keohane, then, hegemony is equated with material dominance. In taking this route Keohane necessarily eschews consideration of ideas as independent sources of power: according to this definition power is seen as an expression of a predominance of material resources. However, the 'power-as-resource' definition that mainstream writers like Keohane employ does little to address the problems associated with the fungibility of such resources: that is to say, mainstream scholars assume, rather simplistically, that material capabilities can automatically be translated into usable power resources. However, as was aptly demonstrated by the US during much of the Vietnam War, material dominance does not always easily translate into strategic or military superiority.[2] A more curious anomaly with the mainstream definition of hegemony centres on its failure to make reference to geo-political sources of power.[3] In fact, the theory of hegemonic stability focuses on the distribution of power within the international economic system, while the role of international power politics is itself neglected. As a consequence, the importance of 'high' politics and alliance solidarity in the post-war economic order is more or less ignored; and even the concept of bipolarity itself is all but overlooked (Haggard and Simmons, 1987: 503). Nevertheless, an attempt has been made to address this problem by linking the debate over international economic regimes explicitly to Kenneth Waltz's more systematic, neo-realist theory of international politics. As we shall see, though, this move comes at the price of moving mainstream IPE even further away from the ideas upon which it was founded.

As is well known within the core discipline of IR, Kenneth Waltz's (1979) *Theory of International Politics* attempted to place realism, and classic balance of power theory in particular, on a more scientific footing by advocating a third image, or systemic, explanation. Waltz's (1979: 79-110) model was built around the idea of an international structure - defined as 'a set of constraining conditions' - consisting of an 'ordering principle' (anarchy), an 'unequal distribution of unit capabilities' and the 'functional non-differentiation of units', which could account for regularities in state behaviour in the international political system. In other words, in a system characterized by an unequal distribution of material capabilities, and in conditions of international anarchy, states would always be compelled to maximize their own security to ensure their ultimate survival. Although Waltz makes little specific mention of political economy (he preferred to rely upon an analogy with microeconomics for much of the basis of his argument), his theory has, nonetheless, had a tremendous influence over the development of mainstream theories of IPE. This, to a large extent, can be attributed to the fact that his focus upon state behaviour in anarchical conditions touched on many of the themes that, as we have seen, were developed concurrently by hegemonic stability theorists. In fact, anticipating much of the subsequent debate that the theory of hegemonic stability was to generate, Waltz's approach dealt specifically with the key issue of co-operation under anarchy. For Waltz, such co-operation is contingent upon the perception that a state stands to gain relatively, as opposed to absolutely, from any agreement. Thus Waltz (1979: 105) writes: 'states that feel insecure must ask how the gain will be divided. They are compelled to ask not "will both of us gain" but "who will gain more?"'

Of course, as again we have seen, Keohane and other neo-liberal institutionalists, who tend to emphasize the role of international institutions as a mitigating factor, reject this position. Yet, apart from this particular dispute, it is important to recognize that neo-liberal institutionalists, in actual fact, accept much of Waltz's neo-realist framework. Once more, Keohane has been the key figure in effecting this rapprochement. In reviewing Waltz's theory, Keohane (1986) put forward his own approach, what he termed a 'modified structural research programme', and attempted to demonstrate that the core assumptions of neo-realism were in fact compatible with international co-operation. In effect, this move by Keohane and others enabled a coalescence of neo-liberal institutionalist and neo-realist research programmes during the 1980s and early 1990s. Within this so-called 'neo-neo' debate the question over relative versus absolute gains became the central point of contention and has generated a series of subsidiary debates dealing with various aspects of the 'co-operation under anarchy' problematic.[4] This coalescence is not without its merits. As David Baldwin (1993: 3) points out, the confluence of neo-realist and neo-liberal institutionalist research programmes has led to 'a more productive debate' by engaging 'one another's arguments directly'. Crane and Amawi (1991) offer a similar line of argument. They suggest that the three main focal points of contemporary IPE - rational action theories of the state, the theory of hegemonic stability and regime analysis - are the result of an evolutionary process of 'cross-fertilization' and 'convergence' among these previously competing paradigms.

Still, in the final analysis, this 'achievement' - if, indeed, that is what it is - has come at a price. As Richard Leaver (1994: 133) has observed, the three focal points of which Crane and Amawi speak are not simply random instances of 'cross fertilization' and 'convergence' but are in actual fact strongly related to, and mutually supportive of, each other. As has been argued, these three discourses have all played a role in the evolutionary movement of mainstream IPE away from ideas associated with transnationalism and interdependence, and towards what Ruggie (1998) has lately described as 'neo-utilitarianism'. Both neo-realism and neo-liberalism, as Ruggie (1998: 3) assesses them, 'share a view of the world of international relations in utilitarian terms: an atomistic universe of self-regarding units whose identity is assumed given and fixed, and who are responsive largely if not solely to material interests that are stipulated by assumption'. Yet the reason for this assumption is not incidental. In fact, it is central to the whole neo-realist/neo-liberal institutionalist approach. By insisting on the analytical primacy of the systemic level of analysis, as Waltz and those who have subsequently adopted his approach do, it becomes necessary to assume that state preferences are given exogenously (Ruggie, 1998; Powell, 1994). For Waltz (1986: 329), it may be recalled, the central aim was to delineate a systemic theory of international politics that would avoid reductionism by locating causal explanations at the level of the state system, in order to explain 'a small number of big and important things'. For this theory to hold, it therefore becomes necessary to assume that states will invariably respond to the external pressure of international anarchy in the same predictable way. But, as Jervis (1988: 324-5) warns us, the advantages of this method are achieved only 'at the cost of drawing attention away from areas that may contain much of the explanatory "action" in which we are interested'. In other words, in adopting a neo-realist framework, as many within mainstream IPE have done, it also becomes necessary to eschew consideration of the source of actor preferences, including, among other things, transnational forces, ideologies, beliefs, experience and knowledge. Despite all of this, given the stark choice between state survival and extinction, which is the only choice that Waltz offers them, it is logical to assume that states will always choose survival. Nevertheless, from our perspective, when Waltz's theory is transposed to situations of political economy - which, in the parlance of game-theoretic IR theory, is often described as a positive-sum rather than a zero-sum game - the choice between the preference for survival over extinction becomes irrelevant. Instead, in this situation, understanding the origins of state preferences becomes absolutely crucial. In the final analysis, then, it would seem bizarre to construct a theory of political economy on the basis of Waltz's neo-realist model, but that, as we have seen, is precisely the route which many within mainstream IPE have taken.

New International Political Economy

The methodological assumptions that currently underpin mainstream IR/IPE theory are not shared by the group of scholars who have coalesced around the term 'new' IPE.[5] In fact, what marks these scholars out is their conscious rejection of the 'methodological orthodoxy' that shapes much of the substantive output of mainstream IPE. In the view of Murphy and Tooze (1991a), this 'methodological orthodoxy' is guided by a largely unspoken commitment to a positivist epistemology and a methodological individualism that maintains a belief in the unproblematic separation of subject/object and fact/value. As they see it, this commitment overrides the competing theoretical claims of each perspective, and, to a large extent, determines the range of questions that can be legitimately addressed in IPE. By way of an alternative to this methodological orthodoxy, Murphy and Tooze pointed to the work of Robert Cox, who argued famously that 'theory is always *for* someone and *for* some purpose' (1996: 87). The target of Cox's statement was IR theory in general and neo-realism in particular. Specifically, Cox sought to uncover the hidden ideological bias of neo-realism, while, at the same time, setting out an alternative theoretical model that could not only explain contemporary social structures, but also conceive of a world fundamentally different from that of the prevailing order. For these purposes, Cox made a distinction between 'problem solving theory' and 'critical theory'. 'Problem-solving' theory, according to Cox, 'takes the world as it finds it, with the prevailing social and power relationships and institutions into which they are organized as the given framework for action' (1996: 88). What this meant, in other words, was that neo-realism, as 'problem-solving' theory, had to assume the immutability of current international structures - including forms of state, international balances of power and capitalist modes of production - in order for the theory to hold. As a result, neo-realism contained no mechanism within its remit for explaining either the emergence of these current international structures, or, indeed, any future transformation that might occur. Cox's preferred alternative of 'critical theory' sought to avoid this limitation by making the understanding of change and transformation its central theoretical goal. In more specific language, 'critical theory...stands apart from the prevailing order of the world and asks how that order came about' (Cox, 1996: 88). In contrast to 'problem-solving' theory, it 'does not take institutions and power relations for granted but calls them into question by concerning itself with their origins and how and whether they might be in the process of changing' (Cox, 1996: 97-8). To these ends, Cox proceeded to outline what were, in his view, the main determinants of continuity and change within the international political economy, which he termed 'historical structures'. For him, historical structures represent a particular configuration of forces - material capabilities, institutions and ideas - which interact reciprocally to reproduce a particular social and political order. It must be stressed, however, that, in Cox's view, these historical structures do not determine action 'in any mechanical way', but impose pressures and constraints upon individuals and groups, who may resist and oppose them but cannot ignore them.

In delineating his method of historical structures, a central aim for Cox was to establish the relationship between hegemony and different configurations of material capabilities, institutions and ideas, as expressed at three different levels: the social relations engendered by different and changing production processes; forms of state, determined by different historical configurations of state-society relations; and types of world order. For this purpose, Cox introduced a Gramscian conception of power that emphasized the ideational and consensual nature of hegemony. It may be recalled that a central component of Gramsci's thinking was the way in which the ruling classes within the Italian state were able to govern with a broad measure of consent. Thus, he wrote: 'the state is an entire complex of practical and theoretical activities with which the ruling class not only justifies and maintains its dominance, but manages to win the active consent of those over whom it rules' (Gramsci, 1971: 244). For Cox, this method of rule was analogous with, and therefore transposable to, hegemony in the international political economy. Upon this basis, hegemony is understood as 'an order based ideologically on a broad measure of consent, functioning according to general principles that in fact ensure the continuing supremacy of the leading state or states and leading social classes but at the same time offer some measure or prospect of satisfaction to the less powerful' (Cox, 1987: 7). Even though this formulation attributes crucial importance to the role of ideology in constructing hegemonic order, it would still be wrong to label Cox ultimately as an idealist. As he has suggested elsewhere (1996a: 132), 'ideas and material conditions are always bound together, mutually influencing one another, and not reducible one to the other'. Hegemony is therefore seen as constituted by both material capabilities and ideas and is thus built upon coercive as well as consensual elements of power. Broadly speaking, the more powerful the position of the leading states and social classes, the less need there is for the use of force in order to maintain rule.

For Cox (1987; 1996), the contemporary world order has its roots in the crisis in US global hegemony, which emerged in the 1970s and has since manifested itself in two related tendencies: the internationalization of production and the internationalization of the state. On the one hand, the internationalization of production refers to a shift in the production process away from a model based on *exchange* between territorial economies, and towards an international, or global, economy based on *production*. In this scenario the key features are the extent to which transnational corporations (TNCs) have increasingly geared their productive capacity to the world market in such a way that key component elements are produced in different territorial jurisdictions, thus generating a new international division of labour. Prior to this, Cox suggests, the mode of capitalist production was seen as subordinate to the requirements of what is referred to as the 'neo-liberal' state.[6] This, in essence, involved the marriage of Keynesian demand-management with Fordist mass-production techniques socially regulated by means of the welfare state and tripartite forms of corporatism centred on business-labour-government coalitions. In contrast, the internationalization of production has signalled a shift towards a form of production that is largely disembedded from the state. Instead, this has generated a newly emerging global class structure, at the apex of which stands a 'transnational managerial class' (Cox, 1996: 111). According to Cox, this class possesses its own ideology, strategy and institutions of collective action, the focal points of which are the Trilateral Commission, the World Bank, the IMF and the OECD, all of which serve as a means to develop frameworks of thought and guidelines for policy.

On the other hand, the internationalization of the state, put simply, refers to the ways in which the powers and prerogatives of the state have been increasingly adjusted to meet the exigencies of the global political economy. For Cox, this process consists of three main elements. First, there is a process of inter-state consensus formation that takes place within a common ideological framework, as advocated by the international institutions described above. Second, participation within this consensus formation is hierarchically structured. Third, the internal structures of states are adjusted so that each state can transform this global consensus into national policy and practice (Cox, 1987: 254). The key to understanding this shift in the role of the state is seen to lie in the transition from an international economy based upon exchange relations between states, associated with the Bretton Woods system, to a global economy, rooted in non-territorial patterns of production and finance. In the former scenario, as Cox describes it, the state generally acted as a 'buffer' between the external economic environment and the domestic economy. Ruggie (1982) has famously referred to this period as the 'compromise of embedded liberalism', because of the degree to which the commitment to economic liberalization and multilateralism was tied to the needs of the Keynesian welfare state in matters of domestic policy. In contrast, the relationship between the state and the global economy in the current juncture is predicated on no such compromise; instead of acting as 'buffer' between the external economic environment and the domestic economy, the state is viewed as a 'transmission belt' for the dissemination of neo-liberalism to the level of the state. In Cox's view, however, these internationalising tendencies, although powerful, are neither necessarily overwhelming nor inevitable. Thus:

> the tendency toward the internationalization of the state is never complete, and the further it advances, the more it provokes counter-tendencies sustained by domestic social groups that have been disadvantaged or excluded in the new domestic realignments. These counter-tendencies could prove capable of reversing the internationalising tendency, especially if the balance tips simultaneously in a number of key countries (1987: 253).

In the absence of such a scenario, however, it is assumed, albeit implicitly, that there is an inexorable logic towards the internationalising process and that the reconfiguration of state-society relations is directed by external pressures and constraints imposed by the global political economy. However, the theoretical foundations for making this claim - in the sense of deploying an explicit theory of the state itself - are not particularly strong in Cox's work. Indeed, despite Cox's preoccupation with the relationship between social forces and the state, such a theory is conspicuous by its absence from his overall theoretical framework.[7] In this vein, Cox has been criticized by Leo Panitch (1994) for offering an 'outside-in' account of the state that is too 'top-down' in its expression of power relations. As a consequence, Panitch argues, Cox's model underestimates the extent to which states directly facilitate processes of internationalization, rather than simply acting as 'transmission belts' for the dissemination of global neo-liberalism. Lilly Ling (1996) has offered a similar line of argument. In her view, Cox is guilty of offering an ethnocentric account of the process of internationalization that presupposes that all states will passively respond to internationalising pressures in the same way. As a result, such an account fails to acknowledge the extent to which reciprocal interaction between the global and the local produces different configurations of state-society relations, which, rather than leading to assimilation for 'Western-states-in-training', create different forms of 'hybridity'.

It should be noted too that, more broadly, the work of Cox and others who have subsequently adopted his approach has been criticized for its alleged misappropriation of Gramscian concepts. This criticism is particularly applicable to the now voluminous writings by 'second generation' neo-Gramscian thinkers, who have attempted to apply Cox's ideas and concepts more rigorously to the context of the global political economy (Gill, 1993; Gill and Mittelman, 1997). Such endeavour has undoubtedly contributed to the enrichment and refinement of Cox's original ideas and concepts, even if sometimes they have been deployed by his followers in a more rigid fashion than by Cox himself. For some, however, attempts to 'internationalize' Gramscian concepts (e.g. hegemony, civil society, historic bloc) risk robbing them of their coherence and explanatory power. In the view of Germain and Kenny (1998), Gramsci only ever used these concepts in the grounding of national social formations, thus raising serious questions over their applicability to the context of the global political economy. From a different perspective, Peter Burnham (1991) has attacked neo-Gramscian political economy for its lack of 'over determination' and 'overall structure' in the sense of a definitive causal reference point, resulting in what he refers to as 'pluralist empiricism'. Burnham proceeds to suggest that Cox's preoccupation with the articulation of ideology neglects the central importance of the capital relation; as a result, we are left with 'an idealist account of the determination of economic policy' (1991: 81). Conversely, Cox has also been criticized for giving insufficient weight to the role of ideas in his empirical work, which, it is argued, has tended to fall back on a straightforward class analysis (Whitworth, 1994).

Whether or not one chooses to accept these mutually incompatible criticisms fully or even partly, what remains undeniable is that Cox's model has contributed to the development of an integrated theory of world order. Quite clearly, neo-Gramscian theories are an important constituent part of this intellectual movement, but Cox has also helped to inspire 'new' IPE in respect of a broader range of ideas, methods and theories, derived from a much more disparate collection of sources. Evidence of this movement was signalled in the UK in the mid 1990s with the launching of two new journals - *Review of International Political Economy* and *New Political Economy* - both of whom have self-consciously sought to promote 'new' IPE. *The Review of International Political Economy*, for its part, committed itself to the 'rejection of orthodox frameworks [that] have been exposed as unsuitable vehicles through which to understand globalization' and, in turn, celebrated 'the rise of heterodox epistemological converges which could take IPE in new directions' (Amin *et al.*, 1994: 2). Similarly, *New Political Economy* sought - more ambitiously - to connect IPE to the older discipline of political economy by means of rejecting the familiar dichotomies of structure and agency and states and markets. In the words of the editors, the aim is to 'build on those approaches in social sciences which have tried to develop an integrated analysis, by combining parsimonious theories which analyse agency in terms of a conception of rationality with contextual theories which analyse structures institutionally and historically' (Gamble *et al.*, 1996: 5-6). Elsewhere, Andrew Gamble (1995) has drawn attention to the fact that a number of highly disparate approaches to political economy - including 'new' IPE, state theory, government-industry relations and even theories of public choice - are increasingly moving towards an insistence upon methodological diversity. Crucially, what connects much of this literature is not so much a consensus upon where the epistemological and methodological parameters of the discipline should lie, but rather a tacit agreement that an eclectic research programme that is genuinely interdisciplinary in nature is the best way for theoretical and empirical investigations to proceed. In the spirit of this endeavour, therefore, the remaining part of this chapter seeks to develop a similar approach by means of an eclectic and open-ended review of some of the key debates concerned with aspects of structural change, and the room for manoeuvre that is left to agents, brought about by the processes of economic globalization. In so doing, it is anticipated that a number of themes and issues salient to the study of the new political economy of US-Caribbean relations will be highlighted in a way that will enable them to guide and inform the subsequent parts of this investigation.

The 'New' International Political Economy of Globalization: Some Key Debates

Undoubtedly, the theoretical and empirical focus of the majority of 'new' IPE scholarship is concerned in one way or another with the issue of economic globalization. As Richard Higgott (1999) has described it, the specific literature in this vein has unfolded through a series of phases. The first phase witnessed a series of 'hyperglobalist' writings, pointing to the inevitable decline of the nation-state in the face of the inexorable logic of global capitalism. This argument, in its strongest form, posits a scenario in which 'nation-states have become unnatural, even impossible business units in a global economy' (Ohmae, 1995: 5). In contrast, the second phase of globalization writings sought to question the veracity of this 'hyperglobalist' thesis by pointing to empirical evidence, which, at best, suggests heightened levels of internationalization between distinct national economies (Hirst and Thompson, 1996; Zysman, 1996; Weiss, 1997).[8] The third and current phase, according to Higgott, reflects greater nuance. Here, what is emphasized is that the onset of globalization does not herald the 'end of the nation-state', as 'hyperglobalists' would have us believe, but nor does it conform to the view of globalization as a 'necessary myth', as sceptics suggest. Instead, what this third version of the globalization thesis depicts is a complex and multi-faceted process that is contingent and therefore by no means inevitable (Higgott, 1999). In this view, the familiar state/global dichotomy, shared by both 'hyperglobalists' and 'sceptics', is discarded in favour of an approach that recognizes that the 'processes of global restructuring are largely embedded within state structures and institutions, politically contingent on state policies and actions, and primarily about the reorganisation of the state' (Amoore *et al.*, 1997: 186).

In light of the proceeding discussion, this view of globalization is clearly one that is consistent with, and partly based on, the Coxian method. As we have seen, this rejects the state/global dichotomy and instead advocates a holistic approach built around his notion of historical structures. In accordance with this approach, what follows is a discussion of global political economy based on three key areas of debate: namely, production, development and governance. As we shall see shortly, these debates are not intended to provide an exhaustive survey of every aspect of global political economy, but rather are designed to highlight those issues of direct relevance to our specific research concerns. In sum, the central purpose of the remainder of this chapter is to review these aspects of the global political economy debate and, in the process, highlight the most pertinent research questions, which will be explored further in a specific geo-political and geo-economic setting in subsequent chapters.

Global Production and the New Spatial Division of Labour

According to Cox, the internationalization of production has resulted in a transnational, or global, mode of production that is served by a new international division of labour. As a theory, the new international division of labour (NIDL) stresses a qualitative shift in the nature of the political economy of North-South relations, away from an 'old' international division of labour wherein developing countries were restricted to the export of raw materials, and towards a situation based on the dispersal of manufacturing away from the core and towards the periphery. In more specific language, Ernst has succinctly set out the NIDL thesis as follows:

> a new capitalist economy has emerged, its main feature being a massive migration of capital from major OECD countries to low-cost production in the Third World. The main purpose of establishing such a new international division of labour is to exploit reserve supplies of labour on a world scale. This type of internationalization of capital requires the existence of world markets for labour and production sites, and of one global industrial reserve army of labour (cited in Gordon, 1988: 26).

The NIDL is thus seen as resulting in global markets for both production sites *and* labour. In the original NIDL formulation put forward by Fröbel *et al.* (1981), the new international division of labour was primarily driven by a capitalist imperative intent on maximising profits in conditions of heightened global competition. Based upon evidence drawn from a study of the West German textile and clothing industry, Fröbel *et al.* claimed that a new international division of labour was being fuelled by the attempts of TNCs to seek out the lowest possible labour costs (the so-called 'Babbage's principle'); and that this was leading to a reallocation of elements of the production process towards those geographical areas where the cheapest and most compliant labour could be found. Fröbel *et al.* went on to suggest that this new international division of labour was not the result of the actions of individual states and the development strategies of particular developing countries, but was an 'institutional' innovation of capital *itself*. 'It is a consequence', they argued, 'and not a cause of these new conditions that various countries...have to tailor their policies...to these new conditions' (1981: 46). In other words, the trend towards a new international division of labour of which Fröbel and his colleagues spoke was conceived to have developed independently of the actions of individual states, with the development strategies of individual developing countries viewed as only incidental to this process.

 The NIDL thesis, in sum, is based on a series on assumptions, the most important of which is the notion that the new international division of labour has been primarily driven by the search by TNCs for lower labour costs in the developing world. While this 'cheap labour' hypothesis has found resonance in popular political discourse in recent years, it can and has been criticized on both theoretical and empirical grounds. First, there lies a danger of overstating the reliance of TNCs' investment decisions on the basis of labour costs alone. As we shall see, even in industries like textiles and apparel, where a reliance on low wages is disproportionately high, investment decisions are as likely to be governed by other factors, such as access to markets and the need for organizational flexibility. Additionally, using low wages as a criterion on which to judge TNC investment decisions is further complicated by the issue of labour productivity, which, in many cases, means that labour unit costs in 'high-wage' countries are often actually lower than in 'low-wage' countries (Jenkins, 1984). This anomaly accounts for the fact most TNC foreign investment is actually concentrated in countries and regions where labour remains relatively costly, but where productivity is high (Mittelman, 1997).

Moreover, this points to a further problem with the NIDL thesis in that not only is the 'cheap labour' hypothesis itself open to question, but also the substantive claims of NIDL theorists regarding the empirical evidence supporting a new international division of labour do not hold up to close critical scrutiny. While it is undoubtedly true that the 1970s witnessed a relative shift in industrial production towards what these theorists referred to as less developed countries (LDCs), this was by no means an unprecedented development. As has been pointed out by Gordon, this most recent shift is not nearly as significant as the gains made by LDCs during the Depression and World War II, and thus merely served to recoup the losses that LDCs experienced during the 1940s and 1950s. More crucially, however, what was most striking about the gain in LDCs' share of industrial production during the 1970s was its concentrated nature. As Hoogvelt (1997: 47) illustrates, citing a 1982 United Nations Conference on Trade and Development (UNCTAD) report, 'fewer than ten newly industrialised developing countries accounted in 1980 for nearly 30 per cent of developing countries' GDP and nearly half of their manufacturing output, even though their share of the population of underdeveloped countries was no more than 10 per cent'. Overall, in the decade of the 1970s, LDCs share of world manufacturing exports increased from 7 per cent to 10 per cent, and two-thirds of this was concentrated in just eight countries (Hoogvelt, 1997: 47).

While these inconsistencies may be put down simply to the overstatement of the NIDL thesis, they are also illustrative of more a fundamental theoretical weakness, which relates to the economistic logic of its core argument. After all, it is important to remember that in the NIDL thesis as put forward by Fröbel *et al.* the new international division of labour is not propelled by the actions of individual states and the development strategies of particular developing countries; in fact, as we have seen, these authors explicitly eschew such a correlation. The point is that this argument fails to recognize the significant role of the state in the process of industrialization in the developing world, evidenced in the lengths to which LDCs have gone in recent years to attract foreign investment (Jenkins, 1984). One such measure is the use of export processing zones (EPZs), which act as economic enclaves, designed to stimulate export performance and attract foreign investment through the provision of investment incentives, such as exemption from import duties and tax holidays (see Chapter Three). The growth of EPZs, located mainly in Asia and the Caribbean Basin, has in fact been particularly pronounced since the early 1970s: Dicken (1998: 131) estimates that, since 1971, over two hundred EPZs have been established, employing over four million people worldwide. The majority of this employment is concentrated in light manufacturing activities, such as textiles and apparel, toys and electronics, all of which rely upon a high degree of labour intensity. Nonetheless, the growth in the EPZ format has facilitated the insertion of many developing countries into the global political economy through a series of transnational production networks. As Held *et al.* (1998) describe it, these networks are not usually characterized by direct ownership by TNCs via foreign direct investment, but rather involve 'regularised contractual relationships'.

Elsewhere, these arrangements have been expressed in terms of a global 'commodity chain', which has been defined as a 'network of labour and production processes whose end result is a finished commodity' (Hopkins and Wallerstein, 1986: 159). In common with the NIDL thesis, the commodity chains approach assumes that an unprecedented dispersal of manufacturing activity towards semi-peripheral and peripheral nations has taken place since the 1970s. But, whereas the NIDL thesis posits a fairly rigid distinction along the lines of the conventional core/periphery and North/South categories, the commodity chains approach points to a more spatially complex form of capitalist reproduction. In the view of Gary Gereffi and his colleagues (1994: 1), 'capitalism today…entails the detailed disaggregation of stages of production and consumption across national boundaries, under the organizational structure of densely networked firms or enterprises'. Accordingly, the most appropriate way of examining this form of capitalism is not through the statist categories of core/semi-periphery/periphery, but by focusing specifically on the various 'nodes' of activity that constitute a particular industry, including raw materials, design, manufacture, marketing and sales.

In so doing, the commodity chain approach helps us to identify the microregional, subregional and macroregional trends in global production, thus serving to enframe one of the key research questions of the book, namely, the identification of core patterns of regionalization in the global political economy. In addressing this research question specifically, Gereffi - utilising a commodity chains perspective - argues that the key to understanding this process lies in the advent of what he calls 'triangle manufacturing'. Put simply, this term describes the contractual relationships between buyers, manufacturers from new industrialising countries (NICs) and affiliated offshore assembly sites located in low-wage countries (Gereffi, 1995: 18-20). This type of arrangement, as we shall see, has been instrumental in the regionalization of apparel production in the Western hemisphere, involving US retailers and branded manufacturers and a variety of *maquiladora* plants and EPZs in Mexico and the Caribbean Basin (see Chapter Five). Bernard and Ravenhill (1995) have identified a similar trend in East Asia. They speak of 'regionalized manufacturing activity in a number of industries…linked by chains of production, exchange, and distribution'. This activity, they suggest, is characterized by 'firms, or even decentralized divisions within firms, [which] maintain a degree of autonomy, but all significant activity is in some way co-ordinated with other organizations in the network' (1995: 183).

In a further elaboration of the commodity chains concept, Gereffi (1994) has delineated two alternative forms of organising and co-ordinating production and distribution within these networks. First, Gereffi speaks of 'producer-driven' commodity chains. Producer-driven chains refer to those industries that typically revolve around TNCs and other large integrated industrial enterprises, which play the key role in co-ordinating production and distribution systems (including forward and backward linkages). The industries characterized by this type of organizational structure, which rely on a high degree of capital and technological intensity, include automobiles, aircraft, computers, semiconductors and heavy machinery.[9] What is most distinctive about this type of arrangement, however, is that organization remains hierarchically structured and power is maintained in the administrative headquarters of the TNC. Second, and in contrast to producer-driven commodity chains, 'buyer-driven' chains are based upon labour-intensive consumer goods, including garments, footwear, consumer electronics, housewares and other furniture and ornaments. Rather than being dominated by TNCs and other large industrial enterprises, buyer-driven chains are often made up of firms which possess no factories, but rather rely upon a complex tiered network of contractors that perform all of the specialized tasks. Profits for these firms are not derived from technological advances and economies of scale, as in producer-driven chains, but from a unique combination of high value research, design, sales, marketing and financial services, which allow the buyers to act as strategic brokers in linking overseas factories and traders with evolving product niches in their main consumer markets.

As will be seen in subsequent chapters, the concept of a buyer-driven commodity chain is particularly well-suited to illustrating the changes that have taken place within the global apparel industry, particularly as manifested in the restructuring of the North American production chain. For, put simply, what has happened here is that large retailers and marketeers have increasingly come to dominate the industry through their role in co-ordinating a global system of manufacture and distribution - often at the expense of marginalizing domestic clothing producers in their own marketplace. Nevertheless, the commodity chains approach can only take us so far. As Mitchell Bernard (1996: 655) warns, 'unless a network analysis is infused with social depth and considerations of power, it offers political economy as a domain limited to state-firm interaction, and the management and locational strategies of corporate managers'. In other words, the commodity chains framework - as well as the NIDL literature more generally - is particularly vulnerable to the criticism that it provides only a largely apolitical understanding of structural change, given the insufficient weight it places on the role of the state. As a useful corrective to this tendency, the next section of this chapter therefore deals more explicitly with the role of the state via a review of some of the debates that have recently taken place within the political economy of development.

The Political Economy of Development

In 1985, David Booth published an influential article, entitled 'Marxism and Development Sociology: Interpreting the Impasse', which seemed at the time to capture the mood of development theory. In this, Booth argued that the predominantly Marxist/neo-Marxist trajectory of development theory in the 1970s had led the discipline into a theoretical cul-de-sac by the end of the decade. It was acknowledged that the Marxist tradition had contributed much to the refinement and progression of development thinking during the 1970s; at its best, this literature helped to delineate an array of possible economic strategies that developing states could pursue, ranging from 'dependent development' and 'national developmentalism' to various forms of 'de-linking' and other types of socialist development. This notwithstanding, Booth (1985) argued that Marxist/neo-Marxist development theory was nevertheless guilty of failings along three dimensions. First, Marxists and neo-Marxists of various persuasions had operated with an essentialist and teleological understanding of economic development, wherein capitalism was defined in terms of concrete laws that produce inescapable and fixed outcomes. Second, and related to this, Marxism/neo-Marxism was guilty of the worst form of economism in so far as the complex of political, social and cultural factors in developing countries was ultimately seen as a consequence of the national and international economic structure. Third, Booth argued that the Marxist and neo-Marxist literature was ignorant of what he referred to as 'mainstream' issues (e.g. the role of the state in the local industrialization process), preferring instead to focus on concepts (such as unequal exchange and exploitation) which were rarely based on empirical research, difficult to quantify and normally clouded in pseudo-scientific jargon.

Yet, for all its insight, Booth's critique of Marxist and neo-Marxist theories of development overlooked one important point: the 'impasse' reached during the early 1980s had less to do with theoretical fallings than with 'real world' events. As Colin Leys (1996: 41) has lately argued, 'if the end of the Bretton Woods system spelled the end of national Keynesianism, it also spelled the end of national development at it had hitherto been conceived'. Even though the collapse of the Bretton Woods system had destabilising consequences for most states, its effects proved to be particularly harsh for developing countries, which were seeking to position themselves as best they could in an increasingly unpredictable world economy. As it later came to be known, the 'lost decade' of the 1980s witnessed a succession of 'debt crises' in the developing world, as one country after another fell into intractable financial difficulties, which ultimately led them into the hands of the IMF and the World Bank. These institutions for their part used the opportunity offered by the conditionality attached to loans to impose 'structural adjustment programmes', which essentially involved substituting 'market forces' for governments as the motor of economic growth. In effect, the successful imposition of IMF 'structural adjustment programmes' in Latin America, Africa and elsewhere led to the inauguration of what was an essentially 'anti-development' paradigm: that is to say, 'by the end of the 1980s the only development policy that was officially approved was not having one - leaving it to the market to allocate resources, not the state' (Leys, 1996: 42).

Despite this, outside of the increasingly narrow remit of development studies, empirical research work conducted in the field of comparative political economy during the 1980s was not generally supportive of the view propagated by the World Bank and the IMF. This was particular true in respect of the East Asian NICs. Although the spectacular economic successes of the NICs were initially proclaimed as testimony of the merits of market-led industrialization, the work of Clive Hamilton and many others convincingly showed that forceful and sustained economic intervention by a strong state over a sustained period of time and within the context of a growing international economy was pivotal to the industrial transformation of East Asia (Hamilton, 1986; White, 1987; Amsden, 1989; Wade, 1990). In the light of the East Asian financial crisis of 1997, some analysts, notably Stephen Haggard (2000), have subsequently called for a fundamental rethink of the alleged benefits of the East Asian development model, particularly with respect to the close relationship between business elites and the state. It is also interesting to note that, in his earlier work on industrialization in East Asia, Haggard (1990) himself had reached a rather unsettling set of conclusions regarding the relationship between authoritarianism and economic development and the improbability of other developing states replicating the NIC experience. Despite this, there is no doubting that the burden of the argument put forward by Clive Hamilton *et al.* is widely acknowledged now within the development community as a whole - it was even accepted, albeit uneasily, by the World Bank in 1993 - even though most Western governments still persist in promoting the case for economic *laissez-faire*.

Besides this, in the last decade or so there have been signals that the core discipline of development studies has itself begun to move beyond the theoretical 'impasse' previously described by Booth (Schuurman, 1993). In fact, Booth (1993) himself has since identified the emergence of a new development agenda associated with the enormous expansion of actual field research carried out in different social, cultural and economic contexts within the last few years. The cumulative effect of this research, Booth has concluded, revealed the thin empirical basis of much of the earlier Marxist and neo-Marxist development literature. In contrast to this work, which, in his view, was for the most part overly deterministic and insensitive to the diversity of local situations within the developing world, the present wave of empirical research has shed light on a range of hitherto under-explored aspects of development, including gender, ethnicity, religion, culture and so on. Lately, Colin Leys (1996) has criticized this work for its tendency to view development theory in essentially idealistic terms: that is to say, the transcendence of the 'impasse' advocated by Booth and other researchers of this ilk merely involves substituting 'development studies' for 'development theory'. Nevertheless, it can be argued that Booth has at least stayed true to his original *World Development* critique, which very much centred on the alleged insensitivity of Marxist and neo-Marxist development theory to 'real world' situations.

Elsewhere, a more ambitious attempt to rethink development *theory* has been made by Björn Hettne (1995). In Hettne's view (1995: 262), the key problem for development theory is that it is 'trapped somewhere between an obsolete "nation state" approach and a premature "world" approach'. Accordingly, there was a need to adopt a mid-point between the two extreme positions of endogenism and exogenism previously exemplified by modernization theory and dependency theory respectively. As Hettne (1996: 263) put it, 'there are in fact no countries that are completely autonomous and self-reliant, and no countries that develop (or underdevelop) merely as a reflection of what goes on beyond their national borders'. Rather, the task is to 'analyse development predicaments stemming from the fact that most decision makers operate in a national space but react on problems emerging in a global space over which they have only marginal control'. In advocating this stance, Hettne self-consciously made the somewhat obvious connection - which had more or less been overlooked by Booth - that the crisis in development theory and practice was evidently related to the onset of economic globalization. For Hettne (1995: 107), the whole phenomenon of economic globalization and, in particular, the emergence of global production systems and a new spatial division of labour, required development researchers to take account of the fact that national economies are now 'penetrated by global phenomena to such an extent as to signify a deepening of the process of internationalization'. In short, the research agenda advocated by Hettne sought to combine 'development theory' and 'new' IPE within a single analytical framework.

Governance, Regions and Regionalism

In his 1977 classic, *The Anarchical Society*, Hedley Bull speculated on the nature of future world orders that might one day replace the Westphalian system. Along with world government, Bull also considered that 'a secular reincarnation of the system of overlapping or segmented authority that characterized medieval Christendom in the Middle Ages' might, conceivably, replace the modern state system. In Bull's view, however, this 'new medievalism' would only prove feasible if five trends within contemporary world politics were to continue: the regional integration of states as exemplified by the European Community; the disintegration of states (with the proviso that secessionism would stop short of the creation of new states); the restoration of private internationalist violence (i.e. terrorism); a growth in the competencies of international organizations; and, finally, unification brought about by technological advances in transport and communications, leading to greater roles for TNCs and non-governmental organizations (NGOs). All of this led Bull ultimately to reject his own hypothesis. Nonetheless, subsequent scholars have once more turned to 'new medievalism' in an attempt to grasp many of the deep-seated changes currently taking place within the global order. Anderson and Goodman (1995), for instance, see in Bull's writings a prescient analysis of the multi-level governance currently unfolding in Europe. In their view, what makes Bull's concept particularly appealing is that it requires neither the 'death of the nation-state' nor a 'Europe of the regions' in order to be proved correct. Rather, they suggest, a 'new medievalism' characterized by 'overlapping and segmented authority' would 'be most likely where the pressures from "above and below" achieve more partial and ambiguous changes, undermining but not relocating sovereignty as presently understood' (Anderson and Goodman, 1995: 605).

Ruggie (1998) has gone even further than this to question the principle of territorial sovereignty itself. For him, the most significant aspect of the medieval period was the extent to which rule was predicated on a non-exclusive form of territoriality, based on a 'patchwork of overlapping and incomplete rights of government' (Ruggie, 1998: 179). Likewise, in the current historical juncture the concept of territorial rule, in the form of state sovereignty, is in his view being rendered increasingly problematical as a result of the non-territorial nature of economic globalization. This can be seen, he suggests, in the increasing untenable distinction between 'foreign' and 'domestic', in a world in which:

> IBM is Japan's largest computer exporter, and Sony is the largest exporter of television sets from the United States. It is a world in which Brother Industries, a Japanese concern assembling typewriters in Bartlett, Tennessee, brings an antidumping case before the US International Trade Commission against Smith Corona, an American firm that imports typewriters into the United States from its offshore facilities in Singapore and Indonesia (Ruggie, 1998: 196).

Building on the arguments of sociologists such as Jameson (1984) and Harvey (1989), Ruggie claims that this is evidence not just of a crisis in the state system, but rather of a more deep-seated crisis in the project of modernity itself. For Ruggie, the notion of territorial sovereignty constituted the quintessential political embodiment of the Enlightenment project, in that it represented an expression of the single-point perspective characteristic of the age of modernity. Conversely, the 'unbundling' of territorial sovereignty brought about by economic globalization is symptomatic of the age of postmodernity. Thus, for this perspective, the EU 'may constitute nothing less than the emergence of the first truly postmodern international political form' (Ruggie, 1998: 173).

Whether or not one chooses to accept this argument fully or even partly, what is undeniable within Ruggie's overall hypothesis is his claim that the notion of territorial sovereignty - both in theory and in practice - has become highly problematical. Nevertheless, as he suggests, systems of rule need not be territorial; even when they are, as with the medieval period, this may not entail the mutual exclusion of different spheres of authority. This point is implied in the very notion of governance which has lately become such a fashionable term of analysis within studies of the new global order. As traditionally understood within the public policy field, the term governance refers to the 'steering' done by governments, but even in this area the term is increasingly been used to refer to governance *without* government (Rhodes, 1996). Within the IPE field, James Rosenau (1997: 145) has been responsible for introducing governance to a wider audience. He defines it as 'spheres of authority...at all levels of human activity...that amount to...systems of rule in which goals are pursued through the exercise of control'. On this basis, then, governance within the global political economy may be conceived as a form of rule that does not necessarily correspond to territorially defined political authority. Like Bull's 'new medievalism', with its 'overlapping' and 'segmented authority', the global political economy is indeed characterized by a complex and multi-layered patchwork of authority, formal and informal, and territorial and non-territorial in character. There is much that could be said in elaboration of this observation, but, for reasons that will become obvious later in the investigation, the remainder of this discussion will focus on just one aspect of the contemporary governance of the global political economy: regionalism.

In a theoretical sense, part of the problem with thinking about regionalism in this way is that much of the most influential debate on this theme has, historically, taken place outside of any consideration of the question of globalization. The theoretical literature in this vein usually takes one of two possible guises. The first follows the enduring, though ultimately false, neo-realist idea that the creation of rival 'trading blocs' must inevitably follow the pattern of the 1930s, where supposedly the outbreak of 'trade wars' led inexorably down the path to actual war. Theoretically speaking, this sentiment is rooted in the hegemonic stability thesis, which, as we have seen, suggests that the openness and stability of the world economy is reliant upon a dominant power, or hegemon, to enforce the 'rules of the game'. For Robert Gilpin, the perceived decline of US hegemony in the 1970s was suggestive of a scenario reminiscent of the 1930s:

> With the decline of the dominant economic power [i.e. the United States], the world economy may be following the pattern of the latter part of the nineteenth century and of the 1930s: it may be fragmenting into regional trading centres, exclusive economic alliances, and economic nationalism (Gilpin, 1975: 258-9).

In a milder form, the notion of mutual antagonistic trading blocs also underpins a similar debate concerned with the compatibility of regional integration with the multilateral trading system, as expressed in commitment to the new World Trade

Organization (WTO). Even in this milder form, though, arguments which posit a dichotomous relationship between regional integration and globalization are fundamentally misconceived. In truth, as Gamble and Payne (1995) suggest, regionalism as a state-led project is just as capable of accelerating globalization, as it is of modifying or reversing it. In practice, they suggest, 'regionalism as a set of state projects intersects with globalisation' (Gamble and Payne, 1995: 250). Others have gone further. Gill (1995), for instance, sees regional integration as a constituent part of an emerging global architecture that seeks to impose disciplinary forms of neo-liberal ideology and economic globalization. Similarly, Andrew Axline has argued that regionalism 'provides a...mechanism for insertion into the global political economy...and serves as a mechanism for globalizing the neo-liberal ideology that defines the form and direction of sub-regional policies chosen for this insertion' (cited in Hout, 1998: 23). From this perspective, then, regional integration is supportive of, rather than antagonistic to, economic globalization.

The second debate to dominate the discussion of regionalism has been that between neo-functionalism and inter-governmentalism which has developed, more or less exclusively, with regard to the European Union over the last four decades. As is well known in this field, the main point of contention for these two opposing camps is the extent to which regional integration is a result of 'spillover' driven by political, economic and bureaucratic elites, or, alternatively, the result of inter-state bargaining. The problem with this debate, as Payne (1999: 209) has rightly observed, is that neither approach is particularly well versed in issues that fall outside of the narrow remit of 'European Community studies'. As such, these discourses have failed to engage with broader questions that have been of such concern in the fields of comparative and international politics, not least the notion of globalization itself. The result has been that both neo-functionalism and inter-governmentalism are still grounded in the traditional, Westphalian assumptions, in which the familiar dichotomies of internal/external, and foreign/domestic remain both central and ultimately unproblematical. Moreover, given that the high degree of institutionalization within the European Union is more or less unique among regionalist projects, generalizations made on the basis of this case are of a rather limited utility (Breslin and Higgott, 2000).

This latter problem is of particular concern when we consider the complex and variegated nature of regional polities that have emerged or been revived in the post-Cold War period. In fact, Andrew Hurrell (1995) has identified a number of characteristics of this so-called 'new' regionalism that differentiate it from previous waves of regional integration. First, regionalism has emerged, more or less for the first time, across the 'North-South divide' (Grugel and Hout, 1998). This trend has been most pronounced in the Americas, both with the launching of the North American Free Trade Agreement (NAFTA) in 1994 and the Free Trade Area of the Americas (FTAA) initiative, scheduled to be implemented by 2005. However, Europe and Asia are also increasingly moving in this direction. Second, Hurrell suggests that 'new' regionalism is distinctive in the wide variation in the levels of institutionalization. In his view, many regional groupings are seeking to avoid the institutional and bureaucratic structure of traditional international organizations and of the regionalist model of the EU. This latter tendency can be most clearly seen in Asia, where, as Richard Higgott (1995) suggests, regionalism has taken the form of 'market-led' integration. While some characteristics of institutionalization are present in Asia, such as the Asia-Pacific Economic Cooperation (APEC) forum, in Higgott's (1995: 365) view these are insufficient in themselves to constitute either a 'regime' or an 'institution'. This idea of 'market-led regionalism' is consistent with the approach taken by Bernard and Ravenhill (1995), who speak of the 'regionalization' of Japanese production networks throughout the East Asian region.

A third and final feature of 'new' regionalism is its multi-dimensional character. In Hurrell's view, the end of the Cold War, coupled with developments in the global political economy, has rendered the distinction between 'political' and 'economic' organizations increasingly irrelevant. Extending this point further, it can added that not only has 'new' regionalism been characterized by political entities that are multidimensional in scope, but it has also led to more complex forms of regional organization than have been previously seen. In the case of the EU, as already noted, the 'unbundling' of territoriality has led to a multi-layered system of rule, incorporating state and substate, public and private, transnational and supranational actors in a complex web of regional governance. Elsewhere the emergence of EPZs, growth triangles, development corridors and dynamic 'micro-states', such as Singapore and Hong Kong, are suggestive of more complex patterns of regionalism developing in other areas as well (Hettne and Söderbaum, 1998). For this reason, a growing number of scholars are beginning to pick up on the term 'microregionalism' as a way of thinking about modes of regionalist governance that involve cross-border integration between geographically contiguous spaces below the level of the state (Breslin and Hook, 2002).

All in all, this brief survey of the nature and character of 'new' regionalism suggests that it is a complex and multi-dimensional phenomenon that defies many of the theoretical categories that traditional discourses have devised in order to account for regional integration. Thus the approach to regionalism that is adopted in subsequent chapters sees it as a part of the emerging world order in so far as it constitutes a response to the consequences of economic globalization and the reconfiguration of state-society relations inherent in this process. To put it another way, regionalism now constitutes a multi-layered, formal and informal, mode of governance that incorporates both public and private actors and increasingly operates across a range of spatial levels - microregional, subregional and macroregional - in complex networks of varying degrees of horizontal and vertical density.

Conclusion

The purpose of this chapter has been to introduce and review critically theories of international political economy. In the process, a number of deficiencies within mainstream approaches have been noted which render them inappropriate tools with which to address the research questions in hand. Specifically, mainstream IPE has largely abandoned the ideas of transnationalism and interdependence, which originally enframed the discipline, and has instead favoured a statist form of political economy, derived from hegemonic stability theory and Waltzian neo-realism, satisfied with examining the rational actions of states within the structural confines of international anarchy. As a rejection of the myopic nature of this literature, we have chosen, instead, to embrace 'new' IPE. This approach, as has been argued, offers several advantages over mainstream approaches. Specifically, the advantages centre on the preference for 'critical theory' over 'problem-solving' theory in so far as the former is concerned with structural change and the possibility of envisaging alternative world orders, while the latter offers a more or less static analysis of the international system. Additionally, it has also been observed that the neo-Gramscian conception of hegemony introduced by Cox offers a considerably more nuanced approach to the question of power in the global political economy.

Perhaps more importantly, however, the 'new' IPE approach pioneered by Cox has enabled us to develop an open-ended and eclectic mode of enquiry. This was clearly shown in the third section of the chapter which introduced three key debates - production, development and governance - of direct relevance to our present investigation. To reiterate briefly, the key points made with regard to these were as follows. First, in relation to production, even though the original NIDL thesis itself is exposed to charges of economism and functionalism, the notion of a new spatial division of labour offers us a useful way of conceptualising TNCs and their global sourcing strategies. Second, in relation to development, it is clear that development theory is now increasingly taking globalization seriously, with some analysts going so far as to seek to effect a convergence with 'new' IPE. Third, in relation to governance, this notion has enabled us to move away from the out-dated idea of rival 'economic blocs' and, instead, to think of 'new' regionalism as an emerging form of multi-layered governance, linked to the dynamics of the global political economy. In sum, then, this framework, developed from the 'new' IPE literature and drawing specifically from these three literatures, shall serve to enframe our study of the restructuring of the global apparel industry and its implications for the new political economy of US-Caribbean relations. It is to this specific study that we now turn.

Notes

1 There were, of course, numerous exceptions to this tendency. See, among others, Russett (1985); Strange (1987); and Nye (1990).

2 Curiously, this was a point on which Keohane and Nye (1977) had earlier criticized realists.

3 Keohane (1984: 137) provides a partial exception to this by speaking of security as a 'prestige good', but then proceeds to explicitly eschew consideration of military-economic linkage, suggesting that geopolitics does not 'impinge directly' on the political economy of advanced industrialized countries.

4 David Baldwin (1993: 4-11) identifies six areas of debate: the nature and consequences of anarchy; international cooperation; relative versus absolute gains; priority of state goals; intentions versus capabilities; and institutions and regimes.

5 The term 'new political economy' is sometimes used to describe the application of the methods and assumptions of economics to politics. It is important to note this usage shares little in common with 'new' IPE, which is clearly founded on quite different theoretical and methodological assumptions. Cf. Caporaso and Levine (1996); and Gamble (1995).

6 It is worth noting that Cox's usage of the term 'neo-liberal' deviates significantly for the ways in which it is more usually employed. For this reason, Ruggie's notion of 'embedded liberalism', which captures the essence of Cox's sentiment, is preferred.

7 Peter Burnham (1999: 37) extends this criticism to include 'new' (or 'heterodox', as he calls it) IPE more generally.

8 For a critique of this literature, see Radice (2000).

9 Useful illustrations of this type of organizational structure can be found in Hill (1989); and Henderson (1989).

Chapter Two

United States-Caribbean Economic Relations Since 1945

Introduction

The purpose of this chapter is to use the framework developed in the previous chapter as the theoretical basis for an alternative reading of the history of United States-Caribbean economic relations since 1945. At the same time the chapter also introduces the specific research questions which shall be fully investigated in subsequent chapters. It begins, in broadly conventional fashion, by describing the significance attached to the Caribbean by the US during the Cold War in geo-political terms (i.e. the need to prevent foreign powers encroaching into its 'sphere of influence'). At this point, it departs from the conventional view by seeking to identify, not simply the material basis of US-Caribbean relations during this period, but also its ideological aspects. Drawing upon neo-Gramscian insights, it demonstrates the extent to which US policy towards the Caribbean during the Cold War was not primarily governed by the fear of foreign invasion, but by the need to use the Caribbean as a 'measure' of the wider manifestations of US global hegemony. Accordingly, it is argued that the ideological significance of the region as a whole during this period came to outweigh the actual strategic importance of even the sum of individual Caribbean states. In turn, it is demonstrated how this perception largely shaped the conduct of US policy towards the region during this time as well as setting the political parameters inside which the policies of individual Caribbean states were necessarily conceived.

On this basis, the second section of this chapter is devoted to the more specific task of examining the impact of the so-called Caribbean Basin Initiative (CBI), which was launched by the US in 1982. The importance of the CBI, it is argued, lay not only with its economic proposals, which were generally designed to integrate the Caribbean more tightly with the US economy, but, more fundamentally, it also acted as a symbolic (though nonetheless highly effective) instrument for the promotion of a 'solution' to the problems of social and economic underdevelopment in the region. In this way the CBI - along with the broader set of economic measures implemented by an array of US and international agencies during the 1980s - facilitated the development of the economic agenda that subsequently emerged in the region after the ending of the Cold War.

This new economic agenda is the subject of the third and final section of the chapter. In addition to supporting the claims already made, this section describes how since the ending of the Cold War the US has increasingly promoted the idea of hemispheric free trade as a means to counter its declining influence in shaping the wider international trading order. At the same time, it is argued that this course of action also constitutes an acknowledgement of a process of 'silent integration' which has been taking place in the hemisphere for some time, and has served to bind Mexico and some - though not all - Caribbean states closer to the US. On the basis of these arguments, a further issue is then introduced: namely, what role is this regionalization of economic activity playing in the integration of the political economies of the Caribbean and the US? This is then explored more fully in subsequent chapters through an examination of the North America apparel industry and the practice of offshore production in the Caribbean.

The United States and the Caribbean, 1945-1989

In many ways, it can be argued that the United States has attempted to pursue a consistent series of political, strategic and economic objectives in the Caribbean since the days of the Monroe Doctrine. The means of achieving these ends have, admittedly, varied enormously, ranging from the 'big stick' diplomacy of Theodore Roosevelt to the 'dollar diplomacy' of William Howard Taft, to the system of 'protectorates' established by Woodrow Wilson to the 'good neighbour policy' of Franklin D. Roosevelt. In each case, however, the underlying motive has remained more or less constant: namely, to prevent any extra-hemispheric powers encroaching into what the US has always proclaimed to be its legitimate 'sphere of influence' in the Caribbean. In this sense, we can suggest that US policy toward the Caribbean during the Cold War was similarly governed by the need to prevent foreign powers, specifically the Soviet Union, from gaining a foothold in its immediate 'backyard'.

From our perspective, however, the Monroe Doctrine is insufficient in itself to able to account for the increased significance that the US attached to the Caribbean during the Cold War. After 1945, as is by now widely acknowledged, the US assumed a position of global hegemony, and was thus largely responsible for the creation and maintenance of the liberal international economic order, on the one hand, and the 'containment' of communism wherever it arose, on the other. For this reason, the significance of the Caribbean during the Cold War stretched far beyond its own shores, as the US came to perceive its own standing as a 'hegemonic power' to be dependent in some measure on its capacity to maintain and demonstrate control in its own backyard (Payne, 1994: 157-8). To put it another way, as Sutton (1988: 41) has done, the primary significance of the Caribbean to the US during the Cold War was 'political - as proof of American power'. The Caribbean mattered, Sutton argued, 'because of what it represents to the people of the US and to the outside world...a belief that if the US cannot deal effectively with events in its own sphere of influence it will not deal effectively with events elsewhere'.

From this perspective, it becomes easier to appreciate the considerable importance which the US attached to the Caribbean during the Cold War, particularly after the Cuban Revolution of 1959, which constituted - at least in the eyes of US policy makers - a direct ideological challenge to the US in its 'backyard'. In the aftermath of the Cuban Revolution successive US administrations thus sought to prevent, by whatever means possible, the extension of the Cuban model to other Caribbean states. In 1965 President Johnson sent 23,000 US marines to the Dominican Republic to prevent the return to power of the democratically elected president, Juan Bosch, precisely in order to avoid a 'second Cuba' in the Caribbean (Lowenthal, 1972). A similar motive lay behind US covert action in British Guiana in 1963, which prevented the return to power of Cheddi Jagan, and attempts to destabilize Michael Manley's Jamaica during the 1970s. Even the more modulated approach of Jimmy Carter (1976-1980), which initially attempted to promote human rights and ideological pluralism in the region, ultimately failed to escape the exigencies of the Cold War and by the time of the 1980 presidential election his administration stood charged with having 'lost' for the 'West' Nicaragua and Grenada, both of which had experienced socialist revolutions the previous year.

When Ronald Reagan assumed the American presidency at the beginning of the 1980s he immediately set himself the task of reasserting US power and international standing after a decade of perceived decline. From his point of view, nowhere was this task seen as more urgently required that in Central America and the Caribbean. Arguably, more than any other US president, Reagan understood the importance of political 'stability' in the Caribbean as a measure of US hegemony elsewhere. As Reagan himself declared in 1983, 'if we cannot defend our selves [in the Caribbean Basin], we cannot expect to prevail elsewhere. Our credibility would collapse, our alliances would crumble, and the safety of our homeland would be put in jeopardy' (cited in Pastor, 1992: 32). This rationale helps to explain the extent of US military involvement in the Caribbean Basin, which led to the militarization of much of the Central American isthmus in the early 1980s and the actual invasion of Grenada in the Caribbean. The invasion of Grenada in October 1983 was particularly revealing of the political rationale behind Reagan's overall strategy in the region. After all, as Payne (1994: 63) has observed, if an island the size of Grenada 'could successfully pursue its chosen revolutionary course, what might be achieved by larger states in the region?' From this perspective, President Reagan clearly recognized that the significance of Grenada was far greater than its best-known export of nutmeg. 'It is not nutmeg that is at stake down there', Reagan declared in March 1983, 'it is the United States' national security' (cited in Payne, 1994: 63). As we shall see shortly, though, Reagan's strategy was not confined to the military sphere: with the launching of the so-called Caribbean Basin Initiative (CBI) in 1982, Reagan set forth a programme which claimed to address economic, as well as political and military, activities within a single policy framework. Before discussing the CBI in more depth, however, it is first necessary to take a brief look at the different development strategies pursued in the Caribbean up until this point.

US Hegemony and Caribbean Development Alternatives, 1945-1980

The development experience of the Caribbean during the post-war period was not only shaped by its geographical proximity to the US, but, more fundamentally, by its peripheral location in the world economy that had been established during the first wave of European colonialism in the seventeenth century. From this time onwards the Caribbean found itself heavily reliant on an economic system based on the production and export of agricultural commodities (Grugel, 1995). In the 1950s and 1960s, therefore, when the notion of 'development' gradually began to enter the vocabulary of elites in the independent, and, in the case of the English-speaking Caribbean soon-to-be independent, Caribbean territories the primary concern was how to overcome the region's longstanding reliance on an agro-export model of development. The dilemma for individual Caribbean governments, however, was to find a method for achieving this within the political parameters that US global hegemony had necessarily established.

The Dominican Republic and Haiti. In the case of the independent territories of the Dominican Republic and Haiti (and Cuba prior to 1959), economic development in the post-war period was, clearly, shaped by the *de facto* sovereignty which was exercised by the US after its occupation of these territories in the inter-war period. In the light of the subsequent developments in both the Dominican Republic and Haiti, the most important consequence of the US occupation was in terms of military organization (Lundahl, 1992). In both countries the reorganization of the military led to the replacement of the various regional armies with national constabularies, and thus facilitated the rise to power of the dictatorships of Trujillo and Duvalier respectively. In the case of the Dominican Republic, Trujillo's rise to power was facilitated by the newly established *Guardia Nacional Dominicana*, which enabled him to exercise absolute control over all aspects - social, economic and political - of Dominican life for over three decades (1930-1961). On this basis, the Dominican Republic pursued a model of economic development that was ostensibly nationalist in orientation, but, in practice, remained heavily tied to the US economy, particularly through its main export crop of sugar. At the same time, however, Trujillo's 'nationalist' economic strategy also enabled the dictator and his family to dominate the Dominican economy, controlling an estimated 50 to 60 per cent of all land on the island, and up to 80 per cent of all trade in the Santo Domingo area (Lundahl, 1992: 300). Upon Trujillo's assassination in 1961 the US, once again, became heavily involved in the Dominican Republic, culminating in its second occupation of the island. In addition to direct military involvement, US aid to the island also grew considerably in this period: during the 1960s, under the Alliance for Progress, the Dominican Republic received US$795 million worth of economic aid - 21 per cent of the total allotted for the Caribbean and Central America (Deere *et al.*, 1990: 127).

As with Trujillo, the dictatorship of François - 'Papa Doc' - Duvalier articulated a nationalist-orientated economic strategy at the same time as attempting to effect a closer economic integration of the island with the US. In essence, this strategy combined attempts to transform Haiti into a 'second Puerto

Rico' (see below), through such measures as tax exemptions, low wages and the suppression of independent labour organizations and the banning of strikes, with a black nationalist ideology intent on marginalizing the island's mulatto elite (Dupuy, 1989). In practice, however, this 'nationalist' ideology merely served the personal aggrandisement of the Duvalier family at the expense of impoverishment of the majority of the Haitian population. The precise tactics for this enrichment were many and varied over time, ranging from the diversion of taxation and foreign aid receipts to extortion, theft and appropriation of property owned by those suspected to be in opposition to the Duvalier regime (Dupuy, 1989). All in all, it is estimated that the Duvalier regime appropriated between US$100 million and US$150 million between 1957 and 1971, while the Haitian economy as a whole stagnated. Moreover, upon Papa Doc's death, the Duvalier family intensified these practices of enrichment - so much so that, by the time that his son, 'Baby Doc', was ousted, the family fortune stood at approximately US$1.6 billion, a figure roughly approximating Haiti's total GDP in 1984 (Lundahl, 1992: 302).

Puerto Rico. As with the Dominican Republic and Haiti, the development path chosen by Puerto Rico after 1945 was overwhelmingly determined by its subordinate relationship to the US. Unlike these countries, however, which had gained formal independence from Spain and France respectively in the nineteenth century, Puerto Rico remained a colony after 1898 when it was ceded to the US by Spain as part of the 'spoils of war'. Despite this, the autonomy of the Puerto Rican state was strengthened after 1945 through the negotiation of 'Associated Statehood', which provided the political basis for its industrialization programme known as 'Operation Bootstrap'. In essence, this strategy sought to tie the island more closely with the US economy through the creation of a 'favourable' investment climate for US corporations, including such measures as low wages; minimum wage exemptions; tax exemptions, including exemptions on US and local corporation taxes, income tax, municipal taxes, licence fees and property taxes; duty-free entry to the US market; and infrastructural provision administered by, among others, the Puerto Rican Economic Development Agency, *Formento* (Deere *et al.*, 1990: 129; see also Dietz, 1986). On the basis of these incentives, Puerto Rico recorded impressive economic growth throughout the 1950s: between 1951 and 1960 gross national product grew annually by 5.3 per cent, while at the same time average real wages of industrial workers grew by 90 per cent (Pantojas-García, 1985: 116-7). Nevertheless, by the early 1960s 'Operation Bootstrap' was already beginning to show signs of exhaustion. In fact, despite the impressive growth achieved during the 1950s, at no time was industrial employment sufficient to offset the rate of agricultural labour-force displacement, which meant unemployment remained consistently above 10 per cent for the entire post-war period, despite the out-migration of an estimated 50,000 Puerto Rican citizens every year. The Puerto Rican model also failed to develop the type of technology transfer and industrial upgrading that the island's political elite had envisaged, as the majority of industrial investment failed to make the necessary linkages with the local manufacturing sector and US firms continued to supply the bulk of the raw materials and capital goods. In fact, throughout the post-1945 period, Puerto Rico remained dependent on US sources for 90 per cent of its manufacturing investment (Pantojas-García, 1985).

The English-speaking Caribbean. Despite these problems, economic planners in the neighbouring English-speaking Caribbean attempted to replicate the 'successes' of the Puerto Rican model in the 1950s and 1960s through their own policies of industrialization, which came to be known, somewhat disdainfully, as 'industrialization by invitation' (Girvan and Jefferson, 1971). The idea of 'industrialization by invitation' is usually associated with the work of the St. Lucian-born economist W. Arthur Lewis, who argued that an industrialization strategy similar to that of Puerto Rico offered the region a means to overcome its longstanding dependence on the production and export of primary commodities, especially sugar (Lewis, 1949; 1950). Accordingly, what followed was an attempt to replicate many of the features of the Puerto Rican model, including the provision of infrastructural services and other investment incentives alongside the establishment of industrial development corporations and development banks (Thomas, 1987: Ch. 5). On the surface, the cumulative effect of these measures was, again, highly impressive: by 1967 manufacturing activity accounted for as much as 16 per cent of gross national product in Trinidad, while in Jamaica, Guyana and Barbados the figures stood at 15 per cent, 13 per cent and 9 per cent respectively (Payne and Sutton, 2001: 4). On closer inspection, however, much of the growth in manufacturing activity in the English-speaking Caribbean in this period was either restricted to assembly industries, wherein foreign firms provided the bulk of raw materials and capital goods, or goods with a higher local value added simply failed to penetrate major export markets. In contrast to the early experience of Puerto Rico, the export-orientated model envisaged by Lewis was never fully established in the English-speaking Caribbean and local firms generally preferred to take advantage of the region's relatively high tariff barriers by producing for the domestic market. In the case of Jamaica, which experienced among the highest levels of industrialization in this period, it has been estimated that only 40 of the 130 firms established between 1950 and 1964 were net exporters. A similar pattern was also noticeable in other parts of the English-speaking Caribbean, to the extent that by 1970 the export of manufactured goods constituted only 4.4 per cent of total production in the English-speaking Caribbean (Deere *et al.*, 1990: 130).

By the mid 1960s, the failure of 'industrialization by invitation' to provide the kind of spectacular results that had, at least initially, been experienced in neighbouring Puerto Rico prompted elites in the English-speaking Caribbean to move towards a strategy of economic integration. The intellectual foundations for this decision were laid in the mid 1960s by William Demas, the then head of the Economic Planning Division of the government of Trinidad, who argued that the failure of 'industrialization by invitation' - both in terms of reducing unemployment and in maximising the use of local resources - could largely be attributed to the relatively small size of the Caribbean islands (Demas, 1965). For this reason, Demas advocated a strategy of regional economic integration, wherein the creation of a custom union among the entire English-speaking Caribbean would enhance market opportunities for manufacturing goods, while also helping to stimulate investment in new industries. Largely on the basis of this thinking, the Caribbean Free Trade Association (CARIFTA) was established in 1968, with the expressed purpose of liberalising intra-regional trade. What followed was a period of impressive intra-CARIFTA trade, particularly in the area of manufactured goods. By 1972, 34 per cent of Trinidad's manufacturing exports were destined for other CARIFTA members, while the figures for Jamaica, Barbados and Guyana stood at 49 per cent, 40 per cent and 66 per cent respectively (Payne and Sutton, 2001: 6). Nevertheless, in the final analysis, because of the particular form of industrialization on which much of this trade rested, the value added in the region remained relatively small. In fact, because of the peculiar rules of origin contained within the CARIFTA agreement, much of the manufacturing activity which constituted intra-CARIFTA trade was made up of goods that were *not* manufactured in the region, but were deemed as such in order to provide the necessary inputs for already established manufacturing industries (Deere *et al.*, 1990). Because of this, Demas was ultimately forced to admit that, despite the impressive growth in intra-CARIFTA trade, regional integration did not prove to be 'all that beneficial to the member countries who [were] exporting' (cited in Payne and Sutton, 2001: 4). For this reason, the Commonwealth Caribbean Regional Secretariat, the administrative agency established to oversee the integration movement, advocated the 'deepening' of CARIFTA, leading to the formation of the Caribbean Community and Common Market (CARICOM) in 1973. Elsewhere, however, under the auspices of the so-called New World Group of the University of the West Indies (UWI), an altogether different prognosis of the failure of post-war Caribbean development was already being articulated. It is to this work to which we now turn.

The Dependency Critique

In 1971, Lloyd Best published an article in a volume dedicated to Caribbean dependency writings that sought to review the policy prescriptions offered by Demas. In this work Best argued that Demas's analysis, as well as the subsequent policies which were adopted, suffered from a basic fallacy in so far as it focused almost exclusively on 'natural' variables, such as size, while 'societal', and therefore 'manipulable', policy variables were all but overlooked (Best, 1971). In Best's view, Demas had manifestly failed to demonstrate that 'smallness necessarily places economies at a disadvantage in the exploitation of their own "endowment" of resources' (Best, 1971: 29). What was therefore required was a mode of analysis derived from 'systematic examination of the instruments that control' Caribbean economies (Best, 1971: 31). For this purpose, Best and other members of the New World Group turned to the concept of economic dependency. Although clearly drawing sustenance from the earlier structuralist and neo-Marxist arguments developed in neighbouring Latin America and elsewhere (O'Brien, 1975; Palma, 1978), the unique character of the Caribbean dependency school lay in its elaboration of what came to be known as the theory of the plantation economy. As initially developed by Best, in collaboration with Karl Levitt (1969), this theory traced the development of the plantation economy in the Caribbean through three distinct phases: (1) 'pure plantation economy' (1600-1838); (2) 'plantation economy modified' (1838-1938); and (3) 'plantation economy further modified' (1938 onwards). In so doing, Best and Levitt drew attention to the fact that, despite high rates of economic growth in the latter period, many features of the 'pure plantation economy' system were in fact being replicated. Despite the prominent role played by the state in most of the major economic initiatives developed in the post-1945 period (e.g. bauxite, petroleum and tourism), the defining feature of Caribbean development remained the high level of foreign ownership and control.

Following the pioneering work of Best and Levitt, other members of the New World Group produced a host of theoretical refinements and case studies, all loosely based around the theory of the plantation economy (Beckford, 1972; Girvan, 1971; Jefferson, 1972).[1] Taken collectively, this work undeniably provided a powerful critique of the condition of economic dependency in the region and of the development strategies that Caribbean governments had pursued. Nevertheless, the Caribbean dependency school was not without its problems. Like the *dependentistas* in neighbouring Latin America, it was vulnerable to the criticism that it had exaggerated the degree of 'exceptionalism' experienced by Caribbean societies in relation to social, political and economic characteristics of other societies, both developing and developed (Oxaal, 1975). Apart from anything else, this weakness pointed to a more fundamental problem with the dependency work of the New World Group, which was identified by Courtney Blackman, the then Governor of the Central Bank of Barbados and former member of the New World Group, in March 1980. As Blackman put it, the New World Group had failed to delineate 'an operational model of economic development..."likely to succeed in real world conditions"' (cited in Payne and Sutton, 2001: 6).

In the context of the 1970s and early 1980s, these 'real world conditions' amounted to a severe economic crisis in the region fuelled by the activity of the Organization of Petroleum Exporting Countries (OPEC), which effectively quadrupled the price for oil during the Arab-Israeli war of 1973. In these circumstances some Caribbean countries, notably the authoritarian and semi-authoritarian governments of Haiti and the Dominican Republic respectively, persisted with the traditional agro-export model of development, whereas others chose to pursue 'radical' economic strategies that, to a greater or lesser extent, drew upon the theoretical work of the New World Group. In 1970 the government of Forbes Burnham committed Guyana to a programme of 'co-operative socialism'; in Jamaica Michael Manley took the similar step in 1974 by announcing his country's attachment to the principles of 'democratic socialism'; while in the tiny island of Grenada Maurice Bishop's New Jewel Movement (NJM), which seized power from the corrupt regime of Eric Gairy in March 1979, attempted to implement a 'non-capitalist' development strategy. In all of these cases, however, the end result highlighted the problematical nature of implementing radical development options in the context of an increasingly hostile geo-economic and geo-political external climate. In Jamaica's case, Michael Manley suffered electoral defeat to pro-US Edward Seaga in 1980 against a backdrop of rising social unrest and political violence at home and barely concealed hostility from the United States and the International Monetary Fund abroad (Kaufman, 1985; Stephens and Stephens, 1986; Payne, 1988); in Guyana 'co-operative socialism' simply turned into a vehicle for the aggrandisement of the ruling elite (Thomas, 1984); finally, the Grenadian Revolution ended in an internecine power struggle within the leadership of the NJM, leading to the execution of Bishop and three of his ministers and the subsequent US military invasion (Heine, 1990). The collapse of the Grenadian Revolution, more than any other single event of that time, symbolized the ending of the 'radical' phase in Caribbean development thinking; significantly, it also coincided with the launching of President Reagan's Caribbean Basin Initiative (CBI), which is discussed below.

The Caribbean Basin Initiative (CBI)

President Reagan officially launched the CBI in his address to the Organization of American States (OAS) on 24 January 1982. In his address Reagan set out a series of innovative trade and investment measures for designated Caribbean states that would, in his words, allow these countries to 'earn their own way towards self-sustaining growth' (cited in Griffith, 1990: 33). During the late 1970s and early 1980s increasing political instability in the wider Caribbean Basin - which had manifested itself in the success of the New Jewel Movement in Grenada in 1979, but also in the Sandinista revolution in Nicaragua, as well as the subsequent growth of revolutionary movements in El Salvador and Guatemala - became intimately linked with the virtual collapse of economic growth in the region. The CBI therefore constituted a belated acknowledgement on the part of the Reagan administration that improving the region's economic performance was central to defusing the perceived security threat posed by the adoption of radical development strategies (previously discussed) in a number of Caribbean countries (Newfarmer, 1985).

     As originally set out by President Reagan, the key elements of the CBI were: (1) the granting of duty-free treatment for eligible items from designated Caribbean Basin states for a twelve-year period; (2) the granting of an additional US$350 million in emergency aid; and (3) the provision of incentives for US corporations investing in the region in the form of a 10 per cent tax credit. Of these proposals, clearly it was the provisions relating to duty-free treatment for Caribbean goods that promised to be the most significant. Nevertheless, in the first instance, it was those aspects of the CBI relating to emergency aid which proved the more controversial. Of US$350 million initially requested, US$128 million was to be allocated to support the right-wing government in El Salvador, while the islands of the insular Caribbean and Belize would have received only 33 per cent of the total. In the end, the requested US$350 million of emergency aid was approved by Congress as the 'Caribbean Basin Economic Revitalization Act of 1982', with El Salvador's share being reduced to US$100 million and that of the insular Caribbean and Belize rising somewhat to 39 per cent. The two remaining components of the original CBI proposal were passed, with significant modification, as a separate piece of legislation, the precise content of which is discussed below.

The Caribbean Basin Economic Recovery Act (CBERA)

The CBERA, which was signed into law by President Reagan on 5 August 1983, granted duty-free treatment to some 6,000 designated products, as well as offering a series of tax-related measures designed to encourage US investment in the region. In essence, the rationale behind the CBERA was built on securing political stability in the region through closer economic integration with the US. In the process, the CBERA also sought to improve the international competitive position of US industries facing deteriorating world market share through the encouragement of 'twin-plant' operations, including those located in Puerto Rico.[2] In practice, however, the means for achieving these ends were severely compromised from the start by a series of exemptions from duty-free treatment, including textiles and apparel, footwear, luggage, leather goods, canned tuna, and petroleum and its derivatives. Moreover, the measures relating to tax provisions, which were originally seen as providing much of the resource-generating potential of the CBI proposals, were also severely diluted during the Congressional bargaining process (Newfarmer, 1985). Nevertheless, as we shall see, despite the relative modesty of the CBERA package as it was ultimately enacted, these measures were still sufficient to re-orientate the Caribbean in a direction more consistent with wider US interests and goals.

In order to be considered eligible for the CBERA programme, potential beneficiaries first had to conform to a series of criteria which reflected the central tenets of Reaganite political economy. Specifically, in order to qualify the CBERA required, among other things, that: (1) the country was not run by a communist regime; (2) that the country had not nationalized, expropriated, or otherwise seized US property without adequate compensation; (3) that the country did not provide preferential treatment to products of developed countries that were likely to have significant adverse effects on US commerce; (4) that the beneficiary county agreed to provide reasonable access to its markets and basic commodity resources to the US; and (5) that certain limits be observed in the degree to which a beneficiary country used export subsidies or imposed export performance requirements or local content requirements that could distort international trade. Significantly, however, the US president could waive any of these requirements if such action was deemed to be in the interests of national or economic security (Anduze, 1990).

Beyond this, eligibility for CBERA preferences was also governed by a series of more specific requirements relating to local content rules. In order to qualify for duty-free treatment, the CBERA required that eligible items 'must either be wholly grown, produced, or manufactured in one or more CBERA country or be "new or different" articles made from substantially transformed non-CBERA inputs in order to receive duty-free entry into the United States' (USITC, 1998: 3). In order to meet this criteria the CBERA stipulated that at least 35 per cent of the direct processing costs and materials produced must be the result of economic activity in one or more CBERA country. Additionally, in an attempt to encourage 'twin-plant' operations between CBERA beneficiaries and Puerto Rico, the CBERA also allowed duty-free entry for articles produced in Puerto Rico that were 'by any means advanced in value or improved in condition' in a CBERA country (USITC, 1998: 3). Finally, and perhaps most crucially, the CBERA allowed up to 15 per cent of the required 35 per cent minimum to be accounted for by the value of US-made materials. In other words, the local content requirement stood at only 20 per cent of the appraised value of the article, provided that an additional 15 per cent of the value came from US-made materials. In the end, then, the most significant aspect of the CBERA local content requirements was the extent to which they were geared towards enhancing the competitive position of US firms (by reducing the production costs of foreign affiliates located in the Caribbean), rather than offering the Caribbean a genuine platform for the export of goods to the US with a high local value added component.

In terms of the specific product categories eligible for duty-free treatment, what is perhaps most revealing about the CBERA in this regard is the extent to which many of these items already enjoyed duty-free treatment prior to the enactment of the CBERA.[3] For instance, under the terms of the General System of Preferences (GSP), which since 1974 has authorized the US president to grant duty-free treatment to exports from selected developing countries, approximately one third of the products covered by the CBERA were already eligible for duty-free treatment.[4] Similarly, product categories eligible for the duty-free provisions under the CBERA also qualified for preferential treatment provided by section 807 of the US tax code, which permitted duty exemption of the value of US-made components that were returned as part of articles assembled abroad (see USITC, 1997). As already indicated, the CBERA also statutorily excluded a number of important Caribbean export categories from the potential benefits of free trade. According to Deere *et al.* (1990: 160), of the fifteen leading product categories from the region, accounting for over 70 per cent of trade with the US, only four were awarded some new exception from tariffs and only one, beef, was granted full duty-free access. Moreover, the level of existing tariffs on these products had previously been as low as 2.6 per cent, rendering the potential benefit from the duty-free provisions relatively minor. All told, Pantojas-García (1991: 33) estimates that a mere seven per cent of Caribbean exports to the US were granted new duty-free access through the CBERA programme. Also, significantly, it has been pointed out that, even in these areas, the major beneficiaries of the programme were likely to be US firms operating in the Caribbean, given that seven of the twelve leading product categories eligible for tariff eliminations were ones where the foreign affiliates of US firms provided the bulk of Caribbean exports (Newfarmer, 1985). Overall, though, the main problem with the CBERA as a means of enhancing Caribbean export growth lay in the fact that the product categories with the greatest potential for expansion were precisely those items which were excluded from duty-free treatment: namely, sugar and apparel.[5]

Sugar. Although the CBERA nominally afforded duty-free treatment to sugar, in practice, its eligibility was severely restricted by quotas and other regulations from the US Department of Agriculture (USDA).[6] In the 1975 to 1981 period, US sugar policy had been governed by a relatively liberal trade regime, as a result of the high commodity prices prevailing in the world market in this period (Hemstad, 1991). However, as world prices for sugar worsened in the early 1980s the US administration took a series of dramatic steps in order to protect domestic producers. First, as part of the 'Agriculture and Food Act of 1981', steps were taken to provide a guaranteed price for domestic raw sugar (initially set at 19.08 cents per pound, subsequently raised to 19.88 cents per pound in mid 1982), while import tariffs were increased by 185 per cent over the 1981 level (Newfarmer, 1985). Second, when these measures failed to halt the worsening value of sugar on world markets in the early 1980s, the administration imposed a quota system for the first time since 1974, which restricted the volume of Caribbean sugar exports entering the US market. Third, the 'Food Security Act of 1985' extended these provisions for a further five years, while also decreeing that the sugar programme be run at 'no cost' to the US Treasury, thus shielding the price support system from budget cuts it might have otherwise faced (Hemstad, 1990).

The cumulative effect of these measures on the Caribbean sugar industry was considerable. With the exception of oil and coffee, sugar constituted the single largest export from the CBI region in the 1980-82 period, accounting for between US$300 and US$500 million annually in exports to the US (Newfarmer, 1990: 71). However, as a result of the changes in US sugar policy outlined above, the sugar quotas for the CBI region as a whole were reduced from an average annual of 1.6 million tons in the 1979-81 period to 260,000 tons by December 1987. Likewise, in the first four years of the operation of the CBERA (1984-88), 78 per cent quota reductions cut potential sugar export earnings by approximately US$500 million. The Dominican Republic, which accounted for 46 per cent of the Caribbean Basin sugar quota in the 1980s, was the major casualty, losing approximately US$210 million in potential export earnings between 1984 and 1987 (Deere *et al.*, 1990: 161). All in all, what this meant for the Caribbean as a whole was that whatever gains may have been achieved in manufacturing and other non-traditional exports through the CBERA were overwhelmed by losses in potential export revenues from sugar.

Apparel. Unlike sugar, apparel was formally excluded from the duty-free provisions of the CBERA. In part, this was due to international obligations under the terms of the Multi-Fibre Arrangement (MFA), which has regulated the international textiles and apparel trade since 1974 (see Chapter Four). As originally conceived, the MFA was intended to create an 'orderly' development of trade in textiles and apparel through a gradual opening-up of developed country markets to exports from developing countries (originally set at an average annual growth rate of 6 per cent). In practice, however, subsequent renewals of the MFA (in 1977, 1982, 1986, and 1991) served to place increasingly restrictive quotas on most of the leading developing country exporters. In the Caribbean, these restrictions manifested themselves in a series of bilateral quotas between the US and the majority of CBERA beneficiary countries, in addition to import tariffs in the range of 25 per cent. As a consequence, the CBERA denied the Caribbean preferential market access in an area with perhaps the greatest potential for export growth. According to one estimate, had these products been eligible for duty-free treatment, trade-related benefits to the region through the CBERA would have increased by 285 per cent (Newfarmer, 1985: 73).

Despite all of this, in the 1980s the Caribbean took substantial advantage of provisions contained within section 807 of the US tax code (it has since been replaced by the Harmonized Tariff Schedule [HTS] 9802.00), which, as indicated, permitted duty exemption of the value of US-made components that were returned as part of articles assembled abroad. Although the 807/9802.00 tax regime was initially developed outside of, and prior to, the CBI, the two schemes were later linked through the Special Access Programme (SAP, but known as 807A), which was established in 1986. The 807A tax regime created relatively generous quotas for CBERA beneficiaries, in addition to those provided by the terms of the MFA, in an attempt to encourage 'production sharing' operations between US clothing firms and Caribbean assembly operations. The impact of these measures on Caribbean textile and apparel exports to the US has, on the surface, been impressive: during the 1980s the export of apparel from the Dominican Republic, Haiti and Jamaica grew annually by more than 20 per cent. In the Dominican Republic itself (the region's leading exporter apparel to the US) this growth was even more spectacular: in 1988 apparel constituted no less than 78 per cent of total manufacturing exports, worth a total of US$183.8 million, and representing an increase of 333.4 per cent since 1981 (Safa, 1994: 251). Still, as we shall see, on closer inspection these gains were not as impressive as initially appeared to be the case. First, it needs to be recalled that, unlike CBERA-eligible items, Caribbean textile and apparel exports were *still* dutiable on the value added in the region, thus leading to the active discouragement of garment exports with a high local value added (Steele, 1988). Second, because of this tendency, the impressive growth in Caribbean textile and apparel exports to the US in 1980s was insufficient to offset the loss of export revenue from traditional commodities, such as sugar (Deere and Melendez, 1992).

In summary, the CBERA manifestly failed to halt the decline in the Caribbean's share of US imports during the 'lost decade' of the 1980s: as the value of US imports increased by 50 per cent between 1984 and 1990, CBERA country exports to the US declined by 13 per cent (Rosenberg and Hiskey, 1994). The reason for this lay, primarily, with the fact that the product categories with the greatest potential for export growth, such as sugar and apparel, were precisely those items statutorily excluded from duty-free entitlement. In addition to this, the original proposal regarding a 10 per cent tax credit for US companies investing in the region, which was envisaged as providing much of the resource-generating potential of the programme, was also omitted from the CBERA as it was ultimately enacted. Instead, the tax investment credit was replaced with tax deductions for business conventions held in the Caribbean, the impact of which, it was claimed by critics at the time, was likely to be more tourist spending than actual industrial investment (Pantojas-García, 1985). Overall, then, to cite a 1988 US General Accounting Office (GAO) report, the trade and investment resulting from the CBERA has 'not been sufficient to generate broadly based economic growth, alleviate debt-serving problems, or create lasting employment' (cited in Anduze, 1990: 190).

In the wider sense, however, despite the obvious flaws in its economic provisions, the CBI served an important political function. As a number of commentators have observed, the CBI, in essence, sought to replicate Puerto Rico's 'Operation Bootstrap' by offering a favourable climate for US investors in exchange for duty-free treatment (Watson, 1982; Pantojas-García, 1985). As such, the notion of the CBI as a 'non-reciprocal' trade agreement is misleading, given the high level of political and economic conditionality which was required in order to qualify for the duty-free benefits of the CBERA. The CBI, from this perspective, can be seen as part of the broader set of macroeconomic and financial strategies implemented by an array of US and international agencies - including the United States Agency for International Development (AID), the International Monetary Fund (IMF) and the World Bank - in the region during the 1980s. In essence, these agencies sought to implement the by now familiar policy prescriptions associated with the so-called 'Washington Consensus': including the liberalization of foreign exchange and import controls; currency devaluations; reductions in social spending; privatization; and tax reform (Williamson, 1990). For some Caribbean states, such as Jamaica under Edward Seaga (1980-89), the adoption of these policies became a matter of conviction; for most, however, it simply represented an acknowledgement of the lack of a realistic alternative to neo-liberalism. Regardless, by the mid 1980s the CBI could be seen to have served its purpose well, in so far as Caribbean elites throughout the region were by then following a political and economic trajectory largely consistent wider US interests and goals. In actual fact, this political and economic trajectory was explicitly acknowledged by Caribbean elites in the so-called 'Nassau Understanding', issued by the CARICOM heads of government at their summit in 1984, which declared their conversion to neo-liberalism as 'a conscious shift to a new development path' (cited in Payne and Sutton, 2001: 10).

The New Economic Agenda: Regionalism and Free Trade

By the late 1980s the original security concerns that had underpinned the CBI had more or less dissipated. In fact, by the time of the 1988 American presidential election, political instability in Central America and the Caribbean had virtually disappeared off the domestic agenda within the US (LeoGrande, 1990). The reasons for this, of course, lay primarily with the ending of the Cold War and the immanent collapse of 'real socialism' in the Soviet Union and Eastern Europe. But, more crucially, these changes also signified a more fundamental process of restructuring within the international political economy. As set out in Chapter One, these changes amounted to a transition from an *international* economy premised upon economic exchange between national economies, towards a genuinely *global* economy rooted in production and finance. At the same time, this process also altered the position of the US itself within the wider world order. As Robert Cox (1987: 299) has described it, these changes imply that US 'hegemony has given way to domination'. What this means is that, while the power of the US unquestionably remains preponderant in the military and ideological spheres, if not quite to the same extent in the economic sphere, its ability to maintain a hegemonic consensual order on its own is no longer possible (Payne, 1994). For the Caribbean, on the other hand, the changes implied by this process of restructuring not only constituted a threat to the relatively privileged position that the region had obtained in US priorities during the Cold War, but have threatened to expose it to an economic order with which it is ill-equipped to cope (Domínquez, 1995).

In the immediate aftermath of the end of the Cold War, the position of the Caribbean within US thinking was fully exposed in the first major policy response to the manifest changes of the late 1980s and early 1990s: namely, the launching of the Enterprise for the Americas (EAI) initiative by President Bush in June 1990 (Payne, 1996). In essence, this scheme sought to combine Latin American and Caribbean debt restructuring, the promotion of regional investment through the Inter-American Development Bank and the launching of a series of bilateral trade negotiations between the US and individual Latin American and Caribbean states that were intended, in time, to lead to a hemispheric-wide free trade area. The EAI, not accidentally, coincided with separate - though closely related - trade talks between the US, Canada and Mexico centred on the negotiation of a North American Free Trade Agreement (NAFTA). In the ensuing period, NAFTA was taken up by President Clinton, who sought and subsequently gained Congressional approval for the agreement in November 1993, with it coming into effect on 1 January 1994.[7] On this basis, President Clinton subsequently set forth his plan for a Free Trade Area of the Americas (FTAA), which was immediately embraced by most elites in Latin America and the Caribbean, who collectively set the ambitious date of 2005 for its implementation at the first so-called 'Summit of the Americas' held in Miami, Florida, in December 1994.

Taken as a whole, the motivation behind the renewed US commitment to Latin America and the Caribbean in the form of hemispheric free trade is not difficult to fathom. Clearly, the US has come to view Latin America and the Caribbean as an area of the world where it has a natural economic advantage, and thus sees hemispheric free trade as working to its particular benefit. In the wider sense, also, the promotion of hemispheric regionalism by the US can be interpreted as a response to the ending of its global - though not regional - hegemony (Payne, 1996). During the 1980s the decline in US global hegemony manifested itself, among other things, in an increasing inability of US policy makers to shape the multilateral trading system through the GATT. For this reason, from the mid 1980s onwards the US began to turn to a 'dual-track' trade liberalization strategy, wherein continued pressure within the GATT process (culminating with the inauguration of the Uruguay Round in 1986) was accompanied by unilateral trade measures, such as 'Section 301' of the 'Omnibus Trade and Competitiveness Act of 1988', and bilateral free-trade agreements with key political and economic partners, such as Israel and Canada, which were signed in 1985 and 1989 respectively (Destler, 1995). In this sense, the launching of the whole EAI, NAFTA and FTAA process, within the context of a post-hegemonic world order, served the dual purpose of 'locking-in' the neo-liberal economic reforms introduced in Latin America and the Caribbean during the 1980s, while, at the same time, providing the US with additional leverage in the multilateral trading arena of the GATT and post-GATT system.

From the perspective of the Caribbean, the most immediate question regarding the EAI and, more specifically, NAFTA was the extent to which these initiatives threatened to undermine the preferential market access offered to the region through the CBI. As Rosenberg and Hiskey (1994) have noted, because the CBI did little to stimulate export growth of traditional commodities such as sugar (as we have seen, it actively inhibited growth in these sectors), the Caribbean has been made acutely vulnerable to competition in areas, such as apparel, where it competes directly with Mexico. As we shall see later, the NAFTA provisions relating to textiles and apparel (which are being phased in over a ten-year period) have indeed seriously threatened the Caribbean's apparel industry by offering Mexico a more competitive and integrated base within the North American supply chain. Nevertheless, despite all of this, the Caribbean has been left with little realistic alternative but to seek accommodation with the concept of hemispheric free trade. In fact, the most immediate response by most Caribbean states to the launching of President Bush's EAI was to sign up to so-called 'framework agreements' in 1991. These essentially stood as expressions of rhetorical support for the principles of economic liberalization and free trade. Some of the larger Caribbean states, including the Dominican Republic and Jamaica, followed this up subsequently by actively pushing for an interim NAFTA agreement designed to pave the way for their eventual accession to NAFTA or participation within a future FTAA; and Jamaica and Trinidad and Tobago went as far as to sign separate bilateral investment treaties with the US.

At the same time, the Caribbean - along with Central America, Colombia, Mexico and Venezuela - responded to NAFTA with the establishment of the Association of Caribbean States (ACS) in 1994. The precise relationship between the ACS and the wider issue of hemispheric free trade is yet to be fully determined and may not turn out to be that significant (Serbin, 1994; Payne, 1998b). Nonetheless, it stands to reason that Mexico does not want to undermine its own privileged access to the US market by sanctioning the use of the ACS as a vehicle for extending NAFTA. More fundamentally, the centrality of the principle of trade reciprocity to the FTAA is likely to expose disparities within the ACS membership. Indeed, the recent and protracted dispute within the World Trade Organization (WTO) between the US Trade Representative (USTR) and the European Union over the latter's banana regime, which is perceived by the US as offering unfair advantages to Eastern Caribbean banana producers at the expense of the 'dollar bananas' produced in Central and South America (Sutton, 1997), has already served to highlight a number of fissures that currently exist between the Caribbean and Central America. Not only does the banana dispute pitch the Caribbean against many of its neighbours in Central and South America; more crucially, it also highlights the increasingly divergent interests *within* the Caribbean. In particular, as Rosenberg and Hiskey (1994: 105) point out, the banana dispute has pointed to the 'widening split [within the Caribbean] between countries still tied predominantly to their former colonial powers and those that have succeeded in establishing a presence in the North American market'.[8]

Beyond this immediate policy dispute, however, the new economic agenda that has begun to unfold in the Americas in the last decade or so points to a more fundamental process of structural change. As described in Chapter One, and already briefly alluded to here, this refers to the process of *de facto* economic integration, derived from emerging patterns of global and regional production and finance, which are now binding many contiguous economic spaces ever more tightly. Within the context of the Caribbean, it is primarily those states standing in closest geographical proximity to the US - Jamaica, Haiti and the Dominican Republic - which are currently experiencing the greatest levels of entanglement, across a range of issues, including trade, finance, drugs and migration (Heron and Payne, 2002). In this way, we can say that the experience of these countries is broadly analogous to the process of 'silent integration' (Weintraub, 1990) that has been integrating the political economies of Mexico and the US for a number of years. In the US-Mexican case, research that has already been undertaken has depicted a scenario in which a newly emerging regional political economy is increasingly reshaping the economic boundaries between North and South (Lowenthal and Burgess, 1993). In more specific terms, the *maquila* industry has, of course, been a dynamic source of economic integration between the US and Mexico since the late 1960s (Sklair, 1988; Wilson, 1992; Gereffi, 1996). In the same vein, the increasingly complex pattern of financial flows between the United States and Mexico has provided an analogous level of *de facto* financial integration. In fact, the 'debt crisis', which erupted in August 1982 when Mexico announced that it could no longer service its debt, served to highlight the degree to which the fate of the largest US commercial banks, and therefore the US economy as a whole, had become inextricably linked to that of Mexico and other Latin American debtor countries (Shepherd, 1994). Likewise, the 1994-95 Mexican peso crisis, and the subsequent US$20 billion rescue package put together by the Clinton administration in the face of considerable domestic opposition, illustrated the high level of economic interdependence that had already been established between the US and Mexico prior to the full implementation of NAFTA.

The extent to which what we have termed the new political economy of United States-Caribbean relations is presently constituted by a similar pattern of *de facto* integration and is the subject of the remainder of this investigation. As with the case of Mexican *maquila* industry, the main focus of economic integration between the US and the northern Caribbean has centred on the 'production sharing' activities between US firms and assembly operations located in export processing enclaves. For this reason the remainder of the study will focus on this area as applied to the specific case of apparel. The remaining four chapters are organized in accordance with the following research questions. What are the economic consequences of the promotion of the so-called offshore development model as a constituent part of the new political economy of US-Caribbean relations? What is the relationship between economic restructuring in the North American apparel industry and the promotion of 'offshore' production in the Caribbean and elsewhere? What is the precise pattern of what we might call the North American apparel commodity chain and how has this been affected by establishment and operation of NAFTA? What is the significance of recent attempts by a range of actors within the US to secure a more equitable production sharing system for the Caribbean in the light of the diversionary consequences of NAFTA?

Conclusion

To sum up, then, on the basis of the 'new' political economy framework this chapter has offered an alternative reading of the history of US-Caribbean political economy since 1945. In the process, it has shown the degree to which US policy towards the Caribbean during the Cold War was primarily governed by the need to use the region as a 'measure' of the wider manifestations of US global hegemony, which accounted for the heightened political, military and economic involvement of the US in the region over this period. In this sense the importance of the CBI can be seen, not only in its economic provisions, which generally served to integrate the region closer to the US economy, but also in its overriding political aims, which were to offer the region an alternative 'solution' to the problems of social and economic underdevelopment in opposition to the 'radical' development options which some Caribbean states pursued in the late 1970s and early 1980s. Thus, the CBI - in conjunction with the broader set of economic measures implemented by an array of US and international agencies during the 1980s - helped to shape the economic agenda which emerged subsequently in the region. In the reminder of the book we will investigate one particular aspect of this new economic agenda, that is, the relationship between export processing in the northern Caribbean and the regionalization of the North American apparel industry. Our first task in this investigation concerns itself with the relationship between the growth of EPZs in the Caribbean and the wider process of economic change, which was briefly introduced in Chapter One. It is to this task that we now turn.

Notes

1 Although the theory of the plantation economy was rarely applied outside of the English-speaking Caribbean, Alex Dupuy (1989) has since used it in his study of underdevelopment in Haiti.

2 The relationship between Puerto Rico and the CBI was a complex one. Although, clearly, the duty-free benefits were surplus to Puerto Rico's needs, the island was connected to the CBI through section 936 of the US tax code, which was originally established in 1976 to offer tax relief to US firms operating in Puerto Rico provided that 10 per cent of their profits were deposited in the local Government Development Bank. In 1984 the scheme was extended so as to allow those deposited funds to be used by CBI beneficiaries to finish semi-manufactured goods of Puerto Rican origin. For more details, see Heine and García-Passalacqua (1993).

3 The twelve-year expiry date of the CBERA was repealed by the 'Caribbean Basin Economic Recovery Expansion Act of 1990' (sometimes referred to as 'CBI II'). For more details, see USITC (1990).

4 For a lengthy comparison of the CBERA and GSP programmes, see Schoepfle (1997).

5 Although, strictly speaking, the greatest casualty of the CBERA exemptions was petroleum and its derivatives, which accounted for 80 per cent of dutiable imports in 1983, the export of these items was restricted to a small number of relatively wealthy Caribbean states.

6 For instance, the CBERA stipulated that, in order for sugar, as well as beef and veal, to qualify for duty-free treatment, the CBERA beneficiary must submit an acceptable stable food production plan to the US, ensuring that these exports would not adversely affect their own nation's food supply or land use or ownership. Thus far, a number of smaller CBERA states (Antigua and Barbuda, Montserrat, Netherlands Antilles, St. Lucia, and St. Vincent and the Grenadines) have not been able to meet this requirement. See Schoepfle (1997: 105-6).

7 For a useful survey of the main NAFTA provisions, see Hufbauer and Scott (1993).

8 The issue of increasing divergence within CARICOM is also discussed in Payne and Sutton (1994); and Segal (1994).

Chapter Three

The Caribbean Offshore Development Model

Introduction

The purpose of this chapter is to take a more specific look at one aspect of the new political economy of US-Caribbean relations that is of particular relevance to our study: namely, the (re-) emergence of the so-called offshore Caribbean as an export platform for US-made manufactured goods that are assembled in the region and then subsequently re-exported to the US market. During the 1980s, as we have already established, many of the region's traditional exports to the US, most notably sugar, witnessed a precipitous decline as a result of both falling commodity prices on the international market and the introduction of punitive import quotas within the US. As a consequence of this, the overwhelming majority of Caribbean countries sought to follow the policy prescriptions offered by the US and international agencies such as AID, the IMF and the World Bank, which advocated the promotion of 'non-traditional' exports - especially light manufacturing industries - as a means to counter the loss of export revenue from traditional commodities. For many of the larger Caribbean islands in close geographical proximity to the US, these policy prescriptions approximated a new economic development model that sought to encourage US firms to outsource the most labour-intensive aspects of the production process to the region in exchange for a range of economic incentives offered by specially designated EPZs.

This chapter seeks to evaluate critically this new economic model. We begin by tracing the origins of this model; we then proceed to outline the specific legislation governing its operation, including both those provisions relating to the use of EPZs in the Caribbean, as well as the special US tariff rules that allow for this type of economic activity. On this basis, we then assess the offshore development model in terms of: (1) the costs and benefits associated with offering preferential treatment to export-orientated investment; (2) the issue of backward linkages fostered between assembly operations and the domestic economy; (3) the extent of technology transfer; and (4) the wider social and economic effects of using EPZs as the basis of a long-term development strategy. Ultimately, it is argued that, even though the offshore development model offers undeniable benefits in terms of employment and foreign exchange earnings, in the longer term it is unlikely to lead to the type of industrial transformation that it is allegedly designed to promote. At the same time, however, we conclude by noting that, despite these limitations, the offshore development model presently constitutes an integral part of the new political economy of US-Caribbean relations, and thus remains central to our ongoing investigation.

The Offshore Development Model

Anthony Maingot (1993) has claimed that, along with tourism and offshore financial services, export-driven light manufacturing is one of the few areas where Caribbean countries have been able to establish and maintain a comparative advantage. Certainly, in light of the previous discussion, it can be argued that the attempt to promote the Caribbean as an export platform for foreign - predominantly US - investment on the basis of the free provision of infrastructural services and fiscal incentives has been a consistent feature of Caribbean development thinking since the 1950s. Indeed, one could go as far as to argue that Puerto Rico's 'Operation Bootstrap' constituted, in embryonic form, precisely the type of EPZ-led industrial strategy that emerged in Mexico and in some East Asian countries during the 1960s. Equally, it could be argued that the economic ideas associated with the work of W. Arthur Lewis, which were partly derived from the Puerto Rican experience, were very much based around the concept of the offshore economy. After all, it is worth noting that, in Lewis's mind, the key to a successful industrialization strategy lay not so much with establishing new external trade links, but rather with persuading manufacturers who were already selling in overseas markets actually to locate their plants in the Caribbean (Payne and Sutton, 2001: 2-4).

Thus, beyond the Puerto Rican experience, development thinking within the Caribbean has, from the onset, been closely tied to the idea of the offshore economy. In practical terms, as we have already briefly mentioned, this initially manifested itself in a series of attempts by Caribbean governments to persuade foreign firms to use the region as a platform for penetrating major export markets, particularly the US. For example, Jamaica enacted the Export Industry Encouragement Act (EIEA) in 1956, which allowed approved firms a tax holiday on profits and dividends for a ten-year period as well as granting duty exemption on capital goods and imported raw materials (Thomas, 1987). Subsequently, with the formation of the Caribbean Common Market (CARICOM) in 1973, similar measures were applied throughout the English-speaking Caribbean, with member states offering exemption from all income taxes for anywhere from 10 to 15 years to firms exporting their products outside of the customs union (Schoepfle and Pérez-López, 1992). Likewise, in the Dominican Republic the Industrial Incentives Act (more commonly known as Law 69) was passed in 1979 and offered similar fiscal incentives and duty exemptions to that of Jamaica's EIEA; Haiti implemented comparable measures in the early 1960s and was the first independent Caribbean territory to establish specially designated EPZs. These EPZs are discussed in more detail below.

Export Processing Zones

In Chapter One we defined EPZs, somewhat broadly, as specially created industrial enclaves, designed to stimulate export performance and foreign direct investment by providing firms with tax exemptions and other fiscal incentives. To this definition, we can add that EPZs are distinct from other industrial districts, such as 'freeports' and 'free trade zones', which are normally associated with warehousing, transshipment and other commercial activities, in so far as they primarily serve to transform primary imported material and components into *manufactured* goods (Dicken, 1998: 130). In more specific terms, we can follow the more comprehensive definition of an EPZ offered by the United Nations Industrial Development Organization (UNIDO) as follows:

> a relatively small, geographically separated area within a country, the purpose of which is to attract export-orientated industries, by offering them especially favourable investment and trade conditions as compared with the remainder of the host country. In particular, the EPZs provide for the importation of goods to be used in the production of exports on a bonded duty free basis (cited in Dicken, 1998: 130).

Although many of the features associated with EPZs - infrastructural provision, duty exemptions, tax holidays and so on - were contained within the first set of industrial policies implemented in the Caribbean in the immediate post-war period, it was not until the late 1960s that specially designated EPZs were established, as regional elites attempted to follow what they took to be the development path set by the East Asian newly industrialising countries (NICs).[1] Having said this, the first EPZs in the Caribbean were actually set up in Haiti as early as 1960 (although they did not become economically significant until over a decade later) when privately owned industrial parks were created in and around Port-au-Prince (Schoepfle and Pérez-López, 1992). More significantly, however, the Dominican Republic opened its first EPZ in La Romana in 1969 and further zones were subsequently established in San Pedro de Macorís (1973), Santiago (1974) and Puerto Plata (1983). Jamaica soon attempted to emulate this strategy when the Kingston Export Free Zone, originally a warehousing and transshipment facility, was converted into an EPZ in 1982. The Kingston Export Free Zone was followed by the creation of two further EPZs in the 1980s - the Montego Bay Export Free Zone in 1985 and the Garmex Export Free Zone (located near Kingston) in 1987.

While the initial impetus for the construction of EPZs emerged mainly in the 1960s and 1970s, it was not until the 1980s that these zones became economically significant for the countries that we are examining. As Buitelaar, Padilla and Urrutia (1999: 143) have argued, during this period EPZs in the Caribbean changed from 'being an exception in an otherwise inward-orientated policy framework', and 'became a spearhead in the change towards an export-led development model'. As we have already established, by the mid 1980s the cumulative pressures exercised by the US and an array of international agencies, notably US AID, the IMF and the World Bank, coupled with the perceived lack of realistic development alternatives in the region, led most Caribbean elites to the conclusion that neo-liberal, export-led growth offered the best means of economic survival in an increasingly competitive global economy. From this perspective, the promotion of the Caribbean as an export platform for labour-intensive and import-intensive industries provided a means by which Caribbean elites could put the principles of neo-liberal, export-orientated development into practice (Pantojas-García, 2001).

All the same, as a number of commentators have pointed out, despite the best efforts of Caribbean governments, the timing of EPZ-related investment growth lay primarily not with these industrial policies, but with a set of factors that were largely exogenous to the region (Mody and Wheeler, 1987). First and foremost among these was the advent and subsequent growth of intra-firm and intra-industry trade associated with the attempts by - predominantly US - TNCs to offset foreign competition by outsourcing the most labour-intensive aspects of the production process to low-wage foreign assembly factories, typically located in the developing world (Fröbel *et al.*, 1981; Grunwald and Flamm, 1985; Sklair, 1988). Although, as we argued in Chapter One, these activities were suggestive of a broader set of structural changes that took place within the world economy during the late 1970s and 1980s, they were also facilitated by a specific set of policies pursued by industrial countries, which actually sought to encourage offshore production. The most important policy instrument in this regard was the US tariff code provisions 806.30 and 807.00, dating from 1930 and 1964 respectively. These provisions offered duty-free treatment to certain metal products and a range of other manufactured goods that were made with US raw materials and then subsequently re-imported into the US, with the importer paying duty *only* on the value added overseas (USITC, 2000). Now known as the Harmonized Tariff Schedule (HTS) 9802.00, these provisions have played a key role in the expansion of a number of Caribbean offshore manufacturing industries, including electronics, footwear, garments and other apparel items. Nevertheless, as we shall see shortly, while the 9802.00 regime has indeed facilitated the vast majority of foreign investment in the Caribbean EPZ sector, it has also brought with it significant costs. Before examining these costs, however, it is first necessary to take a closer look at the specific policy instruments that Caribbean governments have used to persuade foreign investors to locate in their particular EPZs.

Policy Competition for Foreign Direct Investment

According to a number of sources, fiscal incentives designed to attract foreign direct investment to export-orientated industries tend to play a relatively minor role in the locational decisions of TNCs, when compared to other advantages such as market size and growth potential, production costs, skill levels and political and economic stability (Mortimore and Perez, 1998). Nonetheless, as Mortimore and Peres (1998: 54) note, fiscal incentives do tend to be more attractive for footloose, export-orientated investments, such as in the electronics and apparel sectors, which constitute the overwhelming majority of the offshore industries in the Caribbean. The typical range of incentives offered to prospective investors is usually based on a series of fiscal benefits, such as tax holidays and duty-free treatment for imported capital equipment and components that are used in assembling products destined for export. In addition to this, though, most Caribbean governments also offer more general incentives, including the subsidized rental of factory shells, infrastructural improvements, government-supported worker training programmes, reduced public utility rates, credit assistance, guarantees that profits may be repatriated, permission to sell a share of the output in the domestic market and special treatment with regard to foreign currency restrictions (Schoepfle and Pérez-López, 1992: 134).

As specifically related to the cases that we are examining here, the governments of the Dominican Republic, Jamaica and Haiti offer a noticeably similar range of economic incentives to potential investors. Citing a 1988 brochure prepared by the Investment Promotional Council of the Dominican Republic, Schoepfle and Pérez-López (1992: 134-5) have summarized the incentives offered to firms which locate in Dominican EPZs as follows: (1) duty and tax-free importation of all machinery, equipment, spare parts, construction materials and other items needed for the construction and operation of their production facility; (2) duty-free entry of imported raw materials and other goods destined for re-export; (3) complete exemption from all taxes and fiscal charges for periods of 12-15 years; (4) freedom from currency holdings and foreign exchange restrictions; (5) freedom to sell up to 20 per cent of production to the local market; and (6) no financial reporting requirements other than local expenses. A similar package of incentives are offered by both Jamaica and Haiti. Firms operating in Jamaica's EPZs are free from foreign currency restrictions and are exempt from taxes on profits, imports into the zones and exports to countries other than Jamaica, provided that at least 85 per cent of production is exported outside of the customs territory and that wages and other local expenses are paid in Jamaican currency.[2] Likewise, the government of Haiti grants exemption for life from customs duties on imported raw materials and capital goods and all consular fees and administrative charges for firms locating in its EPZ; it also provides for exemption from income, profits and capital gains tax for a period of up to 15 years, depending on the status of the particular exporting firm (Steele, 1988).

The homogeneity in terms of what individual Caribbean governments offer investors in order to persuade them to locate in their particular EPZs does, of course, reflect the widespread policy consensus that currently exists within the region with regard to foreign investment. At the same time, however, this homogeneity also implies a high degree of policy competition within the Caribbean as each country attempts to persuade foreign investors to locate in its EPZs at the expense of neighbouring economies. According to a number of critics, this type of competitive strategy wherein neighbouring EPZ economies compete for foreign investment through 'bidding wars' approximates a fallacy of composition similar to the self-defeating policies that have blighted primary-exporting countries, which have attempted to use such measures as currency devaluations in order to remain export competitive, for a number of years (Kaplinsky, 1993). In other words, while it may make sense for a single EPZ economy to adopt investor-friendly polices, such as tax holidays and duty-free entitlements, the effectiveness of such measures is immediately eroded once neighbouring EPZs choose - as they have done in the Caribbean - to implement similar policies. Ultimately, this can lead to a spiralling competitive 'race to the bottom' as each EPZ economy attempts to out-bid its neighbours by offering increasingly generous incentives to prospective foreign investors.

One manifestation of this competitive logic within the Caribbean has been for governments to transform temporary (10-15 years) fiscal incentives, such as limited-time authorizations to operate under the temporary admissions or EPZ regimes, into permanent ones, whenever a competitor allows for automatic renewal (Mortimore and Perez, 1998: 61). In the Dominican Republic, for instance, the provision of increasingly generous tax holidays for investors choosing to locate in its EPZs has led to a situation where now over 40 per cent of the country's total exports provide virtually no fiscal income for the government (Mortimore, 1999). In the longer term, such measures are likely to have severe consequences for economic development, given that these resources might otherwise have been used to strengthen the local industrialization process via, for example, investment in infrastructure, such as ports, airports and roads. In fact, Mortimore and Peres (1998: 84) go as far as to conclude that the effect of policy competition of this nature has been to limit and distort the nascent industrialization process in the Caribbean wherein continued export growth can only be maintained on the basis of incentive dependent investment.

Beyond fiscal incentives, Caribbean EPZ economies also compete on the basis of exchange rate policy. As we have seen, one of the most important aspects of the Washington Consensus as related to the structural adjustment policies implemented in the Caribbean during the 1980s was the recommendation of currency devaluations as a means to reduce domestic consumption and thus generate sufficient foreign exchange to service debt payments (MacAfee, 1991). One of the most immediate side-effects of this policy was that it led to a significant decline in real wages in the Caribbean and thus made export-related industrial investment in unskilled labour-intensive areas a far more attractive option for foreign capital. Furthermore, while the use of exchange rate policy was not directly aimed at enhancing the international competitiveness of Caribbean offshore industries, the link between the move to more 'flexible' exchange rates and the promotion of EPZs is difficult to ignore. As Williamson explains:

> There is now a very wide consensus in Washington that export-led growth is the only kind of growth Latin America [and the Caribbean] stands any chance of achieving in the next decade. There is equally little controversy over the proposition that the first key prerequisite to export-led growth (or 'outward orientation') is a *competitive exchange rate*. By that is meant one that will promote a rate of growth of exports that will allow the economy to grow at its supply-side potential. It is also fairly widely accepted that, in order to invest in

production for the export market, business needs assurance that the exchange rate *will remain competitive in the near future* (cited in Kaplinsky, 1993: 1860-1, emphasis added).

Within the context of the Caribbean, the adoption of more 'flexible' exchange rate policies went hand in hand with the dramatic expansion of the EPZ sector that took place in the region during the mid 1980s. Kaplinsky (1993) estimates that, in relation to the US dollar, almost all Caribbean Basin EPZ economies - Colombia, the Dominican Republic, El Salvador, Guatemala, Haiti, Honduras, Jamaica, Mexico, Panama and Venezuela - increased their competitiveness measured against the real 1980 exchange rate; and in most cases the effective devaluation exceeded 20 per cent for much of the decade. Citing the specific case of the Dominican Republic, Kaplinsky sees a clear link between these currency devaluations and the dramatic expansion of the island's offshore assembly industries. During the 1980s real wages in the Dominican Republic paid by foreign investors more than halved, at the same time as they rose by 15 per cent in the US. In the same period, the proportion of total manufacturing employment on the island accounted for by EPZs increased from 23 per cent in 1981 to 56 per cent in 1989, by which time EPZ exports were responsible for 20 per cent of the Dominican Republic's total foreign exchange earnings (Kaplinsky, 1993: 1860). A similar pattern has also been observed in other EPZ economies, most notably, Mexico, where the spectacular growth of its *maquila* exports has been accompanied by a recurrent series of currency devaluations, the most recent of which took place during the 1994/1995 peso crisis (Gereffi, 2000).

Taking the region as a whole, the impact of currency depreciation on real wages has been considerable. For example, the hourly compensation costs for Caribbean Basin apparel workers in the late 1980s stood at approximately US$0.95 in Costa Rica, US$0.84 in Mexico, US$0.79 in the Dominican Republic, US$0.63 in Jamaica and US$0.58 in Haiti, while comparable rates in the United States stood in the order of US$13.66 per hour (Kaplinsky, 1993: 1859). Admittedly, these hourly rates still compare favourably to those found in low-cost Asian countries, where unskilled assembly workers generally earn between two to four times less than their Caribbean counterparts. Nevertheless, given the abundance of unskilled low-cost labour in the Caribbean, and the fact that regional EPZs are all primarily geared towards attracting the same prospective investors, harsh policy competition between neighbouring EPZs continues to act as a downward pressure on local wages. Moreover, as more and more regional economies adopt the offshore development model, these competitive pressures are likely to intensify. Since the onset of peace in Central America in the late 1980s and early 1990s, states such as El Salvador, Guatemala and Honduras have become increasingly attractive locations for export-orientated investment (Robinson, 2001). In fact, it is already becoming apparent that the prevailing low wages found in parts of Central America are beginning to lead to the diversion of investment away from the Caribbean and towards the isthmus (again see Chapter Five).[3] This in turn may tempt some Caribbean countries to engage in further 'competitive devaluations' as a means to regain, albeit temporarily, their export competitiveness (Mortimore and Perez, 1998).

Nevertheless, as is already apparent, using exchange rate policy as a means to enhance export competitiveness only works in so far as it offers a temporary advantage until neighbouring economies realign their currencies; after which, such wage depressing tactics become highly contingent upon a continuing fall in local purchasing power for Caribbean workers and a corresponding lowering in their standard of living. Thus, as Pantojas-García (2001: 62) notes, 'it seems clear that maintaining a competitive advantage in labour-intensive *maquiladoras* is a self-defeating strategy for the Caribbean, considering that the key to remaining competitive as a *maquila* export platform means deepening the social and economic disadvantages of the working population'. Conversely, if real wages paid to assembly workers are allowed to rise, as they have done in the Caribbean since the massive currency devaluations of the 1980s, the alternative scenario is that local workers will effectively price themselves out of the market. Mortimore (1999), for instance, argues that increases in hourly labour costs for some of the more established EPZ economies, such as Jamaica and Costa Rica, are growing at a much greater rate than in newly emerging EPZ economies, particularly those located in the Central American isthmus. As a result, we are likely to see a much greater level of trade and investment diversion away from the more established EPZ sites in the Caribbean and towards the lower wage sites of Central America in the near future. More fundamentally, there is no real evidence - at least in the case of Jamaica - that the rise in labour costs in the more established EPZ economies has been accompanied by industrial upgrading or specialization in higher value added tasks. It is these aspects of the offshore development model that we will examine next.

Backward Linkages

From the perspective of the host country, it is often claimed that the most important contribution that EPZs can potentially make to the process of economic development is derived from the degree to which backward linkages (i.e. local inputs used in the production process) are established between EPZ firms and domestic suppliers. The example of the East Asian NICs, which is generally regarded as the archetypal model for successful industrial upgrading through export-led growth, is particularly illustrative of this point. Spinanger (cited in Wilson, 1992: 23) estimates that the proportion of domestic inputs among assembly plants located in South Korean EPZs rose from 13 per cent in 1972 to 32 per cent in 1978; in Taiwan the use of local inputs rose from 5 per cent in 1967 to 27 per cent in 1978. What this all means is that, while export processing in both Taiwan and Korea was heavily reliant on foreign capital and inputs in the initial stages, these zones were able to rapidly establish important economic linkages with the domestic economy. Thus, in the context of the industrial transformation of East Asia, the transition from an initial reliance on foreign inputs to a more integrated form of production can be said to have played a key role in allowing these economies to move into the production and export of goods with a high value added (Gereffi, 1999).

In the Caribbean the most important factor influencing the degree to which local inputs are used in EPZ assembly operations is, clearly, the 9802.00 tariff system. Because this regime provides tariff-free and duty-free treatment *only* for US-made components it effectively penalizes all of the value added outside of the US, and thus discourages the use of local inputs in the production process. As a consequence, this scheme - which accounts for the overwhelming majority of Caribbean EPZ exports - has had the effect on limiting the use of local resources to that of labour costs, for, as Mortimore (1999: 130) aptly puts it, Caribbean inputs are neither 'needed or desired by manufacturer or buyer'. Evidently, the consequences of this for limiting the growth of backward linkages in Caribbean EPZ assembly operations have been considerable: Kaplinsky (1993) cites a study of over 60 EPZs firms in the Dominican Republic carried out by the World Bank in 1990 which could not report a single linkage. Similarly, research conducted in the Dominican Republic by Matthews (1994) found little evidence of the use of local inputs by assembly firms located in the island's EPZs. Peter Steele (1988) has argued, moreover, that the low level of backward linkages between EPZ firms and local Caribbean suppliers is not so much an unintended consequence of the 9802.00 tariff system, but rather a deliberate aspect of US policy. In the case of the Caribbean apparel industry he argues that the strategy has been to 'curb and, in the longer term, effectively to discourage the emergence in the Caribbean of more highly integrated garment enterprises capable of producing items with a higher local added value' (Steele, 1988: 3).

Regardless as to whether or not this is a deliberate aspect of US policy, what remains clear is that the 9802.00 regime has had the effect of limiting the use of local inputs in EPZ assembly operations. What is more, as this accounts for an ever-increasing share of export activity in the Caribbean, the 9802.00 system has begun to distort the evolution of domestic industry by attracting firms which were previously involved in higher value added production for the domestic market (Kaplinsky, 1995). Griffith (1990) cites the example of the Jamaican clothing industry whose retreat into 9802.00 production during the late 1980s had the effect of dramatically reducing the value added in the region, while also limiting the capacity of Jamaican firms to play a decisive role in coordinating the entire garment production chain. At the same time, Jamaica's relatively liberal tariff regime has made its own garment industry increasingly vulnerable to competition from cheap US imports, to the extent that by the mid 1990s local industry was only supplying an estimated 20 per cent of all the clothing purchased by Jamaicans (Willmore, 1994).

The 9802.00 tariff system has had a not dissimilar effect on other Caribbean export industries. During the 1980s, as was argued in Chapter Two, US economic policy towards the Caribbean sought actively to discourage the export growth of traditional commodities such as sugar (particularly through the use of import quotas), at the same time as promoting 'non-traditional' exports, such as garments, whose value added in the region represented a tiny fraction of that which had previously been derived from traditional commodities. Deere and Melendez (1992: 66) estimate that, since 1985, the value added in the Caribbean of 9802.00 exports has never exceeded 32 per cent; and for items entering through the Special Access Program (807A), the figure is as low as 26 per cent. Comparing this with traditional exports, such as sugar and coffee, whose value added component is often as high as 90 per cent, they suggest that a US$1 million decline in sugar exports would have to be offset with a US$3.8 million increase in garment exports to guarantee the same level of foreign exchange. Thus, even with significant growth in 9802.00 exports, such trade is unlikely to compensate for the loss of foreign exchange from traditional commodities.

Still, if the low level of domestic integration between EPZ assembly operations and the local economy can be largely attributed to the exclusionary nature of the 9802.00 tariff scheme, this is not something that Caribbean governments have sought to challenge. Indeed, as Larry Willmore (1995) has argued, the various rules governing EPZs in the Caribbean have, if anything, actually encouraged the exclusion of domestic suppliers from contributing to EPZ assembly operations. According to Willmore, although the 9802.00 regime may indeed limit the scope for backward linkages, not all export processing is carried out through this scheme and, even when it is, this does not prevent local firms from supplying items such as buttons, thread, hangers, plastic bags and cardboard boxes. In Willmore's view, the key difference between the EPZs that took off in some of the East Asian NICs during the 1970s and those in the Caribbean lies not so much with the 9802.00 scheme itself, but rather with the attitude of local customs authorities. When the first South Korean EPZ opened in Mason in 1971, assembly firms were free to use local inputs, which were given duty-free treatment; in contrast, Caribbean assembly operations are prohibited from sourcing locally, either because the use of domestic inputs is explicitly outlawed by EPZ legislation or because complicated bureaucratic procedures discourage potential suppliers from entering the market (Willmore, 1995). All in all, then, the low level of domestic integration between activities in EPZs and the local economy is not only due to the 9802.00 tariff scheme, but also the restrictive nature of the EPZ regimes governing Caribbean offshore industries.

Technology Transfer

In addition to employing large numbers of relatively unskilled workers and generating foreign exchange reserves, advocates often allege that EPZs also act as a vehicle for the transfer of technology, which is defined by the UNIDO as 'the process by which knowledge related to the transformation of inputs into competitive products is acquired by national entities and whose source is foreign' (cited in Buitelaar and Pérez, 2000: 1633-4). Hence, within the context of the Caribbean, it is argued that EPZs introduce workers for the first time to the rigours of industrial employment, including notions of punctuality, quality control and meeting deadlines, while also offering local entrepreneurs a 'low risk' method of entering the export market, which will ultimately enable them to move from simple assembly tasks towards the production of items with a much higher local value added (Willmore, 1994). Once again, the example of the East Asian NICs is broadly illustrative of this argument. Although the economies of Taiwan, South Korea, Hong Kong and Singapore initially relied upon assembly operations for export growth (typically, although not always, utilizing EPZs located near major ports), these countries rapidly progressed to a more generalized system of investment incentives that applied to all export-orientated factories, foreign and domestic, operating in their borders. On this basis, the NICs soon became responsible for original equipment manufacturing (OEM), wherein indigenous firms sourced raw materials locally and manufactured products to the specification of external buyers. Finally, having established a range of technological skills through industrial learning, these firms in the NICs were then in a position to enter original brand name manufacturing (OBM), which was also accompanied by a regionalization of Asian trade and production networks in the late 1980s and 1990s (Gereffi, 1999).

Despite all of this, comparisons between the East Asian NICs and the Caribbean are of only partial relevance (Griffith, 1987). As Kaplinsky (1993) has noted, the key difference between the NICs and the EPZs found in the Caribbean is the dependency of the latter upon the US market. Largely, though not exclusively, because of the 9802.00 tariff regime - which, as we have seen, accounts for the overwhelming majority of EPZ activity - the value added in the Caribbean is limited to that of labour, utilities, port-facilities and building space. What this means is that any potential benefit that EPZs may offer the region in terms of the transfer of technological resources is, to all intents and purposes, confined to the labour aspect alone. This, of course, does not preclude the possibility that EPZs may have positive developmental consequences for the region with regard to certain aspects (i.e. those related to human resources) of technology transfer. In the case of the Dominican Republic, for instance, Willmore (1995) claims that the majority of the 140,000 or so line operators working in the island's EPZs are made up of those entering the labour market for the first time; he also argues that EPZ industrial employment, including supervisors, technicians and plant managers, is constituted by 100 per cent Dominican nationals. As a consequence, EPZ employees are acquiring skills and experience that will be of long-term benefit for the industrial development of the Dominican economy. Finally, Willmore asserts that *prima facie* evidence exists that EPZs have already made a positive contribution to the transfer of technology due to the fact that firms operating within the island's EPZs are considerably more efficient that those producing for the domestic market.

Still, not all analysts share Willmore's optimism. On the basis of a survey of over fifty EPZ firms operating in the Dominican Republic, Matthews (1994: Ch. 4) found that the majority of respondents cited 'prior experience' as the single most important criteria when recruiting workers; he also discovered that in 72 per cent of cases more than half the workforce was drawn from other EPZ firms, thus questioning Willmore's assertion that the island's EPZ workers are those entering the labour market for the first time. On the basis of these figures and his own research, Kaplinsky (1995) has concluded that, rather than introducing workers to the rigours of industrial employment for the first time, EPZs are most likely to recruit from other EPZs or, in the case of jobs requiring a higher skill level, from the domestic economy. Conversely, Kaplinsky sees little evidence of EPZ labour being recruited by non-EPZ employers, thus making it difficult to conclude that EPZs lead to significant technology transfer to the domestic economy.

Even if we accept that Caribbean EPZs may make some positive contribution to the transfer of technology with regard to human resource capital, it still remains unclear how this may lead to the type of industrial upgrading which lay behind the spectacular growth rates experienced by the East Asian NICs from the late 1960s onwards. As Mortimore (1999) has argued with regard to the Caribbean apparel industry, rather than representing the starting point for industrialization, as was the case for some of the East Asian NICs, EPZs in the Caribbean have become an end in themselves, thus leading to a skewed process of industrialization. Despite the rapid explosion of Caribbean apparel exports since the mid 1980s, he argues, this activity does not represent the extension of the national apparel industry into the international market, but rather the 'localization' of the assembly function itself. As a result, this process has not created national leader companies and there has been no transformation of industry to the extent that the assembly country has extended its industrialization process into more technologically complex tasks or more fashion-orientated aspects of the apparel industry.

The Economic and Social Effects of Export Processing Zones in the Caribbean

Despite the dubious nature of EPZ-led growth as the basis for a long-term development strategy, at least as measured by the more limited criteria of creating jobs for Caribbean workers, it can be argued that the offshore development model has been something of a 'success'. Since the late 1980s EPZ employment has come to represent an increasingly greater share of total manufacturing employment. Again, the case of the Dominican Republic is illustrative of this trend. Measured in terms of employment, the Dominican Republic is the fourth largest EPZ economy in the world (the fifth, if China's Special Economic Zones are included), with approximately 430 assembly firms, employing some 160,000 workers, mostly working in the manufacture of garments and other apparel items (Burns, 1995: 39). During the 1980s, as we have already seen, the share of official manufacturing employment accounted for by EPZ firms increased from 23 per cent in 1981 to 56 per cent in 1989, making the Dominican Republic second only to Singapore and Mauritius in terms of the share of the manufacturing labour force employed in EPZs (Kaplinsky, 1995: 1856).

Still, despite the impressive nature of this employment growth, the economic contribution of EPZs towards the generation of employment within the Caribbean has not been as impressive as would seem likely to be the case. In the Dominican Republic, as in other Caribbean EPZ economies, the use of export manufacturing as a means to alleviate unemployment has been largely undermined by the decline of employment in traditional sectors of the economy, most notably sugar. Moreover, the advances made in the EPZ sector have done little to offset decline in these traditional sectors, but rather have incorporated a new social grouping, namely, women between the ages of 18 and 24, into the labour force. According to Helen Safa (1994: 258), EPZ firms in the Caribbean 'have shown a strong preference for women workers, because they are cheaper to employ, less likely to unionize, and have greater patience for the tedious, monotonous work employed in assembly operations'. Certainly, the empirical data seems to support this assertion. In Jamaica, for instance, women occupy 95 per cent of the jobs in the EPZ sector, while outside of the zones they constitute one of the smallest shares of industrial employment in the developing world (Klak, 1995). Similarly, the rest of the Caribbean relies overwhelmingly upon female labour to perform most of the assembly work found in EPZs: Schoepfle and Pérez-López (1992: 14-5) estimate that women workers represent approximately 70 per cent of total EPZ employment in Haiti and the Dominican Republic, while they comprise over 90 per cent of the total EPZ workforce in the English-speaking Caribbean.

The disproportionate number of women employed in assembly factories, coupled with low levels of unionization and the relatively poor pay and working conditions, has led some critics to argue that the zones constitute little more than a means for TNCs to exploit local workers while contributing little to the long-term economic development of the host country.[4] Certainly, some aspects of the Caribbean offshore development model do correspond to this argument. Briggs and Kernaghan (1994) refer to the example of Haiti, where some of the poorest EPZ working conditions in the insular Caribbean are to be found (although the conditions found in Haiti's EPZ factories are by no means exceptional to the region). In a 'model' apparel factory in the EPZ district of Port-au-Prince, the highest paid garment workers receive the equivalent of US$1.48 per day. As of the mid 1990s, these workers' average transportation costs and daily subsistence amounted to approximately 77 cents, leaving them with around 71 cents to take home at the end of the day. Briggs and Kernaghan (1994: 39) estimated that, once rental and other expenses were accounted for, a typical Haitian garment worker was left with as little as US$2.75 with which to feed family members at the end of a six-day working week. All the same, supporters of the offshore development model are quick to point out that pay and working conditions found in Caribbean EPZ factories, while admittedly poor by Western standards, actually compare favourably to conditions found in comparable domestic industries located outside of the zones (Willmore, 1995). Equally, supporters also defend the practice of EPZ factories recruiting disproportionate numbers of non-unionized, women workers. In Jamaica, for instance, despite the opportunities for EPZ employment, women between the ages of 18 and 24 - who often constitute the sole economic contributors to the household - still experience the highest levels of unemployment on the island. Thus, EPZ employment represents one of the few economic opportunities for Jamaican women to earn sufficient money with which to support their families.[5]

These counter-arguments notwithstanding, during the late 1990s the poor wages and working conditions, such as those found in Haiti, led to a series of labour-supported exposés in the US against top brand-name companies (Wal-Mart and K-Mart, Disney, GAP and so on), which were accused of employing EPZ subcontractors engaged in persistent labour abuses, including the use of child and forced labour (Gereffi *et al.*, 2001). Since then, concern over sweatshop labour has been transformed from a relatively minor domestic political issue within the US to a central theme in the so-called 'anti-globalization' movement, which rose to prominence following the disturbances surrounding the opening of the WTO millennial trade negotiations held in Seattle in 1999 (see Green and Griffith, 2001). Partly as a result of the cumulative pressure applied by labour organizations, NGOs and student activists, a number of the leading brand-name companies have since attempted to reassure consumers by setting up (voluntary) codes of conduct and monitoring systems designed to eradicate the labour abuses associated with EPZ employment (Kaufman and Gonzales, 2001). What is more, in 1998 the Clinton Administration, working in conjunction with manufacturers, NGOs and labour groups, established the Fair Labor Association (FLA) designed to implement and monitor a voluntary code of conduct, stipulating that companies must pay at or above the minimum or prevailing local wage, that workers be at least 14 years old, and that employees work no more that 60 hours per week, although they could work unlimited 'voluntary' hours (Gereffi *et al.*, 2001: 61-2).

Despite the well-intentioned nature of these initiatives, however, some within the Caribbean suspect that the 'anti-sweatshop' movement represents in the main a vehicle for domestically orientated labour unions within the US, which are vehemently opposed to the practices of offshore production and preferential trade agreements more generally.[6] Significantly, during the 1990s the opposition of the US labour movement to the practice of offshore production manifested itself in a series of 'shock tactics' designed to expose the labour abuses in EPZ factories, particularly those in Central America (see Chapter Six). In 1992 action of this nature led to the withdrawal of funds from a US AID sponsored project, promoting the establishment of EPZs in Central America, after a '60 Minutes' television exposé claimed - on the basis investigations carried out by the US Department of Labor - that such initiatives were effectively subsidising the export of American jobs (Bradsher, 1992). None of this, of course, detracts from the argument that the Caribbean offshore development model, in which competitive advantage is almost exclusively derived from poorly paid, unskilled labour, does not constitute a sound basis for a long-term industrialization strategy.

Conclusion

According to Michael Porter (1990: 49-51), reliance upon unskilled, poorly paid workers represents what he calls a 'low order' competitive advantage in contrast to other 'higher order' advantages such as propriety technology, product differentiation, brand reputation, customer relationships, and constant industrial upgrading. Similarly, Kaplinsky (2001) sees low wages and other aspects of what he refers to as 'static' comparative advantage as associated with 'immiserizing' growth for developing countries: that is, economic growth contingent upon declining terms of trade and continuous loss of international purchasing power for local workers. Clearly, we have seen evidence for both these sets of claims in our foregoing analysis of the Caribbean offshore development model. To recall briefly, the growth of EPZ employment in the region positively correlates with the decline in the level of real wages paid to Caribbean workers; has been associated with extremely competitive bidding wars between neighbouring EPZs, leading to a drastic decline in the level of fiscal revue available to the host government; and, as yet, has shown little real evidence of promoting technology transfer to the domestic economy or facilitating industrial upgrading to higher value added export activities. Despite these problems - and they are considerable - the offshore development model has nonetheless effected an intensive process of *de facto* economic integration between the political economies of the US and the Caribbean. It is this process of integration which is examined in the next two chapters.

Notes

1 Although a positive link is often made between EPZs and the industrialization of East Asia, it is important not to overstate the case. According to Stephan Haggard (1990), it was only in the larger economies of Taiwan and Korea that EPZs figured prominently and even in these cases export 'take-off' actually preceded the establishment of the zones. It also needs to be recognized that, with the exception of Singapore, the industrial transformation of the East Asian region was accompanied by a secular decline in dependence on foreign sources of capital.

2 Although these provisions relate to Jamaica's EPZ laws, because of policy changes implemented during the 1980s, including the abolition of exchange controls and the removal of import quotas, the same range of incentives are also available through the EIEA (which does not require firms to be located physically within the zones) and many investors now actually prefer to use this system. See L. Willmore (1994).

3 Personal interviews with Peter King, Chairman of the Textiles and Apparel Institute, Kingston, Jamaica, 10-12 November 2001.

4 The general literature on the role of female workers in EPZ factories is now enormous. See, among the many possible sources, Elson and Pearson (1981); Fernández-Kelly (1983); and Safa (1995).

5 Personal interview with Ambassador Richard Bernal, Embassy of Jamaica, Washington DC, 5 October 2000.

6 *Ibid.*

Chapter Four

The Restructuring of the United States Textile and Apparel Industry

Introduction

In global terms, the textile and apparel industries are among the most geographically dispersed of all forms of manufacturing activity and have historically played a key role in the initial stages of economic development for both developed and developing countries (Dickerson, 1999). In organizational terms, these industries are made up of a number of distinct economic activities, each with its own specific technological and structural characteristics, ranging from the supply of raw materials and intermediate inputs (e.g. fibres, yarns and fabrics) at one end of the supply chain to the transformation of these inputs into end-use products (e.g. garments and other apparel items) and their eventual distribution and retail at the other end. Unlike a number of other manufacturing sectors, levels of technological sophistication within the textile and apparel complex remain moderate and, overall, the industry is still characterized by low-cost barriers to entry and high levels of labour-intensive employment. Because of this, the international textile and apparel trade has come to represent an important reference point in the theory of a new international division of labour and in related trade disputes between developed and developing countries.

In this and the two subsequent chapters we examine the ways in which the restructuring of the United States textile and apparel industry complex has impacted on the political economy of the northern Caribbean. The specific purpose of this chapter is to examine this process of restructuring in the US industry against the backdrop of the failure of the international regime that has regulated the textile and apparel trade since 1974, the Multi-Fibre Arrangement (MFA), to protect US industry from low-wage competition. The chapter is divided into two sections. In the first section, we take odds with the dominant account of the MFA offered by mainstream IPE, and theories of hegemonic stability in particular, by highlighting the importance of domestic political processes and structural economic factors in shaping the development of the international textile and apparel trade regime. To be more precise, it is argued that, contrary to the predictions of hegemonic stability theory, the gradual weakening of the MFA during the 1970s and 1980s is best understood in terms of the historical weakness, rather than strength, of the US state *vis-à-vis* domestically-orientated interest groups. Furthermore, it is argued that the illiberal character that the MFA gradually assumed in this period was also due to the unintended consequence of the regime itself, which paradoxically heightened the economic capabilities of developing country exporters as well as intensifying the scope of global competition, thus leading to even greater calls by importing countries for quantitative restrictions to be placed on this trade.

Against this backdrop, the second section examines the impact of low-wage imports on the US textile and apparel complex and the ways in which specific parts of the industry have responded to them. In delineating the competitive strategies adopted by specific parts of the US industry, we re-introduce the concept of buyer-driven commodity chains in order to show how the strategic response of US clothing firms to foreign competition has been driven, not only by the evident failure of MFA, but also by an internally driven process of restructuring within the North American textile and apparel supply chain. Simply put, it is argued that, as buyer-driven chains have come to supplant producer-driven chains, US retailers have chosen to source directly from oversees suppliers at the expense of domestic clothing manufacturers. In consequence, these domestic firms have responded by shifting aspects of the production process - typically, the assembly stages - to Mexico and the Caribbean Basin in order to remain price-competitive in their own market. Hence, it is argued that the regionalization of the North American textile and apparel commodity chain, which is discussed more fully in Chapter Five, is the outcome of the strategic responses that US clothing firms have adopted in the face of the increasing economic power wielded by retailers and major buying groups.

The Politics of Protectionism: The Multi-Fibre Arrangement (MFA)

In 1985 Vinod Aggarwal published what is widely regarded as the most influential study of the development of the international textile and apparel trade regime over the post-war period. In this, Aggarwal (1985) argued that the progressive 'weakening' of the regime that has governed the international textile and apparel trade since 1974, the MFA, was largely consistent with the predictions of the theory of hegemonic stability. As can be recalled from Chapter One, the theory of hegemonic stability correlates the smooth operation of a liberal economic order with the existence of a leader, or hegemon, willing to impose international trading regimes, and at the same time accept a disproportionate share of the cost of providing them. Conversely, in the absence of such leadership or in a situation in which the hegemon loses the capacity to impose these regimes, then the theory of hegemonic stability predicts a corresponding decline in their strength and durability, and hence a weakening in the liberal economic order itself. Within the specific context of *Pax Americana*, then, it is argued that the triple economic crisis of the early 1970s in terms of monetary, trade and energy regimes was directly connected to the loss of US hegemony, which allegedly occurred in this period.

In accordance with this theory, Aggarwal attempts to demonstrate that the weakening of the MFA during this period, which led to increasingly restrictive quotas being placed on most developing country exporters through the course of the 1970s and 1980s, was a direct consequence of the loss of US hegemony. As originally conceived, Aggarwal suggests, the MFA was consistent with the US preference for what he calls 'liberal protectionism' and was intended to create an 'orderly' trade in textiles and apparel through the gradual opening-up of Western markets to exports from developing countries. During the course of the 1970s, however, as US dominance of the international trading system began to dissipate, the MFA gradually came to reflect the preferences of the European countries for a more protectionist regime. At the same time, the loss of US hegemony in the international environment also presaged a corresponding weakening *vis-à-vis* domestic political interests, which pushed for better protection of their national industries. Overall, then, Aggarwal (1985: 4) sees the progressively more protectionist character of the MFA in this period as being consistent with the theory of hegemonic stability, in so far as the latter 'predicts strong regimes when a single power is dominant'.

Even though Aggarwal's narrative is broadly consistent with the theory of hegemony stability, it is important to note that it does actually deviate from the thesis, at least as it was originally conceived, in two important ways. First, Aggarwal qualifies his reference to hegemonic stability by insisting that the theory only provides an accurate explanation of regime strength if it is operationalized in terms of issue-specific capabilities. In the case of textiles and apparel, Aggarwal claims that, because these products tend to be more demand-elastic than other goods, market dominance needs to be measured specifically in terms of consumer power, rather than simply by reference to export/import performance. On this reading, he suggests, the US was overwhelmingly the dominant player in the international textile and apparel trade during the 1950s and 1960s, but by the late 1970s it had been overtaken by the European Economic Community (EEC). Thus, it was the change in the distribution of capabilities measured specifically in terms of textile and apparel consumption, rather than wider sources of geo-economic or geo-political power, that accounted for the weakening of the MFA from the late 1970s onwards.

Second, while Aggarwal's account is broadly consistent with hegemonic stability theory in the sense that it favours a 'systemic' over a 'reductionist' explanation, he is at pains to point out that his account does not neglect domestic factors. Indeed, Aggarwal (1983) specifically argues that in relation to the 1981 MFA renewal domestic interest groups in both Europe and the United States proved to be a 'significant constraint' on the type of regime that was ultimately agreed upon. Despite these caveats, however, one is left with the lasting impression that, in the final analysis, Aggarwal sees the evolution of the post-war textile and apparel regime as closely corresponding to the theory and predictions of the hegemonic stability model, as his ultimate conclusion regarding the 1981 MFA renewal testifies:

> Changes in the strength and nature of the regime appear to be caused by a shift in the distribution of capabilities and increasing competition from newly industrializing countries in the textile and apparel subsystems. In the matter of regime strength, the absence of a hegemon to impose or cajole others into subscribing to an international regime led to an accord that was of necessity a

product of compromise between two key actors - the EEC and the United States (Aggarwal, 1983: 643).

In what follows we offer an alternative reading of the development of the post-war textile and apparel regime. Following Helen Milner (1988: 298), it is argued that the evidence from the textile and apparel industries suggests that a 'sectoral pattern of trade policy cannot be explained by focusing on the loss of hegemony'. Rather, it is suggested that the gradual 'weakening' of the international textile and apparel regime, at least from the perspective of the United States, needs to be understood in terms of the historical weakness of the US state *vis-à-vis* domestically-orientated interest groups. In addition to this, it is further pointed out that, far from being linked to hegemonic decline, a more important factor in the weakening of the MFA was the unintended consequence of the regime itself, which paradoxically heightened the economic capabilities of developing country exporters, as well as intensifying the scope of global competition. This in turn led to even higher levels of import penetration of Western markets by developing country firms, thus leading to calls from domestically-orientated producers for further quantitative restrictions to be placed on these imports.

Within the IPE literature, there is a considerable body of evidence to support the assertion that the ability of a particular state to resist protectionist pressure is largely determined by the strength or weakness of that state *vis-à-vis* domestically-orientated interest groups (Katzenstein, 1978). The case of United States textile trade policy represents a case in point. The US state possesses relatively few independent resources in this area, is political fragmented, both in terms of the separation of powers (executive, legislature, judiciary) and also within the executive (multiple departments with different constituencies), and is vulnerable to penetration by sectional interest groups. In contrast, the textile and apparel lobby has developed a strong political base over the entirety of the post-1945 period through peak organizations such as the American Textile Manufacturers Institute (ATMI) and the American Apparel Manufactures Association (AAMA). Through these peak associations, the US textile and apparel lobby established multiple channels of access to decision-making centres (including both executive agencies and departments and Congress, especially), articulating a broad-based and consistent set of protectionist policies. The end result of this political imbalance between the US state and the textile and apparel lobby has been that the latter has effectively set the tone for US sectoral trade policy since the early 1950s.

The earliest manifestations of this protectionist pressure within the US came with the establishment of voluntary export restraints (VERs) with Japan in the mid 1950s, following the latter's entry into the GATT in 1955, which placed quantitative limits on certain textile and apparel export categories. Despite this, though, these measures did little to protect US domestic textile industries, but merely exposed them to a wider scope of low-wage competition: while Japan's share of US textile imports actually fell from 63 per cent in 1958 to 26 per cent in 1960, this was accompanied by a surge in imports from Hong Kong, whose share of US textile imports rose from 14 to 28 per cent in the same period, and other developing countries such as India and Pakistan (Cline, 1990: 46). This proliferation of low-wage competition in the 1950s convinced industry leaders to press US policy makers towards a more comprehensive programme of quota restrictions, which was ultimately expressed in two separate - though closely related - policy responses. First, at the behest of US trade negotiators, the concept of 'market disruption' - defined as 'instances of sharp import increases associated with low import prices not attributable to dumping or foreign subsidies' - was enshrined in the GATT treaty in November 1960 (Cline, 1990: 147). Significantly, the concept of market disruption departed from normal GATT rules in so far as it stipulated that import restrictions could be enforced even if injury had not taken place, provided that a *potential* threat could be demonstrated. In addition, it further departed from GATT rules in that quantitative restrictions could be placed on a particular country and the most-favoured nation (MFN) principle not applied. Finally, the concept of market disruption also established an important precedent with regard to the price differential between imported and comparable domestic goods. In other words, because developing countries were deemed to possess an 'unfair' advantage over developed countries in terms of lower labour costs, it was reasoned that price differentials constituted sufficient grounds for quantitative import restrictions to be imposed.

The second major policy response to emanate from US textile industry calls for greater protection was the establishment of the Short Term Arrangement Regarding International Trade in Cotton Textiles (STA) in October 1961. This authorized a one-year restriction for 64 categories of cotton textiles in order to avoid market disruption until a more permanent agreement could be reached. The STA was extended in February 1962 when 19 major trading nations adopted the Long Term Arrangement Regarding International Trade in Cotton Textiles (LTA), which was effective until 1973. As with the adoption of the market disruption clause in 1960, the LTA was very much designed to address the alleged peculiarities of the textile and apparel industries without jeopardising trade liberalization in other areas. More specifically, from the perspective of the US, the Kennedy administration saw the LTA as a necessary concession to the textile and apparel lobby, to which it had pledged support in the run-up to the 1960 presidential election, in order to persuade it to acquiesce in the launching of what came to be known as the Kennedy Round of multilateral trade negotiations (Destler, 1995).

At the same time, the LTA was justified by US policy makers in terms of establishing an 'orderly' development of trade in textiles and apparel through a gradual opening-up of its market to developing country exports (originally set at an average annual growth rate of 5 per cent), while simultaneously enabling domestic industry to restructure and modernize. In practice, however, the LTA achieved neither of these goals (Glasmeier *et al.*, 1993). First, although the LTA did manage to regulate international trade in cotton textiles, these restrictions had the effect of pushing low-wage - particularly East Asian - producers towards the manufacture and export of artificial and non-cotton textile products, which were not covered by the agreement. Consequently, despite 83 countries having signed the LTA by 1973, import growth persisted: measured at 1982 prices, Cline (1990: 148) estimates that US textile imports grew from US$1.02 billion in 1961 to US$2.4 billion in 1972; while in the same period apparel imports grew from US$648 million to US$3.5 billion. Taken together, US textile and apparel imports during the 1960s grew at an annual rate of 11.5 per cent.

Second, although supporters of the LTA within the US had argued that trade restrictions would allow domestic industry time to restructure and modernize textile and apparel production, the steps taken by neither government nor industry were sufficient to ensure this. Instead, firms began to shift domestic production from the north east towards the south and west of the US in search of lower wages and less stringent labour regulation. In 1950, for example, six north east states accounted for 40.5 per cent of all textile employment; by 1970 they accounted for only 21.7 per cent. Similarly, in the apparel sector, New York and Pennsylvania alone accounted for 47 per cent of all employment in the industry in 1950, whereas by 1970 the proportion had dropped to 31 per cent; at the same time, South Carolina, Georgia, Tennessee and Alabama increased their share of total apparel employment from 7.4 per cent in 1950 to 22 per cent in 1970 (Aggarwal, with Haggard, 1983: 256-7). As this geographical shift was taking place, the peak associations of the textile and apparel lobby continued to press the US federal government in the direction of further import controls. The outcome of these demands is discussed next.

The evident failure of the LTA to restrict US imports during the 1960s prompted industry leaders and policy makers in Washington to seek an extension of the textile agreement to deal with the rapid expansion in artificial and non-cotton textile imports. For this purpose, the incoming Nixon administration attempted to enlist the support of the EEC for a multi-fibre agreement on textiles and apparel as a means of providing legitimacy for the extension of quota protection to man-made fibres and woollen goods. Initially, however, European governments saw little merit in the extension of LTA coverage, given that these countries had been more successful, not only in terms of restricting their own imports, but also, at least in this period, in exporting a substantial volume of textile products to the US market (see Underhill, 1990). As the US saw it, though, once it proceeded to establish a multi-fibre agreement for controlling textile imports, the subsequent import diversion from the US to the EEC would force European governments to enact regulations that included artificial and non-cotton fibres. In accordance with this logic, in 1971 the United States negotiated bilateral agreements restricting imports of man-made fibre and wool products from Hong Kong, Korea, Taiwan and Japan - the latter only agreeing to further export restraints after President Nixon had threatened to restrict imports of textiles and apparel unilaterally under the 'Trading with the Enemy Act'.[1]

By 1972, the import diversion resulting from the bilateral agreements between the US and Japan and the NICs pressured European governments into accepting a new multilateral framework covering artificial and non-cotton textiles. Thus, following protracted negotiations in 1973, the Arrangement Regarding

International Trade in Textiles, more commonly known as the Multi-Fibre Arrangement, was duly signed and entered into effect on 1 January 1974. Essentially, the MFA constituted no more than a general framework for determining the conditions under which bilateral export restraint agreements could be implemented. Nevertheless, it was seen, at least by US policy makers, as a means of providing legitimacy for the extension of quota protection to artificial and non-cotton fibres without jeopardising the GATT multilateral framework. In practice, these agreements centred on a series of product and category-specific quotas that were set at an annual 6 per cent growth rate (instead of the 5 per cent growth rate stipulated by the LTA). Additionally, several caveats were added to the MFA to make the regime more flexible, including: (1) *'swing'* allowed participating countries to transfer any unfilled quotas to different product categories; (2) *'carry forward'* permitted the exporting country to borrow against a future year's quota; and (3) *'carry over'* permitted the exporting country to add unused quota to the subsequent year's imports.

Between 1974 and 1995 the MFA protocol was re-negotiated four times (in 1977, 1981, 1986, 1991) and on each occasion the quota system became more, rather than less, restrictive. Under MFA II (1977-1981), for example, the EEC successfully negotiated a 'reasonable departure' clause from the terms of the original agreement, which allowed participating countries to establish bilateral agreements that no longer had to comply with the MFA. As a result, for a number of import-sensitive product categories quota growth rates were permitted to fall below the statutory 6 per cent, and in some cases the figure dropped to zero. In addition to this, US fears over imports from Hong Kong, Korea and Taiwan led to a considerable tightening of the 'swing' and 'carry over' provisions, despite the fact that five-year bilateral agreements had only been signed with these countries the previous year. In subsequent MFA renewals, additional restrictions included the establishment of a 'call' mechanism, which required consultations between trading countries if imports exceeded certain levels or threatened to lead to 'market disruption', and the introduction of stricter 'rules of origin' to prevent exporting countries from re-routing goods through a third country in order to circumvent quota restrictions.

In summary, between 1974 and 1990 the MFA oversaw bilateral textile agreements between 43 signatories representing 54 countries. In this period, the US alone established quotas with 34 countries to the extent that quantitative restrictions covered approximately 80 per cent of its textile and apparel imports from developing countries. The scope of the MFA notwithstanding, by the mid 1980s it was seen by many developed and developing countries as having failed in its main objective of creating a more 'orderly' trade in textile and apparel products. Within the US the MFA regime was charged by industry leaders with not having served its primary function of controlling the flow of textile and apparel imports from low-wage countries, particularly in the early to mid 1980s when US imports grew at an annual rate of between 12 and 22 per cent (Aggarwal, 1985). Understanding the persistence of this growth despite the increasingly punitive nature of successive MFA renewals merits further consideration. First, the fact that the MFA was conducted on a bilateral basis tended to encourage non-regulated countries to enter the market, initially as transshipment points for firms which had reached their quota ceiling, but subsequently as textile suppliers in their own right. In this respect, the oversees investment strategies of Japanese textile firms and general trading companies, the *sogo shosha*, were particularly instrumental in encouraging neighbouring economies in Asia to enter the textile and apparel export market. Beginning in the early 1960s as a response to the introduction of the LTA, Japanese textile firms and the *sogo shosha* quickly moved to circumvent quota restrictions by setting up international subcontracting links with other East and South East Asian countries, which were either not signatories to the MFA regime or had not filled their allocated quota. Hence, one of the major, and clearly unintended, consequences of the MFA quota regime was that it led to the internationalization of textile and apparel production in the East Asian region, which in turn widened the scope of low-wage competition faced by developed counties.

A second factor accounting for the persistence of US import growth despite the presence of the MFA relates to the way in which quota levels were calculated. Because the MFA calculated imports on the basis of their physical volume - that is, the total weight or quantity of garments - exporting countries actually had an incentive to produce higher value goods in order to maximize revenue from quantities shipped within the quota restrictions allowed. One dimension of this tendency that occurred among East Asian suppliers during the late 1970s and early 1980s was the shift away from producing textile fabrics and other intermediate goods towards producing finished apparel items. For example, on the basis of International Trade Commission (ITC) figures, Cline (1990: 155) shows a clear pattern between particular product categories and the rate of import growth: while the volume of US yarn imports measured in the standard yard equivalent (SYE) declined from 1.9 billion in 1972 to 1.25 billion in 1985, those of the next stage of processing, fabric, rose from 1.7 billion to 2.4 billion; of the subsequent stage, apparel, imports increased in the same period from 2.2 billion to 5 billion; and for made-up textile items (e.g. carpets) imports grew from 0.4 billion to 1.1 billion. Thus, the corresponding annual growth rates for these four product categories in this period (equalling -3.2 per cent, 2.8 per cent, 6.5 per cent and 8.1 percent respectively) show a clear ascending order by stage of production (which, incidentally, also explains why apparel has suffered more from imports than textiles). In an odd way, then, we can see how the MFA inadvertently heightened the competitive capabilities of developing country firms by encouraging them to upgrade to the production and export of higher value goods.

Despite all of this, however, it remains undeniable that the MFA *still* greatly restricted the rate of export growth from low-wage countries, which has been far lower than would have been the case in the absence of the MFA. After all, it is worth noting that textile and apparel trade between developed countries - which, in 1990, accounted for approximately 43 per cent of total world trade in textiles and 35 per cent of total world trade in apparel - is not subject to the MFA and is thus free from quantitative import restrictions (Cline, 1990: 156). In fact, the MFA is almost completely unique as an international trade regime in that it explicitly discriminates *against* developing countries. However, since the conclusion of the 1995 GATT Uruguay Round, progressive steps have been taken gradually to incorporate textiles and apparel into the multilateral framework, now governed by the World Trade Organization (WTO). As part of the Uruguay Round settlement, on 1 January 1995 the Agreement on Textiles and Clothing (ATC) replaced the MFA as a transitional instrument for facilitating the gradual integration of textiles and apparel into the WTO multilateral framework. Under the ATC, importing countries agreed to phase out MFA quotas over a ten-year period but in four separate stages: 16 per cent between 1995 and 1998; 17 per cent between 1998 and 2002; 18 per cent between 2002 and 2004; with the remaining 49 per cent of import quotas scheduled to be phased out by January 2005. According to Hoekman and Kostecki (2001), the decision of developed countries to agree to the liberalization of the international textile and apparel regime through the ATC was partly due to pressure from different interest groups, including exporting countries, which believed they would do better under a more competitive (i.e. less managed) trade regime, and retailers and consumer organizations in high-income countries which pushed for lower-cost goods. More fundamentally, however, they put the decision to phase out the MFA down to the strategic calculations on the part of developed countries - particularly the US - that the liberalization of the textile and apparel regime would give them significantly more room for manoeuvre with regard to trade liberalization in more controversial areas, such as trade-related intellectual property rights (TRIPS), trade-related investment measures (TRIMS) and services (Hoekman and Kostecki, 2001). Yet, despite the ostensibly liberal nature of this move, the ATC far from guarantees the full opening-up of the textile and apparel trade. In the case of the US, the majority of the product categories scheduled for integration into the WTO framework in the first three phases of the ATC are generally ones that already enjoy quota-free treatment. As a consequence, its ten-year liberalization strategy effectively leaves the elimination of 70 per cent of import quotas to the very end of the transition period. Taking into account the political weight of those interest groups within the US hostile to liberalization, the full implementation of the ATC is, not surprisingly, far from assured (Jacobs, 1995; Williams, 1996).

All in all, then, the evolution of the MFA regime over the period described has led to the emergence of an essentially 'managed' - albeit imperfectly so - trade system in the textile and apparel industries. While, clearly, this system has important consequences for developing countries in terms of limiting the market opportunities available to their low-cost exporting firms, for our more immediate purposes the question that primarily concerns us is its effects on US industry. In the light of the foregoing discussion, it is tempting to see the current level of foreign competition faced by US industry as resulting from the actions of firms and governments in other countries seeking to develop their own US-targeted export industries, the MFA notwithstanding. As will be argued, however, this interpretation overlooks the somewhat paradoxical situation whereby much of the recent growth in textile and apparel imports entering the US market has in fact been organized and co-ordinated by its own firms locating production overseas (Dicken, 1998). In accordance with this trend, the following section of the chapter will show the extent to which the industrial restructuring within the US textile and apparel industries has been also tied, not only to the geographical dispersal of these industries from developed to developing countries, but to the specific reconfiguration of the US production complex as retailers and branded marketeers have gradually come to supplant manufacturers in terms of controlling and coordinating the entire supply chain.

Buyer-Driven 'Commodity Chains' and the Restructuring of the US Textile and Apparel Complex

In Chapter One we introduced the concept of a global 'commodity chain' and defined it as a network of labour and production processes (e.g. research and design, raw materials, manufacture, marketing and sales) whose end result is a finished commodity. In a further delineation of this concept, we then introduced Gereffi's distinction between those commodity chains that are primarily 'producer-driven' and those that are primarily 'buyer-driven'. That is to say, in industries that rely on a high level of capital intensity and technological sophistication (e.g. automobiles, computers and semiconductors), it is generally the manufacturing firms which play the key role in co-ordinating production and distribution, including taking responsibility for both backward (sourcing) and forward (marketing) linkages. In contrast, light manufacturing industries that produce labour-intensive consumer goods (e.g. garments, footwear and electronics) are more likely to be organized around a decentralized system of production wherein retailers and marketeers, as opposed to those firms actually responsible for producing the goods, play the key co-ordinating role.

In what follows, we will attempt to utilize the commodity chains framework and, more specifically, the concept of producer/buyer-driven chains as a means of discerning the major structural changes currently underway in the US textile and apparel industries. Clearly, these changes - which include the utilization of new technology and the rationalization of domestic production, as well as investment in offshore manufacturing - reflect to a large degree the failure of the MFA to protect US industry from foreign competition. At a more fundamental level, however, these changes need to be understood as part of the reconfiguration of the US textile and apparel complex as retailers and branded marketeers have gradually come to supplant manufacturers in terms of controlling and coordinating the entire supply chain. For this reason, it is incumbent upon us to begin this part of our investigation by examining the specific actions of US retailers and marketeers before moving on to look at the activities of manufacturing firms and the ways in which they have impacted upon the broader political economy of the US-Caribbean apparel trade.

The Role of Retailers in the United States Textile and Apparel Complex

Although, traditionally, the US retailing sector was seen as the main customer of the domestic apparel industry - and thus indirectly of the textile industry, which supplies the bulk of its fabrics and other intermediate components - it is now increasingly perceived as a major source of competition. In 1975, for example, US garment retailers relied upon imports for only 12 per cent of the apparel consumed by US customers; by the mid 1990s, this figure had risen to well over 50 per cent and, in some product lines, virtually all apparel consumed in the US is now imported (Dickerson, 1999). According to the US Customs Service's Net Import File, US retailers were responsible for 48 per cent of the total value of imported apparel sold by the top hundred US clothing firms in 1993; branded apparel marketeers (i.e. those firms which perform design and marketing tasks but outsource the actual production of apparel to foreign and domestic contractors) were responsible for a further 22 per cent of the value of these imports, while branded apparel manufacturers (not including 9802.00 production-sharing activities, which are discussed later) made up an additional 20 per cent of the total (Jones, 1995: 26). In short, US retailers and branded marketeers have come to assume an important role in heightening the competitive pressures faced by domestic textile and apparel producers.

According to Gereffi (1994), the changing relationship between retailers and domestic clothing producers is the result of a fundamental process of restructuring within the textile and apparel supply chain as a whole. Over the last several decades, he argues, a 'retail revolution' has taken place in the United States, as clothing chains and retail outlets have responded to changing consumer preferences by adopting 'flexible specialization' marketing strategies that are based on small-scale and just-in-time production, rather than the traditional pattern of mass production associated with Fordism (Piore and Sabel, 1984). To be more precise, the oligopolistic pattern that typified the US retail sector during the late 1960s and 1970s, wherein large department stores and mass merchandisers (e.g. J.C. Penny, Sears and Montgomery Ward), offering a broad selection of general merchandise suitable for 'family shopping', were able to use economies of scale and mass advertising in order to deal with competition from independent retailers, came under increasing strain in the 1980s as this mass market fragmented into distinct, if overlapping, retail constituencies. In the process, traditional department stores and mass merchandisers found themselves increasingly squeezed between large-volume discount chains (e.g. Wal-Mart, K-Mart and Target), on the one hand, and a wide variety of newly emerging speciality clothing retailers (e.g. Gap, The Limited and Liz Claiborne), on the other (Gereffi, 1994).

One of the major consequences of this process was that it led to a further concentration of the US retailing sector in the hands of small number of key retailing chains and buying groups. In 1995 the five largest US retailers - Wal-Mart, Sears, K-Mart, Dayton Hudson and J.C. Penny - accounted for approximately 68 per cent of all apparel sold in the US, while the next 24 retailers represented an additional 30 per cent of these sales. In the burgeoning non-traditional retail sector (e.g. large-volume discount stores, off-price retailers and factory outlets), the level of market concentration is particularly striking. As of the mid 1990s, Wal-Mart, K-Mart and Target (a division of Dayton Hudson) were alone responsible for over 70 per cent of the booming discount-store business, which itself accounted for approximately 25 per cent of all apparel consumed within the US (Gereffi, 1999: 44). The growing concentration of buying power in the US retailing sector among large-volume discount chains such as Wal-Mart and K-Mart and the increasing tendency of these retailers to establish fewer, but closer, relationships with suppliers have significantly intensified competition among apparel producers, both domestic and foreign. This has manifested itself in considerable downward pressure on apparel manufacturers in terms of lower unit prices, shorter orders and faster product turnover. At the same time, traditional mass merchandisers, such as Sears and J.C. Penny, which now focus on private label (i.e. store-brand) goods as a means of competing directly with the national brand-name goods sold by discount stores, have begun to assume many of the entrepreneurial functions hitherto carried out by apparel manufacturers, including product design, fabric selection, procurement and even production (Jones, 1995).

At the other end of the US retail market, the activities of branded marketeers - so-called 'manufacturers without factories' - have had a comparable effect on domestic apparel production. Unlike the standardized apparel sector, where high volume production very much remains the norm, the fashion-orientated end of the US retail chain is highly vulnerable to changing consumer preferences, with many of today's top retailers adopting six or more buying seasons every year (Gereffi, 1994). Because of this, the most dynamic aspect of the fashion end of the US apparel market in the late 1980s and 1990s was not to be found among established retailers, but rather from hybrid firms (e.g. Gap, Liz Claiborne and The Limited) which do not actually possess manufacturing facilities, but operate a decentralized system of offshore manufacturing, wherein overseas contractors perform all specialist tasks apart from research and design, marketing and sales. The advantage of this particular strategy is that it enables the coordinating firm - that is, the branded marketeer - to maximize organizational flexibility in terms of utilising quick response and just-in-time production techniques, while at the same time shielding itself from responsibility and legal liability for the workers employed in overseas factories (Appelbaum and Gereffi, 1994). From the perspective of domestic producers, on the other hand, the particular disadvantage of this type of manufacturing system is that it more or less eliminates the need for domestic suppliers in the overall production chain.

All things considered, then, the strategic reorientation of the US retailing sector in the last two decades has had an enormous effect on the configuration of the textile and apparel commodity chain. Whereas in the past US clothing firms have primarily relied upon the retail industry for their main source of income, the actions of US retailers and branded marketeers are now increasingly at odds with the needs of these domestic suppliers. To put it another way, the US textile and apparel commodity chain is becoming progressively transformed into a *buyer-driven* chain in the sense that it is now predominantly the retailers and branded marketeers, as opposed to those firms actually responsible for producing the goods, which play the key co-ordinating role. As we shall see shortly, this transformation has had particularly deleterious consequences for domestic apparel manufacturers, which have been effectively marginalized within their own market place. Before examining these consequences and the strategic responses that US apparel firms have adopted, however, it is first necessary to take a brief look at the textile sector, which has also been affected - albeit indirectly - by the changing dynamics of the apparel supply chain.

Restructuring in the Textile Industry

The textile mill industry consists of those firms responsible for transforming natural and synthetic fibres into yarns used in the production of garments and other end-use products by apparel manufacturers. Although these firms are only indirectly affected by changes at the retail level, the shift from producer-driven to buyer-driven commodity chains has nonetheless had important consequences for the textile mill industry, given that approximately 50 per cent of all textile production goes into the manufacture of garments. According to Glasmeier *et al.* (1993), textile firms have tended to pursue one of three broad, in some cases overlapping, strategies in their response to the threat posed by low-cost imports fuelled by the global sourcing activities of US retailers. First, by investing heavily in new technology, some US textile firms continue to produce highly standardized goods for large markets and use the economies of scale associated with high volume production in order to reduce marginal costs and compete on the basis of price. Second, other textile producers have chosen to supply these very same markets, but, rather than investing heavily in new technology, have done so through establishing links to extremely low-cost labour sites found offshore in neighbouring countries (e.g. Mexico and the Caribbean Basin). Third, and at the opposite extreme, some generally smaller textile firms have been able to remain competitive by specialising in the production of small quantities of high-quality goods for specific niche markets, which are sold at a premium in order to offset the additional costs of constantly switching the specifications of small-scale production. For the most part, then, the strategic response of the textile sector to competition from low-wage countries has been built on a combination of capital intensification and offshore investment for larger firms, while smaller firms have been inclined to pursue niche market opportunities overlooked by their larger domestic rivals. In other words, the size of a particular textile firm and, more importantly, its overall position within the production chain has tended to shape its strategic options and hence its ability to respond to competition, both foreign and domestic.

Taken as a whole, the US textile mill industry is among the most heavily fragmented of all manufacturing sectors, with an estimated 6,000 firms employing approximately 707,000 workers in 1992, predominantly located in the south eastern part of the country (Finnie, 1992). In many cases, the traditional pattern of textile mill employment remains: that is, small rural establishments that dominate the economic base of the local community, but typically employ less than 50 or so workers. Yet, while this general pattern still prevails, in a number of significant product areas the US textile industry has in recent years become increasingly dominated by a handful of vertically integrated corporations (e.g. Burlington

Industries, Guilford Mills and Cone Mills), and it is principally these firms that have made the most use of new technologies and offshore manufacturing, as well as protectionist government policies, in order to offset competition from low-wage sources.

Unlike apparel, where, as we shall see shortly, technological innovation has had a relatively minor part to play in the industrial restructuring process, the advent of new technology in the US textile sector (or at least parts of it) has played an integral part in its strategic response. Broadly speaking, there are two kinds of technological change within the textile industry that have been especially important - those which increase the speed and efficiency with which a particular manufacturing process can be carried out and those which replace manual labour with mechanized and automated operations - and in both cases the impact of these developments has been extensive. For example, Dicken (1998: 297) estimates that the advent of open-ended yarn spinning, which combines what were formerly two separate processes into one by using rotors instead of spindles, has contributed to a fourfold increase in spinning speeds while reducing labour requirements by approximately 40 per cent. In the same way, parallel developments with regard to textile weaving, knitting technology and in finishing have further led to the increased speed and efficiency of textile operations and a consequent reduction in the number of workers required by the industry. The cumulative result of these technological innovations has been to enhance greatly the competitive capabilities of US textile mill operations, both in terms of productivity and lower labour costs. Again, however, these developments have not been evenly distributed throughout the industry, as the ability of individual textile firms to utilize these new technologies depends on their ability to afford capital investment in the first place, which in turn is shaped by their overall position in the textile production chain.

Equally, the ability of US textile firms to offset foreign competition by utilising low-wage labour through offshore investment is also shaped by the position of the individual firm in the overall production chain. In recent years a number of larger, vertically integrated US textile firms have sought to combine capital intensification with offshore investments in Mexico and the Caribbean Basin, although, as we shall see, this strategy is still far less commonplace in textiles than in apparel. This latter point notwithstanding, for a number of these firms the ability to tap into the low-cost labour found in Mexico, in particular, has come to represent a central component in the revitalization of parts of the US textile industry.[2] Since the implementation of the tariff-free and quota-free 'yarn forward' ruling as part of the NAFTA agreement (which is discussed further in Chapters Five and Six), a number of US textile firms, including Burlington Industries, Guilford Mills and Cone Mills, have looked to strengthen their overall presence in Mexico through joint ventures, acquisitions and other arrangements with local firms (Gereffi and Bair, 1998; Millman, 2000). According to Gereffi and Bair (1998: 27-8), the strategic rationale behind this move has been three fold. First, it has enabled US firms to improve their competitive standing in the region by taking advantage of the weakness of the Mexican textile industry in certain areas, especially in the manufacture of natural and synthetic fibres; second, it has allowed US textile suppliers to establish more of a presence near the country's rapidly expanding apparel sector; and, third, it has allowed US firms to take advantage of low-wages and Mexico's geographical proximity to the US, in order to supply the home market via direct imports.

As we have already noted, however, the twin competitive advantages of capital intensification and offshore production are not currently available to all sectors of the US textile production chain. Although the textile sector is now dominated by a handful of vertically integrated firms, the industry as a whole is still made up of small rural establishments that generally lack access to sophisticated technology and links to low-cost labour. Even though, as previously suggested, some of these smaller firms have managed to remain competitive by specialising in the production of small quantities of high quality goods for specific niche markets, the opportunities for other firms to replicate this strategy are generally constrained by the high costs involved in constantly updating product specifications in order to meet changing market conditions. Moreover, since the late 1980s many of these smaller textile firms have found themselves increasingly caught between the oligopolistic practices of vertically integrated textile firms (e.g. predatory pricing, establishing customer loyalty through brand reputation and eliminating competition through acquisition), on the one hand, and competition from low-cost foreign imports, on the other. Thus, even as vertically integrated textile firms have successfully offset 'foreign' competition by investing in new technologies and offshore manufacturing, the small business sector has had to bear the brunt of industrial restructuring in the US textile industry, which has manifested itself in approximately half a million job losses since 1973.

Restructuring in the Apparel Industry

In common with textiles, the US apparel sector - that is, those firms responsible for transforming yarns and cloth into garments and other apparel items - has been historically and remains characterized by a high level of industry fragmentation. In 1999 the US International Trade Commission (USITC) estimated that, of the approximately 18,000 apparel establishments in operation in the United States, 60 per cent employed less than 20 workers, and only 10 per cent of the total number of firms employed more than 100 workers. At the same time, however, in certain product areas the industry has come to be increasingly dominated by a handful of firms. In 1998, for instance, VF Corporation (26.1 per cent) and Levi Strauss & Co. (14.8 per cent) accounted for 40 per cent of the US jeans market; while Sara Lee and Fruit of the Loom were responsible for more than two-thirds of the sale of men's and boys' underwear and for around one half of those for women and girls (USITC, 1999a). The apparel sector thus shares much in common with textiles in that, even though it is predominantly made up of small, mostly rural, manufacturing plants, the industry as a whole is essentially oligopolistic in structure.

Nevertheless, while the apparel industry shares much in common with textiles in terms of industry structure, the two sectors contrast sharply in their respective levels of technological sophistication. As we have just seen, major textile firms have to a large degree been able to offset competition from low-wage countries by investing in new technologies, which have greatly enhanced the speed and efficiency of textile operations at the same time as dramatically reducing the number of workers required by the industry. In contrast to this, capital intensification has played a relatively minor role in the restructuring of the US apparel industry. For example, even though the introduction of computer-assisted design (CAD), coupled with the application of micro-technology to the grading and cutting process, has led to significant increases in speed and efficiency in relation to the pre-assembly stages of production (Hoffman, 1985), the result of these innovations has been somewhat double-edged. Because these changes generally relate to the pre-assembly stage of the production process, any improvements that have been made in terms of speed and efficiency extend to less than five per cent of total labour costs, but at the same time affect the most highly-skilled members of the industry's workforce (Parsons, 1988). In the same way, technical innovation in peripheral sewing operations (e.g. pocket stitching and belt loop construction) and improved machine flexibility, both of which have partially automated production, especially in the standardized product market, have yet to be fully extended to the main sewing operations (Mody and Wheeler, 1987). All told, when it comes to the actual sewing and assembly of garments, which still accounts for approximately 90 per cent of total labour costs, the impact of technological innovation in the apparel industry has been minimal.

The consequences of the failure of capital intensification within the apparel sector in terms of bankruptcies and attendant job losses have been considerable: between 1970 and 1997 apparel employment in the US fell from 1.4 million, or the equivalent of seven per cent of the country's manufacturing workforce, to 0.8 million, or four per cent of the country's manufacturing workforce; and the industry currently has the highest attrition rate of any US manufacturing sector, accounting for 9 per cent of all business failures in 1997 (ECLAC, 2000: 55). Of course, many of the problems that the apparel industry has faced in this respect can be put down to the peculiarities of the MFA regime, which, as we have already seen, have tended to encourage importing firms to switch from textiles to apparel in order to maximize revenue from their quota allowance. Added to this, the apparel industry has suffered disproportionately from the costs of adjustment due to its relatively weak domestic position *vis-à-vis* the retail and textile industries. Not only has the apparel industry had to bear the brunt of the increasing concentration of market power on the demand side, which has manifested itself in calls by the major retailing chains and buying groups for lower prices, shorter orders and faster product turnover, but it has also had to deal with the growing power of textile suppliers pushing for larger orders, higher prices for inputs and favourable (to the textiles firms, that is) payment schedules.[3] Thus, in the shift from producer-driven to buyer-driven commodity chains the apparel industry has found itself increasingly squeezed between the growing power of retailers, on the one hand, and the growing power of the textile industry, on the other.

Yet, at the same time as this transformation has produced numerous casualties in terms of business failures and job losses, as with textiles, these costs have not been evenly distributed throughout the apparel industry. In fact, among the major apparel producers which dominate the US clothing market (e.g. VF Corporation and Levi Strauss & Co; Sara Lee and Fruit of the Loom), the process of industrial restructuring has turned out to be quite beneficial: between 1993 and 1997 the top 10 apparel firms in the US, each with annual sales in excess of US$1 billion, increased their sales by on average 26 per cent (USITC, 1999a). The contrasting fortunes between these firms and those which, numerically at least, make up the US apparel industry can partly be explained in terms of the capacity of the former to use economies of scale in order to make the most of technical innovation (especially in the production of highly standardized apparel items, such as jeans and T-shirts) and to acquire rival companies through merger and acquisition (VF Corporation, for instance, acquired no less than 6 of its major rivals between 1969 and 1998). Nevertheless, the key to understanding the economic buoyancy of parts of the US apparel sector at a time when the rest continues to experience industrial decline lies not in the first instance with economies of scale or technological innovation, but rather with the fact that these larger firms have chosen to invest in offshore assembly in order to remain competitive in their own market.

As we have already noted, the paradox at the heart of the politics of US textile trade policy is that much of the growth in imports - which has been of such concern to domestically-orientated interest groups - has in fact been organized and co-ordinated by US firms locating production overseas. In the past, this activity has been predominantly based on the global sourcing strategies of US retailers and garment importers; now, however, a growing proportion of this trade is accounted for by branded apparel manufacturers seeking to reduce costs by locating production overseas. During the late 1980s and 1990s, many of these firms, including VF Corporation and Sara Lee, began to adopt a 'if you can't beat them, join them' attitude towards international subcontracting, as they sought to avoid competing directly with low-cost importers - and by extension US retailers - and instead outsource their own manufacturing activities to these countries. At the same time, a process of domestic restructuring accompanied this strategy, which involved the 'de-verticalization' of production in favour of moves towards marketing and retail. As a Sara Lee executive explained in the mid 1990s, 'the operating model for today's exemplary [clothing] companies no longer needs to include significant manufacturing assets...we've determined that we no longer need to own all the assets needed in manufacturing the products we sell' (cited in Gereffi, 1999: 48). Thus, it has been precisely companies, such as VF Corporation (which cut its staff from 68,000 to 62,800 between 1994 and 1998), Levi Strauss & Co (from 36,500 to 30,000) and Fruit of the Loom (from 37,400 to 28,000), which have been shedding jobs in the US while simultaneously investing in offshore assembly operations (ECLAC, 2000).

That said, the actual pattern of offshore sourcing and subcontracting more generally within US apparel industry often varies according to the overall market position and the individual strategy of the firm in question. Broadly speaking, there are three primary options available to apparel firms seeking to reduce costs through outsourcing aspects of the production process, either domestically or overseas (Taplin, 1994). First, generally smaller apparel firms have tended to retain production within the US but to outsource the assembly stages of production to independent contractors. This practice of domestic subcontracting is particularly prevalent in the fashion-orientated sector located near to major cities such as Los Angeles, New York and Miami, where a high concentration of low-skilled female and immigrant labour allows 'flexible' working practices and other wage-depressing tactics to exist. Because this trade invariably centres on the use of illegal and undocumented workers - for whom work in the apparel industry often constitutes employment of 'first and last resort' - contractors have been able to use a 'third world' labour force in what amounts to *de facto* 'third world' labour market conditions (Taplin, 1994). Thus, not unlike the geographical dispersal of the apparel manufacturing at the global level, the reconfiguration of the apparel supply chain domestically has led, among other things, to a changing geographical division of labour within the US heavily reliant on immigrant labour, largely composed of workers of Caribbean or Hispanic origin.

Second, firms may choose to outsource the entire production process to an overseas firm, whereupon local enterprises accept responsibility for procuring the raw materials and then manufacture the product to the strict specifications of the buyer. In the past this type of contract manufacturing has been the sole preserve of major retailing chains, which have used a variety of first (Hong Kong, Taiwan, Korea and China) and second (Malaysia, Philippines, Indonesia and so on) tier East Asian firms to supply the US market. This option is now, however, becoming progressively more popular with 'up-market' branded apparel manufacturers as well (e.g. Ralph Lauren, Donna Karan and Tommy Hilfiger), as it allows these firms to combine cost-competitiveness and organizational flexibility without compromising the high quality required by the non-standardized fashion end of the US retail sector. Significantly, also, from the perspective of the recipient offshore firm, this type of arrangement has a number of advantages in that it gives it a crucial stake in co-ordinating backward linkages (e.g. fabric, buttons and thread) with the domestic economy, enabling these firms to engage in the process of industrial learning that ultimately facilitates their own country's process of economic development (Gereffi, 1999).

A third option available to apparel firms seeking to utilize offshore production - and one that is of the greatest significance to our study - entails taking advantage of specific tax benefits available to US firms through the HTS 9802.00 tariff scheme. As we have already discovered, the 9802.00 scheme permits duty exemption on US-made components that are returned as part of articles assembled abroad. Although this scheme discriminates against the type of 'full package' contract manufacturing described above, it has nevertheless proved to be a highly attractive option for those US apparel firms which have sought to outsource only the most labour-intensive aspects of the production process. In more specific terms, the HTS scheme has enabled US apparel firms producing highly standardized apparel items, such as jeans, T-shirts and underwear, to supply intermediate inputs (e.g. cut fabric, thread, buttons and other trim) to 9802.00 beneficiary firms (almost exclusively located in either Mexico or the Caribbean Basin) which are then responsible for assembling the garment to be subsequently re-imported into the US with tariff charged only on the value added by foreign labour. From the perspective of the US apparel industry, the advantage of this particular scheme over other forms of contract manufacturing is to be found in the fact that it allows the higher value added activities (e.g. cutting, grading and dyeing), which require greater skill levels, to be retained within the US. Unfortunately, though, from the perspective of the 'beneficiary' country, the 9802.00 production-sharing model is distinctly less advantageous than contract manufacturing in terms of creating opportunities for the overseas firm to establish backward linkages with its domestic economy, or upgrade to higher value added manufacturing activities (Heron, 2002). Despite these problems - and they are considerable - the HTS 9802.00 regime has nonetheless played a key role in integrating the northern Caribbean into an extended North America apparel commodity chain, as we shall soon discover.

Conclusion

This chapter has sought to examine the process of industrial restructuring within the US textile and apparel complex against the backdrop of the historical failure of the MFA to protect US industry from low-wage competition. In so doing, it has argued that the gradual weakening that the MFA experienced during the 1970s had less to do with the changing position of the US within the wider international political economy than it did with its specific sectoral weakness *vis-à-vis* textile interest groups, which pushed for better protection for their own industries from newly emerging sources of global competition. Because of the peculiarities of the MFA, however, once enacted the regime actually exacerbated the problems faced by US firms by paradoxically heightening the economic capabilities of exporting countries, as well as intensifying the scope of the competition faced by domestic industry. Against this backdrop, the second section of the chapter examined the impact of low-wage imports on US industry and at the same time illustrated the ways in which specific parts of the industry have responded to these competitive pressures. Here it was shown that, as buyer-driven chains have come to supplant producer-driven chains, US retailers have chosen to source directly from overseas suppliers at the expense of domestic clothing manufacturers. In consequence, domestic apparel manufacturers have responded by shifting aspects of the production process - typically, the assembly stages - to Mexico and the Caribbean Basin in order to remain price-competitive in their own market. Hence, the regionalization of the North American apparel commodity chain, which we will examine in detail in the next chapter, is, in the main, the outcome of the strategic responses that US clothing firms have adopted in response to the growing economic power wielded by retailers and major buying groups, given that the MFA has generally failed to contain the global sourcing activities of these firms.

Notes

1 The Trading with the Enemy Act was originally passed in 1917 to enable the US president to 'prohibit, restrict, licence or regulate' any transactions by citizens or corporations of 'enemy' countries operating within the US during the First World War. Despite the ensuing peace the Trading with the Enemy Act was never revoked and even today it is used to prevent US firms from trading with 'enemy' countries (e.g. Cuba).

2 Personal interview with Douglas Bulcao, Deputy Executive Vice President, American Textile Manufacturers Institute (ATMI), Washington, DC, 15 September 2000.

3 Personal interview with Steve Lamar, Senior Vice President and Director of Government Relations, American Apparel Manufacturers Association (AAMA), Arlington, Virginia, 29 September 2000.

Chapter Five

The North American Apparel Commodity Chain

Introduction

Over the course of the last decade regionalism has emerged as one of the most important areas of study within the field of international political economy. Within the literature dedicated to this topic (reviewed in Chapter One), most analysts have chosen to make a clear conceptual distinction between the notion of regionalism as a state-sponsored project, on the one hand, and regionalization as an informal process of integration, on the other. The distinction offered by Gamble and Payne serves to illustrate the point. Regionalism, they suggest, refers to a 'state-led project designed to reorganize a particular regional space along defined economic and political lines' (Gamble and Payne, 1996: 2). By contrast, regionalization, like globalization, is characterized not as a state project but as a combination of historical and emergent structures - 'a complex articulation of established institutions and rules and distinctive new patterns of social interaction between non-state actors' (Gamble and Payne, 1996: 250). In this sense, then, regionalization is best understood as a *de facto* process of integration, in contrast to the agency-orientated political strategy implied by regionalism.

This chapter examines the regionalization of the North American apparel commodity chain in a manner that is mostly consistent with the definition offered by Gamble and Payne. In common with their approach, it argues that the regionalization has come about not as a direct result of state sponsorship, but is due to the particular strategic responses that US apparel firms have adopted in the light of increasing competition from low-wage countries. At the same time, however, the chapter acknowledges the extent to which these strategies have themselves taken place within a particular political and institutional context. In other words, although the regionalization of apparel production can be largely understood in terms of the strategic and locational decisions of US apparel firms, this trade has in turn relied on the particular institutional mechanisms provided by governments in the US, Mexico and the Caribbean Basin respectively. Hence, regionalization for our purposes needs to be understood as both a process of *de facto* integration *and* as the logical consequence of the region-building schemes articulated by various political elites within the region.

The chapter proceeds in the following order. In the first section we provide an overview of the regionalization of the North American apparel commodity chain, measured in terms of the changing composition of US imports. In so doing, the chapter highlights two significant, though not necessarily correlated, trends: (1) a relative decline of apparel imports from East Asia; and (2) a relative rise in HTS 9802.00 imports, which come almost exclusively from Mexico and the Caribbean Basin. Focusing specifically on this latter trend, the chapter advances three inter-related arguments in order to account for the regionalization of North American apparel production. First, it argues that particular policies promoted by the US federal government have played a key role in encouraging US clothing firms to outsource their most labour-intensive manufacturing activities to low-wage assembly factories located in Mexico and the Caribbean Basin. Second, the chapter suggests that the reciprocal packages offered by host governments within the region have also played an important part in persuading apparel firms to invest there. Third, the chapter focuses on the apparel firms themselves and shows the extent to which the 9802.00 production sharing option has become a central component in the strategic reorientation of US industry, as it seeks to remain price-competitive in its own market place.

In the second section of the chapter we examine the issue of competition among host governments for apparel-related investment. Advancing a claim first put forward in Chapter Three, it suggests that zero-sum policy competition among neighbouring EPZ economies constitutes an inherent part of the offshore development model, at least in so far as it has evolved in the Caribbean. On this basis, the chapter considers the degree to which our case studies - Jamaica, Haiti and the Dominican Republic - now compete directly with Mexico and Central America, as well as with non-9802.00 beneficiaries, for apparel-related trade and investment. It then seeks to map briefly the newly evolving regional division of labour within the North American apparel commodity chain and to locate the Caribbean within this emerging nexus.

Against this backdrop, the third and final section of this chapter examines the implications of the establishment and subsequent operation of the North American Free Trade Agreement (NAFTA) in terms of the differential roles of Mexico and the Caribbean in the newly emerging division of labour described above. It begins by considering the major advantages offered to Mexico through NAFTA, which include both greater access to the US market, as well as more flexible rules of origin. It then goes on to examine both the short- and long-term consequences of these measures for apparel production in the Caribbean. Here, it will be argued that, since its implementation, NAFTA has led to significant trade and investment diversion away from the Caribbean and towards Mexico and is facilitating the latter's move away from simple apparel assembly towards higher value added activities in the form of vertically integrated, full-package garment production.

The Regionalization of the North American Apparel Commodity Chain

According to Garry Gereffi (2000: 17), the global apparel industry has undergone a number of significant migrations of production since the 1950s. The first migration of the industry took place from North America and Western Europe to Japan in the 1950s and 1960s, when Western apparel production was displaced by a sharp rise in imports from Japan. A second shift in apparel production occurred when the 'big three' East Asian NICs - Hong Kong, Taiwan and South Korea - gradually replaced Japan as the most important source of apparel exports in the 1970s and 1980s. Finally, in the last 10 to 15 years there has been a third migration of production away from the Asian 'big three', initially towards other Asian countries such as China and Malaysia, and more recently towards Mexico and the Caribbean Basin. Clearly, these migrations in production have had a number of important implications for US industry. As was argued in the previous chapter, the US apparel sector has historically been defined by a high level of import penetration, particularly from the low-cost exporting countries of East Asia. Over the last decade or so, however, there have been a number of significant changes in the composition of US apparel imports (see Table 5.1). In 1987, the 'big three' NICs, plus China, were responsible for 56 per cent of total US apparel imports; by 1998, this figure had declined to just 22 per cent. At the same time, the proportion of US apparel imports derived from the Caribbean Basin and Mexico increased from 8 per cent to 24 per cent and from 2 per cent to 15 per cent respectively. These changes merit further consideration.

Table 5.1   United States apparel imports by region, 1987 and 1998

Source	1987 (millions of square metres)	Import Share (%)	1998 (millions of square metres)	Import Share (%)	Growth 1987- 1998 (%)
Big Four	3,040	56	2,853	22	-6
ASEAN	709	13	1,469	11	107
South Asia	547	10	1,858	14	240
CBI	436	8	3,066	24	603
Mexico	134	2	1,985	15	1381
All other countries	593	11	1,655	13	179
Total apparel imports	5,459	100	12,886	100	136

Source: Adapted from American Apparel Manufacturers Association (1999).

At a glance, the changing composition of US apparel imports described above would seem to support the new international division of labour (NIDL) thesis, first put forward by Folker Fröbel and his colleagues in the early 1980s. To recall from Chapter One, this thesis advanced the idea that, in the context of heightened conditions of global competition, the most labour-intensive aspects of the production process would inevitably fall to those countries with the lowest wages. Certainly, the North American apparel commodity chain provides a degree of evidence to support this assertion. During the 1980s, the East Asian 'big three' experienced above average increases in production costs associated with rising wage levels, which contributed to a reduction in their share of the US apparel market (Bonacich and Waller, 1994). At the same time, the sharp appreciation of Asian currencies *vis-à-vis* the US dollar after the signing of the Plaza Accord in 1985 also played a critical role in arresting the growth of apparel exports from these countries, at a time when other newly emerging apparel producing countries, such as Mexico and the Caribbean Basin countries, were experiencing rapid export growth due to currency *de*valuations against the dollar.[1] Overall, then, the combination of rising wage levels and currency realignments can be said to have contributed significantly to a reduction in the competitive advantage of garment production in the 'big three' Asian NICs.

Despite this, a closer inspection of the relevant arguments reveals the 'cheap labour' hypothesis to be less than convincing in its account of the changes which have occurred in global apparel production in the last decade or so. First, despite the fact that Mexico and the Caribbean Basin have come to assume significant competitive advantages over the Asian 'big three' with regard to low wages, it still remains the case that average earnings in the Mexican and Caribbean garment industries are significantly higher than those found in China and other emerging East and South East Asian suppliers. Second, although the share of US apparel imports represented by Hong Kong, Taiwan and South Korea has declined significantly in the last 10 to 15 years, these economies still rank among the top six apparel exporters to the US, despite having the highest labour costs of all major suppliers (Gereffi, 2000). Clearly, a more thorough investigation of the Asian apparel production complex would be required in order to account for these anomalies. Nevertheless, it should be noted, albeit in parenthesis here, that the continued viability of garment production in the 'big three' owes much to the constant industrial upgrading of local firms and to the establishment of a multi-layered sourcing hierarchy within Asia which takes advantage of the low-cost production sites offered by a second and third tier of low-cost suppliers, including Indonesia, Malaysia and the Philippines. Hence, the emergence of new sources of garment production in Asia is not unrelated to the continuing economic significance of the 'big three' in the global apparel industry (Gereffi, 1999).

For our more specific purposes, however, it is those issues directly related to the increasing significance of Mexico and the Caribbean Basin that are of most concern. The regionalization of the North American apparel commodity chain, with regard to local production in Mexico and the Caribbean Basin, can be understood in terms of three inter-related causes. These are: (1) the promotion of production sharing incentives by the US federal government, designed to reassert the global competitiveness of its national textile and apparel industries; (2) the promotion of reciprocal legislation in the *maquila* and EPZs platforms of Mexico and the Caribbean Basin aimed at attracting US firms to their particular assembly sites; and (3) the strategic responses that US apparel firms have adopted in the light of the particular competitive advantages offered by state-sponsored offshore manufacturing. Although all of these factors have, to a greater or lesser extent, already been discussed in previous chapters, there is a need to reaffirm the importance of each in turn here, given their centrality to the whole issue that is being investigated.

The Impact of US Government Policy

Broadly speaking, the attempts of US policy makers to promote the global competitiveness of the domestic apparel industry can be characterized in terms of two sets of policy instruments. The first set of policy instruments centres on the use of import quotas and tariffs in order to restrict the threat posed by low-cost apparel exporting nations. Of course, the most significant policy mechanism in this respect has been the MFA. As this was discussed at considerable length in the previous chapter, there is no need to restate its importance here, suffice to say that this regime patently restricted the rate of export growth from low-wage countries but, at the same time, had a number of unintended consequences, which were mainly to the detriment of apparel production in developed countries, especially the US. In addition to the MFA, US policy makers have also sought to penalize apparel goods entering the US market through the use of punitive import tariffs. According to the USITC (1999: 29), apparel enjoyed a 15.5 per cent *ad valorem* trade-weighted rate of import duty in 1997, compared to just 3 per cent for other comparable products. Significantly, also, while the tariff cuts agreed to as part of the GATT Uruguay Round settlement led to significant reductions for most manufactured goods, apparel was much less affected by this round of trade liberalization: tariff cuts for US apparel amounted to a mere 9 per cent trade-weighted average, compared to a 34 per cent reduction for manufactured products as a whole (USITC, 1999a). Thus, even as the US apparel industry is having to come to terms with the gradual phasing-out of the MFA, import tariffs remain a considerable weapon with which to deal with competition from low-wage countries.

A second series of instruments employed by US policy makers in order to deal with competition from low-wage countries is derived from tax measures which act to encourage offshore sourcing among US apparel firms. As was briefly outlined in the previous chapter, the strategic rationale underlying these measures is to enable domestic firms to remain globally competitive - in the way the Asian 'big three' have done - through the establishment of low-cost supply links with offshore *maquila* and EPZ platforms in Mexico and the Caribbean Basin. The specific entitlements offered to US apparel firms engaging in this type of economic activity come from two specific legislative packages (already discussed in previous chapters), which are summarized below.

Harmonized Tariff Schedule (HTS) 9802.00. The HTS 9802.00 combines the previously separate US tax code provisions 806.30 and 807 and permits duty exemption to the value of US-made components returned in articles assembled abroad; the value of US-made components entered under 9802.00 is also exempt from the merchandise-processing fee (the so-called 'customs user fee', normally charged at 0.21 per cent *ad valorem* with a US$485 per entry cap). Although - nominally at least - these entitlements are available to any exporting country in any industrial sector, in practice they have tended overwhelmingly to favour apparel production sharing in Mexico and the Caribbean Basin. In 1995, for example, these countries alone accounted for something in the order of 90 per cent of the total value of goods entering the US market through 9802.00; in the same period, apparel accounted for approximately 60 per cent of the total duty savings from the production sharing scheme (USITC, 1997).

    Special Access Program (SAP). Launched on 1 January 1986 and related to the Caribbean Basin Initiative, the SAP (also known as 807A and super 807) is designed to offer preferential treatment to textile and apparel imports from CBI-beneficiary countries, thereby giving additional encouragement to apparel production sharing operations involving US manufacturing firms.[2] Essentially, SAP offers the same duty-free entitlements as the HTS 9802.00 scheme, but with the added requirement that eligible goods must be constituted with fabric that is entirely made *and* cut in the US (the 9802.00 only requires fabric to be cut in the US). Despite this, the SAP has a significant advantage over 9802.00 in that it provides market access above and beyond that permitted by the MFA. Notwithstanding these differences (which are examined more critically in Chapter Six), the two schemes combined have come to assume a prominent role in the regionalization the North American apparel commodity chain by encouraging US apparel firms to establish low-cost supply links with Mexico and the Caribbean Basin, as we shall see shortly. Before turning to this, it is first necessary to reconsider briefly the importance of the reciprocal EPZ preferences offered by host governments and the impact of these on offshore production in the region.

The Impact of Caribbean Government Policy

The broad range of policy measures that have been advanced by Caribbean governments in order to attract US firms to invest in their particular EPZ platforms has already been discussed at considerable length. However, what remains to be fully examined is the extent to which these measures have impinged directly on the apparel industry. As with the 9802.00 production sharing scheme previously described, EPZ policies promoted by Caribbean governments have not, in the main, set out directly to target the apparel industry. Yet it is this industry that has overwhelmingly taken advantage of the investment incentives offered in the region. In 1995, apparel accounted for 90 per cent of the value of US 9802.00 imports from the Caribbean Basin (excluding Mexico); whereas no other manufacturing sector (e.g. electronics) accounted for more than 5 per cent of the total (USITC, 1997: 2-5). What all this means is that, while the EPZ-led development model in the Caribbean was originally conceived as a means of attracting a range of labour- and import-intensive industries to the region, for most countries it has manifested itself in practice in an acute reliance on apparel as the only significant source of industrial investment - Kaplinsky (1993) refers to this practice as 'industrial monocropping'.

    When we take into account some of the evidence regarding the restructuring of the US textile and apparel industry complex presented in Chapter Four, the disproportionate interest in the Caribbean offshore option shown by US apparel manufacturers becomes easier to fathom. Clearly, there are a number of industry-specific factors that make this option more favourable to apparel than to other manufacturing sectors. Two of these are worth highlighting. First, due to low-cost barriers to entry associated with low-skilled, labour-intensive production, the apparel industry has suffered disproportionately from competition from low-wage countries. As a consequence, the offshore sourcing option has proved to be more attractive in apparel than it has in other manufacturing sectors, which have been able to remain competitive via industrial upgrading and capital intensification (Mody and Wheeler, 1987). Second, and related to this, because of the low level of mechanization within the apparel industry, low-skilled - and therefore low-waged - labour constitutes a relatively high proportion (roughly 25-40 per cent) of total production costs. Therefore, the option of outsourcing to geographical areas with large pools of low-skilled labour (of which there is an abundance in the Caribbean Basin) and thereby reducing dramatically production costs represents an effective means of remaining competitive.[3]

None of this, of course, explains precisely why US apparel manufacturers have chosen to invest heavily in Mexico and the Caribbean rather than in other low-wage regions such as China. The reason for this is to be found in the specific advantage that the Caribbean Basin has over other low-wage areas: namely, proximity to the US market. In the same way that the Mexican *maquila* industry was initially established in the border areas of Ciudad and Tijuana, close to leading apparel-producing districts in Texas and California, the Caribbean offshore garment industry is heavily tied to distribution points on the US east coast, including New York, Baltimore and Miami. Significantly, also, the US textile mill industry - which, as we have seen, supplies the bulk of the fabrics used in Caribbean assembly operations - is heavily concentrated in the south east US with just four states - North Carolina, South Carolina, Georgia and Tennessee - accounting for roughly one third of all employment in the industry. Because of this, the Caribbean is particularly well positioned to respond to rapidly changing market conditions through swift production turnover. According to one estimate, the product turnover time (including production, transportation and distribution) for apparel sourced in the Caribbean is approximately three to five weeks, whereas apparel sourced from East Asia can take anywhere up to four months to reach the US market (Taplin, 1994). All things considered, then, the geographical proximity of the Caribbean to the US market, coupled with the relatively low wages and a range of other fiscal benefits, offers US apparel manufacturers a significant number of distinctive advantages. In the next section we will briefly examine how US clothing firms have responded to the opportunities afforded by these advantages.

The Strategic Responses of US Apparel Firms

According to the USITC, the rationalization of production through the 9802.00 regime has become an increasingly integral part of the strategic efforts of US manufacturing firms to remain globally competitive (USITC, 1999). Certainly, the quantitative evidence presented so far in this chapter supports this claim: the increasing proportion of apparel imports entering the US market from Mexico and the Caribbean Basin via the 9802.00 production sharing scheme would suggest that that US apparel firms have come to assume a decisive role in the reconfiguration of the North American apparel supply chain. A more qualitative measure of this trend can be gained through briefly examining the competitive strategies of some of the leading US apparel firms that have lately turned to offshore production as a means of enhancing competitiveness in their own market place. The examples of VF Corporation and Sara Lee will serve this purpose.

VF Corporation. VF Corporation produces the popular Lee and Wrangler jeans, as well as a number of other lesser-known apparel brands, including Vanity Fair and Vassarette (intimate apparel), Jantzen (swimwear) and Healthtex (children's apparel). In 1998, VF Corporation, with annual sales in the range of US$5 billion, was the largest selling denim manufacturer in the US, accounting for 26.1 per cent of the domestic jeans market (USITC, 1999a). This success has been built on a competitive strategy combining the strategic acquisition of major rivals (briefly outlined in the previous chapter) with the rationalization of domestic production (approximately 5,000 jobs were cut between 1994 and 1998), while simultaneously investing in offshore assembly operations. In 1995, VF Corporation closed 14 plants in the US and shifted 35 per cent of its production to Mexico (eight plants) and the Caribbean Basin (six plants in Costa Rica and one in Honduras). By 1998, 57 per cent of its production was located offshore and the stated aim of VF Corporation is that this figure should eventually rise to 80 per cent of its total sewing operations (USITC, 1999a).

Significantly, the success achieved by VF Corporation during the 1990s stands in marked contrast to its major rival, Levi Strauss & Co., which saw its share of the US jeans market decline sharply from 31 per cent to 14 per cent in the same period. In the all-important men's jeans sector, Levi's market share dropped from 48.2 per cent in 1990 to 25 per cent in 1998; at the same time VF Corporation increased its market share from 22.1 per cent to 31.9 per cent (USITC, 1999a). Significantly, industry sources put the loss of competitiveness by Levi Strauss in the 1990s partly down to its long-standing commitment to retain production in the US, while its major competitors like VF Corporation were busy moving offshore in order to take advantage of the lower production costs (Gereffi, 2000). Levi Strauss was later forced to restructure along the lines of the offshore model pioneered by VF Corporation. Between 1998 and 1999, Levi Strauss closed 23 of its 32 US plants (reducing its domestic workforce by 38 per cent), while investing heavily in offshore assembly factories in Mexico and the Caribbean Basin, which now supply the majority of its apparel goods (ECLAC, 2000).

Sara Lee. In 1998, Sara Lee, with popular brands such as Hanes, Playtex, Bali and L'eggs, represented 32 per cent of the US market for brassieres, 36 per cent of the market for women's and girls' pants and 38 per cent of the market for men's and boys' underwear. During the mid 1980s, Sara Lee was among the first US apparel firms to shift production offshore, with much of its early activity centred on Mexico. Since then, it has consolidated its operations in Mexico via a number of high profile acquisitions (including Rinbros, Mexico's leading manufacturer of men's and boys' underwear, and Mallorca, the country's second largest producer of hosiery) and has extended its offshore operations into other parts of the Caribbean Basin, including a US$45 million investment programme in Puerto Rico (where it is the island's largest employer), as well as other contract operations in Jamaica, Honduras and El Salvador. By late 1997, 42 per cent of its apparel output was produced at foreign assembly factories, with these operations responsible for 47 per cent of it profits (USITC, 1999a).

It is interesting to note that, like Levi Strauss, Sara Lee's major rival in the US underwear market, Fruit of the Loom, was initially slow to react to the potential benefits of offshore production. In fact, up until the mid 1990s Fruit of the Loom's outspoken chairman, William Farley, was one of the fiercest critics of offshore production: as a major financial contributor to both the Republican and Democratic parties, Farley had actually opposed legislation designed to enhance market access for sewing operations undertaken in the Caribbean Basin (see Chapter Six). However, in 1995 Fruit of the Loom took the decision to reverse its position on offshore sourcing and thereafter began outsourcing its sewing operations to the Caribbean Basin at a very fast rate: by 1998, approximately 95 per cent of its sewing operations had been moved offshore to Mexico and the Caribbean Basin, by which time its headquarters had been relocated to the Cayman Islands (Franklin, 2000). In December 1999 Fruit of the Loom declared bankruptcy. Ironically enough, this was largely attributed to its decision to move offshore, which according to industry sources was undertaken too quickly and in too few countries to save the company from financial ruin.[4]

This latter case notwithstanding, what this necessarily brief survey of the competitive strategies of some of the leading US apparel firms has shown is the degree to which the competitive standing of the US apparel industry has come to rely on offshore manufacturing in Mexico and the Caribbean Basin. The cumulative offshore activities of firms such as VF Corporation and Sara Lee have clearly made a significant contribution to the reconfiguration of the North American supply chain as a progressively greater share of the US clothing market is sourced via 9802.00 imports. After all, it is no coincidence that the top ten leading apparel firms in the US in 1997 - each with sales in excess of US\$1 billion - were reliant upon offshore factories (mostly, though not exclusively, located in Mexico and the Caribbean Basin) for anywhere between 50 and 95 per cent of total assembly-related production (USITC, 1999a). There is thus a clear link between the continuing economic buoyancy of the US apparel industry (or at least parts of it) and regionalization of the North American apparel commodity chain. The impact of this process upon individual supply countries within this newly emerging regional commodity chain is the issue that is taken up in the next section of the chapter.

Competition and Hierarchy in the North American Apparel Commodity Chain

In many ways, it can be argued that the intensification of competition between participating countries is a logical consequence of the encouragement of production sharing operations between US apparel firms and offshore assembly sites in Mexico and the Caribbean Basin. Indeed, as was shown in Chapter Three, the offshore development model in the Caribbean Basin (although not to the same extent in Mexico, which is discussed separately in the following section) is very much predicated on a competitive rationale wherein neighbouring EPZ economies compete for more or less the same investment. In the same manner, it can be argued that the peculiarities of the HTS 9802.00 regime itself add to this predicament by encouraging these economies to engage in zero-sum policy competition in order to convince US apparel firms to invest in their particular EPZs. That is to say, because of strict rules of origin stipulated by 9802.00 (i.e. requiring the use of US fabrics), production sharing of this kind is only really viable for the handful of countries situated within close geographical proximity to the US.[5] This geographical imperative has had a number of important consequences for the region as a whole. First, because the 9802.00 system effectively discriminates against those countries which are not situated within close geographical proximity to the US, this trade is increasingly dividing the northern Caribbean (and Central America) from the southern Caribbean, which has generally failed to establish a presence in the North American market (Rosenberg and Hiskey, 1994). Second, even though 9802.00 does shield participating countries from direct competition with other apparel producing countries (e.g. East Asia), it nevertheless heightens the competitive pressures between individual participating countries *within* the region.

The various manifestations of these pressures have already been discussed in Chapter Three, with regard to policy competition for foreign direct investment. A further indication of the degree of competition within the North American apparel commodity chain can be gained through an examination of the changing hierarchy among apparel supply countries within the Caribbean Basin. During the 1980s, just four countries - Jamaica, Haiti, the Dominican Republic and Costa Rica - dominated the US-Caribbean Basin apparel trade, to the extent that by the end of the decade they were jointly responsible for more than 80 per cent of 9802.00 exports from the CBI region (Steele, 1988: 68). Despite this, competition among supply countries has intensified considerably in the ensuing period as more and more Central American countries have come to adopt the offshore development model.

Table 5.2   United States 9802.00 apparel imports from selected CBI countries, 1992-1998

Country	1992 (US$ millions)	1994 (US$ millions)	1996 (US$ millions)	1998 (US$ millions)	Growth 1992-1998 (%)
Dominican Republic	1,031	1,377	1,601	2,154	109
Honduras	244	451	970	1,586	550
El Salvador	130	303	588	1,006	674
Costa Rica	418	587	646	791	89
Guatemala	322	450	579	706	119
Jamaica	217	371	437	382	76
Haiti	63	30	96	211	235
All other	398	493	649	599	50
CBI total	2,823	4,062	5,566	7,435	163

Source: Adapted from USITC (various years).

As Table 5.2 shows, states such as Honduras and El Salvador are rapidly becoming major players in the North American apparel commodity chain. What Table 5.2 also reveals is the degree to which these advances have come at the expense of the more established EPZ platforms, such as those found in Jamaica and Haiti. The Dominican Republic, for its part, remains the dominant source of apparel exports within the CBI region, accounting for US$2.1 billion (31 per cent of the CBI total) of apparel exports to the US in 1998. Significantly, however, it is among the new entrants from Central America that the highest growth rates are to be found: Honduras increased its apparel exports by 550 per cent from US$244 million to almost US$1.6 billion (25 per cent of the CBI total) between 1992 and 1998; while El Salvador increased its apparel exports by 674 per cent from US$130 million to US$1 billion (13 per cent of the CBI total) in the same period. In contrast, Jamaica - which was second only to the Dominican Republic in terms of 9802.00 apparel exports for much the 1980s and early 1990s - has seen its relative share of US apparel imports fall dramatically: although its exports rose by 76 per cent from US$217 million to US$382 million (7 per cent of the CBI total) between 1992 and 1998, this still represented the slowest growth rate of any major CBI supplier. Finally, although Haiti has also enjoyed an increase in apparel exports during the 1990s (from US$63 million to US$ 235 million) due to the lifting of the UN trade embargo (see below), this, again, suffers from comparison within the spectacular rises enjoyed by the isthmus states.

Understanding the emerging hierarchy among apparel supply countries in the Caribbean Basin requires us to consider two sets of factors. The first of these, which we might call location-specific advantages, refers to the precise benefits (e.g. better infrastructure, more competitive wage rates, etc.) that Central American states offer foreign investors in order to persuade them to invest in their particular EPZs rather than in the more established zones found in the insular Caribbean. In this respect, wage rates may be said to be a key factor. Even though we have already expressed doubt over the theoretical and empirical veracity of 'cheap labour' arguments associated with the NIDL thesis, there are still considerable grounds for claiming that, when other factors are held constant, labour costs may prove critical in determining the locational decisions of foreign investors, particularly in 'footloose' industries such as apparel (Mortimore and Perez, 1998). In specific relation to 9802.00-related investment in the Caribbean Basin, a comparison of average wages rates found in Central America and the Caribbean is highly instructive. In the mid 1990s, hourly compensation rates for garment workers for Jamaica and Costa Rica, the countries which have experienced the most rapid decline in apparel-related investment, stood at US$1.09 and US$0.91 respectively; while comparable rates for El Salvador, Guatemala and Honduras were, in that order, US$0.67, US$0.45 and US$0.48 (Mortimore, 1999). Furthermore, in addition to the disparity between 'old' and 'new' EPZ sites with regard to labour costs, industry sources suggest that the *de facto* pay and working conditions found in much of Central America (although not Costa Rica) are even worse that official figures reveal.[6] On this basis, we may conclude that inferior pay and working conditions found in most parts of Central America offer these countries a number of location-specific advantages over their Caribbean counterparts.

An additional set of location-specific advantages available to the Central American platforms comes from the productive capacity of the assembly factories themselves. As will be recalled from the previous chapter, a central part of the restructuring process within the US apparel industry has been for some of the larger clothing firms, such as Sara Lee, to engage in 'de-verticalization': that is, the shift away from direct responsibility for garment manufacture to focus only on the design, marketing and retail aspects of production. At present, this process has only gone as far as is permitted by the 9802.00 regime (i.e. the outsourcing of assembly tasks); nevertheless, pressure is mounting within the industry for the extension of these provisions to cover the entire manufacturing process, so as to allow US apparel firms to remain globally competitive. Gary Gereffi, for instance, claims that one of the major consequences of the regionalization of the North American apparel commodity chain has been to create a supply gap for 'full package' garments (i.e. ready to wear apparel), previously filled by East Asian suppliers (Gereffi, 2000). Because of this, there is now an increasing need on the part of the US apparel industry to establish low-cost supply links within the Caribbean Basin capable of carrying out the entire array of manufacturing tasks (i.e. raw materials, yarns and fibres, fabrics, apparel manufacture and distribution) required to produce 'full package' apparel (Jacobs, 1998). At the moment, only Mexico comes anywhere near meeting this requirement. Nevertheless, it is not insignificant that, unlike the insular Caribbean countries where the development of 'full package' infrastructure has been effectively truncated by the 9802.00 system, many Central American countries, including Guatemala, Honduras and El Salvador, do possess a history of textile production, which could be utilized in order to meet the 'full package' requirements of the US apparel industry. Hence, it may be argued that, in addition to its location-specific advantages associated with lower wages, Central America holds a further advantage over the insular Caribbean due to the potential productive capacity of its domestic textile and apparel industries.

A second set of factors, which we might refer to as security-related issues, relate to the underlying political and military imperatives that impinge upon the otherwise rational locational decisions of US apparel firms. As was shown in Chapter Two, security-related issues have played a key underlying role in the political economy of the US-Caribbean apparel trade, given that the CBI - which gave rise to production sharing - was itself founded on the need to solve perceived security problems associated with political and economic instability in the region. In another important sense, security-related issues - in particular, the estimation of 'political risk' by US investors - have been an important consideration in determining which particular EPZ sites represent viable investment opportunities and which do not. Steele (1988), for instance, suggests that the main factor inhibiting apparel-related investment growth in Central America (with the obvious exception of Costa Rica) during the 1980s was the perception of political risk associated with left-wing insurgency in El Salvador and Guatemala and the inability of the US government to overthrow the Sandinistas in Nicaragua. This was clearly to the benefit of the insular Caribbean at the time, in so far as it led to a considerable amount of trade and investment diversion, which might otherwise have been destined for the isthmus.

By the same token, however, now that relative peace and stability has returned to most parts of Central America political anxieties draw attention more to the insular Caribbean. In this respect, the experiences of Haiti and Jamaica during the 1990s represent cases in point. Following the violent overthrow of Jean-Bertrand Aristide by disaffected elements of the Haitian military in September 1991, the United Nations imposed a multilateral trade embargo (leading to the withdrawal of all CBI and 9802.00 entitlements) on the island, which was effective until September 1994, by which time a US-led mission had restored the constitutional government to power (see Dupuy, 1997). Since the embargo was lifted, however, apparel and other sources of US investment have been slow to return to the island, with investors opting for the safer option represented by Haiti's most immediate neighbour, the Dominican Republic (Willette and Overstreet, 1994). For its part, Jamaica has suffered in the last decade from its debilitating image as a centre for international drug trafficking that is out of all proportion to its tiny size.[7] It is estimated that approximately 5 per cent of worldwide marijuana production takes place in Jamaica and the island is also widely believed to be one of the most important transshipment points for Colombian cocaine destined for the shores of Miami (Heron and Payne, 2002). In some cases, Jamaica's drugs problem has come to impinge directly on apparel-related investment in that 9802.00 garment shipments have been implicated in narcotics-smuggling operations.[8] The net effect of this has been to turn a considerable amount of investment away from the island and towards neighbouring EPZ economies, which do not suffer from these problems to anything like the same extent (Bernal *et al.*, 2000).

In sum, then, the various economic and security-related issues outlined above take us some way towards understanding the evolving supply hierarchy within the North American apparel commodity chain, whereby Central America has begun to supplant the insular Caribbean as the favoured destination for 9802.00 apparel-related trade and investment. However, there are a number of caveats to place upon this generalization. First, despite this trend, the Dominican Republic still constitutes the dominant source of apparel production in the Caribbean Basin (although it is rapidly being overtaken by Honduras and El Salvador). This is due to a combination of its competitive wage rates, its close proximity to the US market and the fact that it is the principal beneficiary of trade and investment diversion from Jamaica and Haiti (USITC, 1999). Second, evidently, Costa Rica does not correspond to the characterization of Central America presented above: unlike states such as Honduras and El Salvador, Costa Rica's export success in the regional apparel industry has not come about predominantly as a result of low wages; rather it has been based on a relatively high-wage and high-skilled labour force. Because of this, Costa Rica has been able to compensate for the loss for 9802.00 apparel exports by upgrading into more integrated forms of garment production and by attracting non-US sources of foreign direct investment (Mortimore and Zamora, 1999).

The third and final caveat to the above account of the evolving supply hierarchy within the North American apparel commodity chain relates to the (deliberate) omission from the discussion to this point of Mexico. Prior to the implementation of NAFTA in 1994, Mexico had competed more or less equally for apparel-related US investment through the 9802.00 scheme and the Special Access Program. Since then, however, Mexico has begun to develop a more competitive and integrated form of apparel production due to the special preferences contained within the NAFTA treaty, which are denied to both the Caribbean and Central America. The impact of these special preferences on garment production in the Caribbean Basin is addressed in the remainder of this chapter.

The Impact of NAFTA

Launched on 1 January 1994, NAFTA offers a number of significant advantages to the Mexican apparel sector, which are not afforded to either Central America or the Caribbean via the much more restrictive 9802.00 system. These advantages come from two main provisions contained within the NAFTA treaty.[9] First, NAFTA provides for tariff-free and quota-free treatment for trade among member states in apparel goods that originate from within the NAFTA trade area. In the case of Mexico, virtually all tariffs on apparel had been phased out by 1 January 1999. The US eliminated import quotas for originating apparel from Mexico upon NAFTA's implementation, while those for non-originating apparel are scheduled to be phased out by 1 January 2004. Second, the Mexican apparel sector also benefits from the NAFTA rules of origin, which are designed to encourage the use of regional yarns and fabrics in all garment production as means of consolidating the North American supply chain. In this respect, most Mexican apparel enters the US market via the so-called 'yarn forward' ruling, which stipulates that all manufacturing stages, including yarn formation, must take place in the NAFTA trade area in order to qualify for tariff and quota-free treatment. Additionally, however, in certain 'short supply' product categories (e.g. silk, linen, corduroy, etc.), Mexican 'non-originating' apparel is permitted to enter the US market duty-free via Tariff Preference Levels (TPLs), provided it is cut and sewn in the NAFTA trade area.

What all this means is that, while NAFTA permits Mexican apparel (both originating and, in some cases, non-originating apparel) to enter the US market quota- and duty-free, Caribbean and Central American apparel entering though the 9802.00 regime is *still* dutiable on the value added offshore (i.e. labour costs). A simple example will serve to illustrate the point. Suppose a typical CBI garment entering the US market through the 9802.00 scheme is worth, say, US$10; approximately US$6.40 of this is made up of duty-free US materials and the remaining US$3.60 of dutiable, local value added. Applying the 1996 trade-weighted tariff for apparel of 16.1 per cent to this would result in an *ad valorem* equivalent duty of US$0.60, an equivalent duty of 6 per cent for CBI garments (Kornis, 1997: 8). Hence, as a result of NAFTA, Mexican apparel qualifying for duty- and quota-free treatment - which in 1996 accounted for approximately 88 per cent of the total value of its apparel exports - is at a distinct advantage *vis-à-vis* Caribbean and Central American apparel exports to the US, which are still subject to duty on the value added offshore.

In addition to this, Mexico's relatively privileged position within the North American apparel commodity chain was considerably enhanced as a result of the devaluation of the peso that took place between December 1994 and January 1995. Although this was not directly related to NAFTA or even to the promotion of its *maquila* exports, it nevertheless had the effect of heightening Mexico's economic advantage over the Caribbean Basin, which has itself experienced steady increases in the value of local currencies *vis-à-vis* the US dollar since the dramatic devaluations of the 1980s. Specifically, the Mexican devaluation amounted to a 50 per cent drop in the value of the peso against the US dollar; in relation to the apparel industry, this manifested itself in a reduction in labour costs for local assembly workers from approximately US$2.47 in 1994 to US$1.23 in 1996 (USITC, 1997: 4-5). According to some estimates, the reduction in local labour costs caused by the devaluation of the peso was sufficient to effect a threefold increase in the cost-competitiveness of the Mexican apparel industry in relation to the higher cost countries of the Caribbean Basin, including Costa Rica and Jamaica (USITC, 1997: 4-5). Clearly, these changes in themselves can be said to represent a significant challenge to the viability of apparel production in the Caribbean Basin; moreover, when we take into the account the additional effect of the duty- and quota-free provisions contained within the NAFTA treaty, then we can say that the challenge is all the more significant. The impact of these changes is examined below.

There are a number of ways in which we can estimate the impact of NAFTA on the North American apparel commodity chain. Clearly, it would be difficult to sustain the argument that NAFTA has inhibited apparel export growth from *all* Caribbean Basin countries, given the spectacular rates of growth achieved by newly emerging export platforms, such as Honduras and El Salvador. Nevertheless, if we compare Mexico's post-NAFTA apparel export growth with the CBI region as a whole, we get some measure of the extent to which the former's competitive position has been enhanced at the expense of the latter. Between 1992 and 1998, Mexico's apparel exports grew by approximately 517 per cent; while in the same period the CBI total increased by 163 per cent. An even more impressive measure of Mexico's export success can be gained by looking at its overall volume of apparel exports and its increasing share of the US market: in 1998 Mexico exported approximately US$5 billion of apparel to the US, which accounted for roughly 15 per cent of the total value of US apparel imports in that year. By way of comparison, even though the total for the Caribbean Basin region was slightly higher that this at approximately US$7 billion, or 17 per cent of the total value of US apparel imports, no single CBI beneficiary exported more than US$2 billion or 4 per cent of the total of US apparel imports (ECLAC, 2000: 184).

Table 5.3   Total United States apparel imports from Mexico, 1992-1998

1992 (US$ millions)	1994 (US$ millions)	1996 (US$ millions)	1998 (US$ millions)	Growth 1992-1998 (%)
840	1523	3033	5187	517

Source: Adapted from USITC (various years).

Of course, not all of this can be put down to the impact of NAFTA, or even to the peso devaluation - Mexico's apparel export boom evidently preceded both of these events. Nevertheless, given the highly competitively environment that we have already described in this chapter, we can at least claim that both NAFTA and the peso devaluation have been contributing factors in Mexico's emergence as the number one supplier in the North America apparel commodity chain (Jacobs, 1999). Precisely how this has impacted upon garment production in the Caribbean, however, remains an unresolved issue. According to the Caribbean Textile and Apparel Institute, based in Kingston, Jamaica, the closure of 250 Caribbean apparel plants, with the loss of some 123,000 jobs, in the 1995-96 period alone was directly attributable to trade and investment diversion caused by NAFTA (Rohter, 1997). Further to this, there is sufficient anecdotal evidence in respect of US investors shifting production from the Caribbean to Mexico to support the claim that NAFTA has come to threaten the viability of apparel manufacturing in the region.[10] Beyond this, however, there is a great deal of ambiguity regarding the degree to which trade and investment towards Mexico is a *direct* result of NAFTA. The case of Jamaica illustrates this. Without a doubt, Jamaica is the Caribbean country hardest hit from competition from Mexico (and elsewhere): In April 2000, East Ocean Textiles, hitherto one of the island's largest and most successful garment manufacturers, announced its closure with the loss of some 2,800 jobs (out of a total of 36,000 employed in the industry). Revealingly, however, although East Ocean did cite the loss of investment to Mexico due to NAFTA as one of the major reasons for its closure, they saw this as secondary to the mounting security problems in and around the Kingston Free Trade Zone, associated with drug-related violence.[11] This, of course, is not to suggest that NAFTA has had negligible impact on apparel production in the Caribbean; what it does show is the inherent difficulty of attributing the loss of trade and investment solely to NAFTA when other contributing forces are clearly also at work.

Be this as it may, the case against NAFTA does not simply revolve around trade and investment diversion due to the more favourable terms of access to the US market offered to Mexico through this arrangement. In a more fundamental sense, NAFTA can be said to threaten apparel production in the Caribbean Basin, not primarily because of better market access, but rather due its specific rules of origin provisions, which are expressly designed to encourage *integrated* production across the NAFTA trade area. Crucially, NAFTA neither requires fabric to be cut in the US or necessarily to be of North American origin in order to qualify for quota- and tariff-free treatment. What this means is that NAFTA offers Mexico considerably more scope for co-ordinating backward linkages with the domestic economy than is allowed to the Caribbean Basin under the much more restrictive 9802.00 regime (Welling, 2000).

The emergence of full package apparel production in Mexico is particularly evident in the blue jeans sector, which has entailed the development of a *locally*-based supply chain (ECLAC, 2000). By 1998, Mexico was responsible for approximately 60 per cent of US imports of blue jeans, the bulk of which were manufactured in the booming industrial district of Torreón, located in the northern state of Coahuila, which was responsible for the weekly export of an estimated 4.5

million pairs of jeans in the same year. The most noticeable aspect of jeans production in Torreón, however, is the degree to which it no longer conforms to the conventional *maquila* stereotype: Gereffi and Bair (2001) estimate that roughly 50 per cent of Torreón's denim exports are made with Mexican textiles of which approximately half could be accurately described as full package. The remainder, they suggest, is mostly made with of 9802.00 fabrics, but nevertheless entails manufacturing tasks not normally carried out in the *maquilas*, including cutting, laundering and the finishing of the jeans.

Clearly, the type of industrial transformation represented by Torreón's jeans industry has much to do with the relatively - that is, to the 9802.00 regime - liberal rules of origin contained within the NAFTA agreement, which have sought to encourage precisely this type of integrated production. Analysed in these terms, it becomes easy to understand exactly how NAFTA has altered the nature of competition between Mexico and the Caribbean Basin: not only has it enhanced Mexico's attractiveness as an investment location due to the tariff and quota-free provisions, but, measured in the longer term, it offers Mexico the opportunity of industrial upgrading and technology transfer via the establishment of local supply chains. Even though the long-term benefits of NAFTA in terms of fostering integrated production and industrial upgrading in the Mexican apparel industry are yet to be fully determined, it is difficult to disagree with the findings of a recent report by the Economic Commission for Latin America and the Caribbean (ECLAC), which concluded that the operation of NAFTA was leading to the emergence of a new model of competition within the North American apparel commodity chain: the *Mexican model* (ECLAC, 2000: 191-3). According to ECLAC, this emerging - although by no means consolidated - model involves an ongoing transition from 9802.00 assembly, which still characterizes garment production in most Caribbean Basin countries, to a more full package type of production. Hence, from this perspective, NAFTA can be said to be leading to the bifurcation of the offshore development model in Mexico and the Caribbean Basin, with the former increasingly moving away from traditional *maquila*-led industrialization, whereas the latter remains tied to this type of growth strategy.

In the following chapter, we will examine the attempt that has been to reconcile these two competitive models, by examining the events leading up to, and including, the enactment by the US Congress in May 2000 of the Caribbean Basin Trade Partnership Act (CBTPA), which was designed to address the diversionary consequences of NAFTA in terms of apparel-related trade and investment in the Caribbean Basin. Focusing on the events leading up to the enactment of the CBTPA, we will attempt to show the extent to which the implementation and subsequent operation of NAFTA not only impacted upon the Caribbean countries themselves, but also upon an otherwise disparate set of US actors who had a subsequent collective interest in the establishment of a more equitable production sharing system for the Caribbean garment industry. In doing so, we will attempt to uncover some of the political manifestations of the regionalization of the North American apparel commodity chain and assess the implication of these for the future direction of US-Caribbean political economy more generally.

Conclusion

In the meantime, to sum up, this chapter has served to map out the process of regionalization in the North American industry and the implications of this for garment production in the Caribbean. In this manner, we have been able to discern three inter-related aspects of this newly emerging regional political economy. The first of these centred on the issue of regionalization itself. Here, it was argued that the regionalization of the North American apparel commodity chain - witnessed both in terms of the changing composition of US apparel imports and the intensification of 9802.00 production sharing operations - is presently being driven by a combination of the specific set of policies pursued in the US and the Caribbean Basin and by the particular strategic responses that US apparel firms have set in train in the light of increasing competition from low-cost apparel exporting countries. The cumulative effect of these activities, it was concluded, has led to the emergence of a regional political economy covering the entirety of the apparel commodity chain (i.e. from the procurement of raw materials through to the marketing and distribution of garments) and incorporating a number of supply countries across the Caribbean Basin.

On this basis, the second section then went on to explore the implications of this in terms of the evolving hierarchy of supply countries within the Caribbean Basin. Advancing a claim first put forward in Chapter Three, it argued that, because of the underlying rationale of EPZ-led industrialization, the regionalization of apparel production has tended to foster zero-sum policy competition between neighbouring states. Accordingly, it was argued that over the last decade the newly emerging EPZ economies of the Central American isthmus have come increasingly to dominate the supply hierarchy because of the prevailing low wages and other location-specific advantages that these countries hold over the insular Caribbean.

Extending this argument to Mexico, the third and final section of the chapter then went on to examine the implications of NAFTA in terms of the differential roles of Mexico and the Caribbean in the evolving supply chain previously described. Here it was concluded that NAFTA has led to a significant amount of trade and investment diversion away from the Caribbean and towards Mexico and, more fundamentally, is facilitating the latter's move away from simple apparel assembly operations towards higher value added activities in the form of vertically integrated, full-package garment production.

Notes

1 The Plaza Accord refers to the initiative launched by the Group of Five (France, Germany, Japan, UK and US) in September 1985, designed to devalue the US dollar against the currencies of its major trading partners. In practical terms it led to the revaluation of the Japanese yen by 40 per cent, the Taiwanese dollar by 28 per cent and the South Korean won by 17 per cent. For more details on this, see Bernard and Ravenhill (1995: 179-80).

2 At the time of writing six CBI beneficiaries were eligible for the Special Access Programme: Costa Rica, the Dominican Republic, El Salvador, Guatemala, Haiti and Jamaica. Prior to the implementation of NAFTA, Mexico had benefited from a parallel agreement under the terms of the so-called 'special regime' (United States Office of Textiles and Apparel, 2001a).

3 Personal interview with Steve Lamar, Senior Vice President and Director of Government Relations, American Apparel Manufacturers Association (AAMA), Arlington, Virginia, 29 September 2000.

4 Personal interviews with: Laura Rodriguez, Trade Analyst, United States International Trade Commission (USITC), Washington, DC, 14 September 2000; and Douglas Bulcao, Deputy Executive Vice President, American Textile Manufacturers Institute (ATMI), Washington, DC, 15 September 2000.

5 Approximately 20 per cent of all HTS 9802.00 production sharing activity takes place outside of Mexico and the Caribbean Basin, and is mostly located in South East Asia; however, in the case of apparel, the figure is much lower (7-10 per cent). See USITC (1997).

6 Personal interviews with Peter King, Chairman of the Textiles and Apparel Institute, Kingston, Jamaica, 10-12 November 2001.

7 Undoubtedly, Jamaica's image has worsened considerably as a result of the sensationalist reporting by influential newspapers, such as *The Economist* and *New York Times*, which have come to portray the island as an almost ungovernable 'narco-state'. See, for example, 'The Caribbean's Tarnished Jewel' (1999).

8 Personal interview with John Struble, Economic Officer, United States Embassy of Jamaica, Kingston, Jamaica, 7 November 2000.

9 This section is based on United States Office of Textiles and Apparel (OTEXA) (2001).

10 Personal interview with L. Rodriguez.

11 See 'Jamaica Suffers from Competition with Mexico', http://www.emergingtextiles.com/ cg.../more.Cgi/garments06400print.html, retrieved 22 September 2000.

Chapter Six

The Politics of NAFTA Parity

Introduction

The purpose of this penultimate chapter is to assess the wider political significance of the regionalization of the North American apparel commodity chain by examining the issue of NAFTA parity for the Caribbean, which culminated in the enactment by the United States of the Caribbean Basin Trade Partnership Act (CBTPA) in May 2000. In focusing on this issue the chapter will attempt to address three inter-related aspects of US-Caribbean political economy. First, in drawing attention to the coalition of forces within the US which pushed for equal treatment with Mexico for the Caribbean garment sector after 1993, it is anticipated that the chapter will allow us to gauge some of the wider political implications of the process of *de facto* integration that has taken place in the North American apparel industry. Second, the chapter seeks to untangle the relationship between this political process and apparel production in the Caribbean through an examination of the specific entitlements offered to the region by the CBTPA. Third, and finally, it is hoped that these findings will provide us with a broader measure of the new political economy of US-Caribbean relations, which is the ultimate purpose of the study as a whole.

The chapter begins by attempting to understand the politics of US trade policy against the backdrop of the broader set of structural changes within the global economy that were outlined in Chapters One and Two. More specifically, it attempts to show how the advent of intra-firm and intra-industry trade - in our case the apparel industry - has effected a qualitative change in the relationship between the state and competing interest groups in terms of the process and outcome of US trade and economic policy more generally. Drawing on the work of Helen Milner and Robert Cox (among others), it argues that the internationalization of production has led to a shift in the trade preferences of the most important interest groups within the US, but at the same time suggests that this has not been easily translated into a coherent free trade agenda. Rather, it is shown that the attendant contradictions associated with intra-firm/intra-industry trade and economic integration more generally have tended to exacerbate the existing fissures within the US state/society complex. Because of this, it is argued, US trade policy is now characterized by a new political economy that reflects the deep divisions within the US between domestically-orientated and internationally-orientated groups.

Against this background, the second section of the chapter looks specifically at the issue of NAFTA parity. It begins by briefly setting out the background to the debate and then proceeds to identify the coalition of forces within the US which assumed a collective interest in the continued viability of apparel production in the Caribbean Basin after the passage of NAFTA. It then seeks to disaggregate the NAFTA parity coalition in terms of the specific interests of individual interest groups and attempts to show how the divisions within the coalition as a whole accounted for both the timing and character of the CBTPA as it was eventually enacted.

The third section of the chapter focuses on the specific entitlements offered to the Caribbean apparel industry by the CBTPA. In this section we will compare the CBTPA with NAFTA and seek to highlight the ways in which the former is likely to affect the degree of competition within the North American apparel commodity chain. This section of the chapter then gives attention to the likely short- and long-term consequences of the CBTPA in terms of fostering industrial development in the Caribbean via the encouragement of more highly integrated forms of garment production. Finally, the chapter concludes by way of setting out a number of generalizations, drawn from the process and substantive outcome of the NAFTA parity campaign, regarding the broader political economy of US-Caribbean relations.

The (New) Political Economy of US Trade Policy

In Chapter Four, we took odds with the dominant account of the MFA offered by mainstream IPE, and theories of hegemonic stability in particular, by highlighting the importance of domestic political institutions and structural economic factors in shaping the development of the international textile and apparel trade regime. In the first part of this chapter we will attempt to show how these arguments are just as applicable to US trade policy making more generally. As can be recalled from our discussion in Chapter Four, part of the problem with hegemonic stability as a theoretical explanation of the MFA was that, for the most part, it failed to account for the numerous industry-specific factors, which meant that textiles was more vulnerable to protectionist pressure than other industrial sectors. An additional problem for hegemonic stability theory - and mainstream IPE more generally - relates to its insistence upon a 'systemic' as opposed to a 'unit' level of analysis. For hegemonic stability theory, it is the international distribution of power between states that is the main determinant of the degree of openness within the world trading system: that is to say, whether a nation pursues liberal or protectionist trade policies is not primarily determined by national institutions or by the balance of power among domestic social forces, but rather by the prevailing structure of international governance.

However, as Helen Milner (1988) has shown in her comparative study of selected global industries in the 1920s and 1970s, the problem with this line of argument is that it fails to explain those cases where ostensibly similar international structures have led to markedly different policy responses. In order to account for this anomaly, Milner has herself developed an alternative theory of international trade, which focuses on the level of integration of global industries and on the changing trade preferences of domestic social forces. More specifically,

Milner argues that the degree of openness within any particular industrial sector is mainly determined by the degree of export dependence and multinationality of domestic firms. In industries characterized by a high degree of export dependence and multinationality, protectionist pressures are likely to be resisted; whereas in industries characterized by low levels of export dependence and multinationality, protectionism and other forms of economic nationalism are more likely to be found. Hence, the major reason why the global recession of the 1970s and early 1980s did not presage a return to the 'beggar-thy-neighbour' policies of the 1920s and early 1930s was to be found in the heightened degree of economic integration among advanced industrial countries in the latter period, which meant that domestic firms and industries had more to lose from protectionism than they did from free trade (Milner, 1988; see also Helleiner, 1977).

Applied to our particular case study, this line of argument is not without its merits. Certainly, the course of action described in the previous two chapters - whereby US textile and apparel firms have entered into international subcontracting via offshore sourcing in Mexico and the Caribbean Basin - raises questions as regards the entire rationale behind US textile trade policy as it has hitherto been conceived. After all, it is not insignificant that the peak associations of the textile and apparel lobby, the American Textile Manufacturers Institute (ATMI) and the American Apparel Manufactures Association (AAMA), both took a broadly favourable view of NAFTA (for obvious reasons) when they had opposed more or less every other previous post-war free trade agreement.[1] From this perspective, one could even argue that the multilateral Agreement on Textiles and Clothing (ATC) agreed as part of the 1995 GATT Uruguay Round can be linked to the changing trade preferences of textile and apparel producers in the US and other developed countries.

Despite all of this, however, an analysis based solely on the interests and changing trade preferences of producer groups does not necessarily lead to a satisfactory explanation of the changing political economy of US textile trade policy. Although, as we shall see, many constituent parts of the US textile and apparel lobby have indeed adopted a far more favourable attitude towards freer trade in the last decade or so, this has not easily translated itself into a coherent free trade agenda. What also needs to be taken into account is the decentralized and fragmented nature of power within the US state and the changing political sociology of its contemporary society as a whole. In this respect, a brief examination of the legislative passage of the original NAFTA treaty is of some relevance. Although NAFTA was eventually passed in November 1993 by relatively healthy margins in both the Senate (by 61-38 votes) and the House of Representatives (by 234-200 votes), the broader attendant debate which accompanied its passage did much to expose the many cross-cutting cleavages underpinning US politics and society. As Payne (1996: 118-24) has described it, these cleavages centred not primarily on the traditional capital versus labour split (although this was also in evidence), but on a far more complex set of divisions, ranging from differences between internationally-orientated and domestically-orientated capital to those between the 'sunbelt' states of the south and west and the 'rustbelt' states of the north and east, to disputes between producers, consumers and environmentalists to those between *and* within the Democratic and Republican parties. All things told, the passage of NAFTA was not grounded domestically on a firm social and political basis.

In more theoretical terms, the social, political and economic cleavages of which Payne speaks are consistent with Robert Cox's (1987; 1996) notion of the internationalization of the state. To recall briefly from the discussion in Chapter One, the internationalization of the state refers to the ways in which national political practices have been adjusted in order to meet the exigencies of the global political economy. What Cox also explicitly acknowledges with this notion is the degree to which these internationalizing pressures tend to provoke counter-movements sustained by domestically-orientated groups that have found themselves disadvantaged or marginalized by these adjustments and which thus seek to reverse the internationalization of the state. Placed in language that is more directly applicable to our case study, the internationalization of the US state with respect to textile trade policy has been expressed in terms of increasing support for those internationally-orientated textile and apparel firms which have sought to take advantage of offshore sourcing in Mexico and the Caribbean Basin. This in turn has generated a significant constituency among domestically-orientated textile and apparel firms and labour unions, which are opposed to the practice of offshore sourcing. The ultimate result of this is that US textile trade policy has been increasingly attempting to meet two separate and irreconcilable constituencies. It is against this backdrop that the politics of NAFTA parity will be examined.

The Politics of NAFTA Parity

As was argued in the previous chapter, the creation and subsequent operation of NAFTA has had negative consequences for garment production in the Caribbean in at least two important ways. First, through the extension of duty-free entitlements to the local value added, NAFTA considerably enhanced Mexico's competitive position in the North American apparel chain *vis-à-vis* the Caribbean and Central America, where the local value added was still subject to import duty of around 16 per cent. Second, the Mexican garment industry also benefited from the relatively liberal rules of origin contained within the NAFTA treaty, which allowed for the use of non-US fabrics, provided that they were cut and sewn in the North American free trade area. This meant that Mexico gained considerably more scope for co-ordinating backward linkages with the domestic economy than was allowed to the Caribbean Basin under the much more restrictive 9802.00 regime. As a consequence of this, by the mid to late 1990s it was becoming increasingly evident that Mexico was firmly establishing itself as the first choice investment location for US textile and apparel firms, which were by then gearing their sourcing activities increasingly towards offshore sites capable of producing 'full package' apparel.

However, as NAFTA came to threaten garment production in the Caribbean Basin in the mid to late 1990s, it also came to undermine the competitive privileges of those US apparel firms which were either directly involved in 9802.00 production sharing or otherwise had a strategic interest in the continued viability of apparel assembly in the region. In this respect, what was particularly important about the regionalization of North American apparel production with regard to the Caribbean was the degree to which it tied the region, not only to the US textile and apparel industry complex, but also to specific geographical areas within the US. Thus, in the same way that the Mexican *maquila* industry has become heavily tied to the south west of the US (e.g. Texas and California), the Caribbean offshore industry is now most closely connected to the south east and in particular to Florida and the city of Miami. It is for this reason that that the NAFTA parity coalition, which we are about to examine, needs to be understood, not simply as a random alliance of interest groups sympathetic to the Caribbean, but in essence the first political manifestation of a newly emerging regional political economy that actually straddles the border between the US and the Caribbean.[2]

In the following section we will attempt to map out the politics of NAFTA parity by identifying the aims and objectives of the each of the main protagonists within the coalition that collectively served to ensure the passage of the CBTPA in 2000. In this manner, the aim is to draw attention to the ways in which closer *de facto* economic integration between the US and the Caribbean (at least in the area that we are investigating) is generating new forms of interest groups politics *across* the new regional political economy that we have previously described. Before moving on to this, a final preliminary task needs to be addressed concerning the nature of the US state. Although much of the subsequent analysis is based mainly on the activities of various regional and sectional interest groups, it is important to note that, notwithstanding its historical weakness *vis-à-vis* domestic social forces, the US federal government and its various administrative agencies have pursued their own narrowly-defined interests with respect to the issue of NAFTA parity for the Caribbean. It is worth recalling that the CBI - which gave rise to production sharing - was originally conceived on security-related grounds that essentially served the independent interests of the US state. In this sense, it needs to be made clear that, despite the fact that the CBTPA was in essence a Congressional initiative sponsored by various regional and sectional interest groups, its passage not only served the needs of these groups but also the more broadly defined interests of the US state itself.

On the other hand, because of the Caribbean's comparative lack of resources, the region was never likely to launch the type of spectacular public relations effort that was mounted by the government of Mexico at the time of the NAFTA debate in the US. Over the entirety of the Clinton period, nevertheless, the Caribbean did manage to articulate effectively the view in Washington that the region had been hurt by the implementation of NAFTA, causing particular damage to its apparel sector. Generally speaking, also, the region was able to exploit its relatively healthy relationship with President Clinton to push his administration in the direction of NAFTA parity legislation. In actual fact, Clinton backed such a bill on numerous occasions - most notably, during a historic meeting in Bridgetown,

Barbados, attended by the President and 15 Caribbean states, in May 1997 (Payne, 1998a). Despite the enthusiastic rhetorical support that the President offered, however, his ability to deliver parity for the Caribbean was highly contingent on gaining sufficient support within Congress for the enactment of such legislation. For this reason, as far as the Caribbean was concerned, the successful passage of NAFTA parity legislation was ultimately determined by the domestic coalition of forces within the US which actively lobbied Congress from 1993 onwards. It is this coalition to which we now turn.

The Textile and Apparel Lobby

For much of the post-war period the textile and apparel lobby had shown itself to be among the most formidable protectionist forces within the US and is still often considered by many to be the 'benchmark' industry against which the activities of other 'special interests' measure their success (Stokes, 2000). Nevertheless, for reasons that we have already established, the peak associations of the industry took the decision in the late 1980s and 1990s to revise their long-standing resistance to foreign imports by seeking to embrace the benefits of offshore production. The reasons for this change in position are not difficult to fathom. As previously discussed, the shift from producer-driven supply chains to buyer-driven ones generally came about at the expense of US textile and apparel manufactures, as retailers increasingly turned to 'full package' East Asian imports. For the textile and apparel lobby, therefore, the option of production sharing through the 9802.00 programme allowed the industry to respond in two ways: (1) it enabled US textile and apparel manufacturers to reduce production costs by relocating their most labour-intensive activities offshore; and (2) it ensured that a growing proportion of US apparel imports were constituted with fabric made and cut in North American textile mills.

In this light, it would have made sense for the textile and apparel industry to support NAFTA parity legislation in so far as this would have led to further increases in 9802.00 production activities and would have strengthened the competitive position of those US firms with existing assembly operations in the Caribbean Basin. Nevertheless, it is important to note that the practice of offshore production - and therefore the 9802.00 system - has not served the same strategic purpose in the US textile industry as it has done in apparel. Whereas the decision of US apparel firms to move offshore to Mexico and the Caribbean Basin has been mostly dictated by the need to reduce dramatically production costs in order to remain price-competitive in their own domestic market, the textile industry has been much more guarded in its attitude towards the 9802.00 system and has tended to favour it only in circumstances where it has been guaranteed to boost the sale of yarns and fabrics made and cut in US textile mills. Overall, then, while broadly supportive of NAFTA parity for the Caribbean, it is important to disaggregate the textile and apparel lobby in terms of the competing interests of different constituencies within this coalition. In doing so, we should go some way towards accounting for the reasons why the CBTPA took the shape it did when it was eventually enacted in May 2000.

Textiles. In order to understand the position of the textile lobby towards the issue of NAFTA parity for the Caribbean, it is first necessary to consider the particular role that offshore production has played in the overall restructuring of the industry. Unlike apparel, which has come to rely heavily on the 9802.00 system as the predominant means of remaining price-competitive in its own market, offshore production in the textile industry represents only one of a number of strategic options potentially available to larger domestic firms. Others include technological upgrading, product specialization and the like. Because of this, the ATMI has generally taken a cautious approach towards offshore sourcing and has tended to support legislation designed to promote this only in circumstances where it has clearly been in the interests of its members to do so. Hence, the ATMI took a fairly unambiguous line in favour of the passage of the original NAFTA agreement, given that the yarn-forward provisions and the general weakness of Mexican industry meant that US textile mills were likely to be a major beneficiary of freer trade between these two countries.[3]

In contrast, the ATMI was generally more hesitant towards legislation designed to enhance production sharing in the Caribbean Basin. This hesitancy was mainly expressed through the issue of yarn-forward (Nitschke, 1995). As discussed in the previous chapter, yarn-forward refers to the provisions contained within the original NAFTA agreement which stipulates that all manufacturing stages, including yarn formation, must take place in the North American free trade area in order to qualify for tariff- and quota-free treatment. What this means is that, even though Mexico is now supplying a growing proportion of the yarns and fibres used in local garment production, yarn-forward has essentially consolidated the position of the US textile mill industry within the reconfigured North American apparel commodity chain. By the same token, the position of the ATMI with regard to production sharing in the Caribbean Basin has been to ensure that it remains the principal supply source of yarns and fibres, irrespective of what specific entitlements are offered to the region.

Moreover, it is worth noting that the issue of yarn-forward with respect to the Caribbean has been part of a broader attempt by the textile industry to ensure that a growing proportion of US apparel imports are constituted with fabrics made and cut exclusively in US textile mills. For instance, in 1995 the Committee for the Implementation of Textile Agreements (CITA), a US Department of Commerce agency that is in theory responsible for overseeing the implementation of international textile agreements but in practice tends to serve the interests of the domestic textile industry, issued a series of 'calls' (temporary quotas) against a number of Caribbean Basin exporters of underwear and pyjamas on the pretext of 'market disruption' (Jacobs, 1997). Although ostensibly concerned with protecting US industry from rapid import expansion, the real motive behind these calls was an attempt to shift Caribbean countries away from 9802.00 production (formerly 807, which permits the use of non-US fabrics) and towards SAP (807A, which only permits the use of fabrics made and cut in US textile mills). Significantly, at the time that these calls were issued, the overwhelming majority of Caribbean underwear and pyjama shipments to the US entered via the 807 regime and were thus inconsistent with the interests and goals of the textile industry lobby in regard of offshore sourcing and the production sharing system more specifically. [4]

Against the backdrop of this episode, the subsequent position of the US textile industry lobby in respect of NAFTA parity for the Caribbean was to ensure that legislation would follow strictly the yarn-forward rules of origin, stipulated by the original NAFTA agreement. Indeed, as it turned out the position of the ATMI actually hardened after 1995 when parts of the industry lobby began to insist upon rules of origin even stricter that those specified by yarn-forward. In 1997, for example, a legislative proposal offering the Caribbean 'parity' with NAFTA along the lines of yarn-forward had been put before Congress in the form of the 'Caribbean Basin Trade Enhancement Act (CBTEA)', but this was rejected by the textile industry lobby and their representatives in Congress on the grounds that it would have threatened textile employment in the US south east. Accounting for the discrepancy between Mexico and the Caribbean Basin with respect to the issue of yarn-forward, industry sources suggested that stricter rules of origin were required in the case of the latter in order to prevent competitors for East Asia taking advantage through the practice of illegal transshipment, which allegedly costs the domestic textile industry approximately US$2 billion every year.[5]

In addition to this, a further concern for the ATMI in respect of legislation designed to enhance production sharing in the Caribbean centred on the issue of knit fabric made in the region from US yarns. As part of both the original CBTEA proposal and the draft bill that subsequently became the CBTPA, measures were included that would have allowed knit fabric made in the Caribbean from US yarns to enter the US market duty-free. However, the ATMI objected to this proposal on two principal grounds. First, it argued that allowing knit fabric made in the Caribbean to enter the US market duty- and quota-free would enable East Asian fabric suppliers to gain a foothold in the North American supply chain.[6] Second, the ATMI pointed out that it would be less inclined to support legislation containing knit fabric provisions for the additional reason that this would substantially reduce the economic benefits of NAFTA parity to the domestic textile industry. According to its own research, the ATMI had concluded that, whereas NAFTA parity legislation consistent with yarn forward would deliver an increase in textile shipments to the Caribbean Basin in the order of US$8.8 billion, knit fabric provisions would more than halve these shipments, generating an increase of only US$4 billion with US knitters losing approximately US$4.8 billion of orders (ATMI, 1999). Overall, then, the position of the textile industry lobby with respect to the granting of NAFTA parity to the Caribbean was supportive of legislation *only* in so far as it was predicated exclusively on the use of fabrics both made and cut in US textile mills.

Apparel. As with the ATMI, the position of the AAMA with respect to the issue of NAFTA parity for the Caribbean was largely governed by the particular role that offshore production played in the overall restructuring of the US apparel industry. Unlike the textile industry, which was, to a considerable degree, able to offset competition from low-cost countries by investing in new technologies, capital intensification played a relatively minor role in the restructuring of the US apparel sector. Instead, the apparel industry came to rely heavily on the 9802.00 system - and NAFTA - as the predominant means of remaining price-competitive in its own market. More to the point, by taking advantage of low wages in Mexico and the Caribbean Basin, government-sponsored production sharing via 9802.00 and NAFTA constituted a far more effective means of enabling domestic apparel firms to respond to foreign competition than either technological upgrading or trade protectionism through the MFA. Because of this, not surprisingly, the position of the AAMA regarding NAFTA parity for the Caribbean was to seek the most comprehensive package possible, given that it was clearly in the economic and strategic interests of its members to do so.

A further issue for the apparel lobby regarding NAFTA parity for the Caribbean centred on the particular position of the industry within the overall North American commodity chain. The advent of 9802.00 production sharing not only enabled the domestic apparel industry to meet the standards set by US retailers and buying groups for cheaper garments, shorter orders and faster product turnover, but it also served as a response to the increasing demands of the textile industry. As we discovered in Chapter Four, by the mid 1980s the demands placed upon domestic apparel firms by the textile industry had manifested themselves in a drive for larger orders, higher prices for inputs and favourable payment schedules.[7] On this basis, then, the apparel industry lobby favoured the passage of NAFTA parity legislation for two principal reasons: (1) NAFTA parity for the Caribbean would strengthen the competitive position of the domestic apparel industry *vis-à-vis* low-wage foreign competition by providing further fiscal incentives for US firms investing in the region; and (2) if the bill contained relatively liberal rules of origin permitting the use of yarns and fabrics not exclusively formed in US textile mills, it would lessen the dependence of apparel manufacturers on the textile industry and would allow them to source inputs at more favourable prices from either the Caribbean or from a third country (e.g. East Asia, Mexico). The aim of the AAMA was therefore to persuade Congress to enact legislation that would not only provide for the elimination of tariff duty on the value added in the Caribbean but also permit the use of yarns and fabrics not exclusively formed in US textiles mills, provided that these were consistent with either yarn-forward or the Tariff Preference Level (TPL) provisions contained within the original NAFTA agreement.[8]

To sum up, then, even though the textile and apparel industry lobby as a whole broadly favoured the enactment of NAFTA parity legislation, it was evident that the support shown by different sections of this coalition was governed by the particular role that offshore sourcing played in the restructuring of different parts of the industry. Placing this within a wider analytical context, it is clear that, while the general support of the textile and apparel lobby for NAFTA parity for the Caribbean was evidence of the process of *de facto* economic integration between the political economies of the US and the Caribbean previously described, it was also illustrative of the changing configuration of power *within* the US textile and apparel industry complex. Later in this chapter, we will attempt to show how these two aspects of the new political economy of US-Caribbean relations, when combined, go some way towards accounting for the nature and character of the CBTPA as it was ultimately enacted. Before doing so, however, it is first necessary to consider the other major political constituency shaped by the regionalization of the North American apparel commodity chain: that is, the state of Florida.

The Florida Connection

One of the most important manifestations of the regionalization of the North American apparel commodity chain with respect to the Caribbean has been the degree to which the attendant process of *de facto* integration has tied the region - economically and politically - to particular geographical parts of the US. As previously stated, in the same way that the US-Mexican *maquila* industry led to closer patterns of economic integration between northern Mexico and south western US states such as Texas and California, the Caribbean offshore garment industry is now most closely connected to the south east and in particular to Florida and the city of Miami. What makes this example particular significant in terms of our case study is the extent to which the state of Florida and the city of Miami have actually sought to take advantage of their geographical location and to position themselves politically as a 'gateway to the Caribbean' (Maingot, 1988) and a 'Caribbean city' respectively (Grosfoguel, 1995). This positioning is evident in a number of ways. First, the state of Florida represents the Caribbean's largest economic partner in the US and as such constitutes a major trading link between the US and the Caribbean. In 1999 total Caribbean trade with Florida was worth US$22.8 billion (much of which was facilitated by either the CBI or the 9802.00 production sharing system) and 40 percent of total US exports to Latin America and the Caribbean passed through the state.[9] Second, Florida's identity as a 'gateway to the Caribbean' has been evident in the emergence of a more active political stance on the part of its political representatives and private sector organizations located within the state. This stance has been most clearly expressed with respect to the NAFTA parity campaign (see below), but has also emerged more generally through the articulation of Florida's very own 'foreign policy' regarding the wider issue of hemispheric free trade as agreed in principle by heads of state at the first FTAA summit held in Miami in December 1994 (Rosenberg, 1996).

With specific relation to our case study, since the mid 1980s Miami has established itself as the hub for US-Caribbean 9802.00 production sharing operations: in 1994, Balkwell and Dickerson (1994) estimated that between 3,500 and 5,000 apparel-related firms were active in south Florida, including contract cutting, warehouses and sewing machine supply. Much of this activity takes advantage of the fact that - in contrast to Mexico and some parts of Central America - the Caribbean generally lacks textile infrastructure (partly as a result of the restrictive nature of the 9802.00 regime), so much of the cutting is done in Miami, prior to the fabric being sent offshore for assembly. The city of Miami is also responsible for the co-ordination of much of the 9802.00 'remake' industry, which repairs defective garments arriving from the Caribbean before they reach US retailers (Gereffi, 2000a). All things told, the state of Florida and the city of Miami have received significant economic benefits from the regionalization of the North American apparel commodity chain that has been facilitated by the 9802.00 system. So, in the same way that NAFTA has threatened to undermine Caribbean assembly operations and the competitive privileges enjoyed by US apparel firms, Florida as a principal beneficiary of these linkages was also threatened by this legislation. For this reason, in the mid to late 1990s the state of Florida sought to assert itself as an autonomous actor and pushed for NAFTA parity for the Caribbean as a means of maintaining its own privileged position in the 9802.00 apparel trade. Admittedly, much of this effort was disparate and, at times, incoherent, involving a variety of actors, such as the state's Senate and House representatives, the state governor and his executive agencies and various government/business partnerships, such as Enterprise Florida and the Florida Partnership of the Americas (Payne, 2000: 78-9). Nevertheless, it was not ineffective, with the state's Congressional representatives unquestionably taking an aggressive position in the Congress in favour of both CBI enhancement and NAFTA parity.[10]

Still, as with the textile and apparel industry lobby, the support of Florida for NAFTA parity for the Caribbean was by no means unconditional. Even though south Florida, in particular, has received undeniable economic benefits due to its position in the 9802.00 production system, the practice of offshore sourcing has also brought with it significant costs: according to one journalistic account, textile and apparel employment in Miami fell by 28 per cent during the 1990s as jobs migrated to the Caribbean and Central America (Fields, 1997). In addition to this, Florida has also had to come to terms with increasing competition from other south eastern states seeking to gain access to the lucrative 9802.00 trade. For example, in the late 1990s the city of New Orleans began to market itself an alternative transport hub for US-Caribbean 9802.00 production sharing operations; in particular, political representatives of New Orleans cited the city's closer geographical proximity to US textile mills as a major strategic advantage over Miami (Bussey, 1997). In fact, this latter claim actually proved to be quite well founded and certainly persuaded many of Florida's political representatives to stop short of advocating a more comprehensive NAFTA parity agreement for the Caribbean. Specifically, it was feared that a more comprehensive agreement, containing cutting as well as sewing provisions, might have undermined Florida's own role in 9802.00 apparel transshipments, as fabrics would then be free to go straight from the textile mills in other parts of the south east directly to the Caribbean, effectively ruling Florida and the port of Miami out of the North American apparel commodity chain (Bussey, 2000).

Social Forces Against NAFTA Parity

The numerous tensions that existed inside the NAFTA parity coalition were undoubtedly exacerbated by the actions of those domestically-orientated social forces that were opposed to the passage of Caribbean trade enhancement legislation. As we have already shown, the debate that accompanied the passage of the original NAFTA agreement did much to expose the fissures that had come to define US politics and society by the mid 1990s. In a more specific way, the political fall-out from the NAFTA debate actually had a number of important consequences for the Clinton administration's post-NAFTA trade agenda in respect of Latin America and the Caribbean. In the aftermath of the NAFTA debate the Republican-dominated Congress refused a request from President Clinton to have so-called 'fast-track' trading authority - the executive provision set forth in the 'Trade Act of 1974' that allows the US president to negotiate free trade agreements with foreign governments without Congressional interference - reinstated after its original expiry date passed in June 1993. The failure of Clinton's administration to gain Congressional approval for the renewal of 'fast-track' trading authority, which had previously enabled the president to secure the legislative passage of both NAFTA and the GATT Uruguay Round, meant that the ownership of future US trade policy was effectively ceded to an increasingly sceptical Congress (Destler, 1995).[11] In actual fact, by the late 1990s the increasing hesitancy of US trade policy (as shown by the fact that no significant piece of trade legislation was passed between 1993 and 2000) was not only evident in Congressional scepticism but also in regard of President Clinton himself, who had adopted a less than unambiguous position regarding free trade by the end of his term in office.[12]

Against the backdrop of this hostile political climate, the idea of extending NAFTA provisions to the CBI region was most vehemently opposed by US labour organizations. Because the US textile and apparel industries tend to rely heavily on a typically non-unionized, female and immigrant workforce, the labour movement has not wielded the degree of influence over government policy that is found in other US industries, such as steel. This notwithstanding, as part of the AFL-CIO coalition, the Union of Needle Trades, Industrial and Textile Employees (UNITE), which represents what remains of the workers employed in the US textile and apparel industry, still took a particularly assertive role in opposing parity for the CBI region, as it had done the original NAFTA agreement. The opposition of the US labour movement towards offshore production and the 9802.00 system more specifically is centred on the perception that US textile trade policy in the 1990s increasingly came to serve the interests of those internationally-orientated textile and apparel firms which have sought to take advantage of offshore sourcing in Mexico and the Caribbean Basin, at the expense of domestically-orientated manufactures that lack the necessary links to low-cost supply. As one critic aptly put it, 'a domestic apparel producer can get far more US assistance for contract garment manufacturing in Haiti than for manufacturing in North Carolina' (Rothstein, 1989: 55).

In specific terms of the NAFTA parity issue, the opposition of the US labour movement manifested itself in a skilfully articulated campaign, which attempted to tie the interests of its members to a broader critique of the 9802.00 system and offshore production more generally. Specifically, the AFL-CIO and UNITE opposed the passage of legislation designed to promote further production sharing in the Caribbean by reference to three inter-related core arguments.[13] First, parity legislation was questioned on the grounds that NAFTA had not actually inhibited the growth of apparel exports from the CBI region, given that Caribbean and Central American apparel exports rose steadily even after the implementation of NAFTA. Second, the US labour movement raised objections to the underlying rationale of the CBI/9802.00 development model by arguing - not unreasonably - that production sharing had delivered neither equitable growth nor economic prosperity to the region, even though it had effectively subsidized the export of American jobs. Third, and relatedly, UNITE raised the issue of local labour rights and the degree to which both the CBI and 9802.00 had jointly contributed to a *de facto* working environment that failed to recognize even the most basic labour rights of those workers employed in the assembly factories.

This latter point proved to be a telling one. The issue of labour standards in respect of international trade agreements had found resonance throughout US politics and society ever since the Clinton administration (in deference to the Democratic Party and the US labour movement) had committed the original NAFTA signatories to a 'side agreement' providing for basic worker rights (e.g. health and safety legislation, job training, protection against child labour, labour law and worker rights). In its opposition to the passage of NAFTA parity legislation for the Caribbean the AFL-CIO coalition was thus able to draw upon the support of a broad range of groups, including NGOs and 'anti-sweatshop' organizations, as well as powerful agencies, such as the Department of Labor and the National Labor Committee, which were all ostensibly committed to promoting workers rights in the developing world. As we have already seen, in the early 1990s the opposition of this 'anti-sweatshop' movement had manifested itself in a series of 'shock tactics' designed to expose the appalling working conditions found in EPZs and thereby undermine the practice of government-sponsored offshore production. In the same way, the AFL-CIO coalition, and UNITE more specifically, viewed the passage of NAFTA parity legislation for the Caribbean as nothing less than a referendum on whether the US government was willing to tolerate, not less promote, sweatshop labour in its immediate backyard.

For different reasons, the idea of extending NAFTA provisions to the CBI region was also opposed by domestically-orientated capital - representing both textile and apparel firms - which had found itself increasingly marginalized by the offshore sourcing activities of the larger firms that dominate the industry. On the apparel side, organizations such as the New York-based National Knitwear and Sportswear Association and the Contractors Alliance of California argued that, if enacted, parity legislation would merely serve to enrich a handful of US corporations at the expense of smaller firms which would have to bear the brunt of further economic restructuring.[14] On the textile side, opposition to NAFTA parity came not only from smaller firms but also from some larger vertically integrated enterprises, which were opposed to both the principle of free trade and the practice of production sharing (even the more moderate version of this advocated by the ATMI). Roger Milliken, head of the South Carolina-based Milliken and Co., one of the largest privately owned textile firms in the US, was typical of this position. As a prominent figure in the Republican Party and the textile caucus, Milliken is a passionate advocate of trade protectionism (in 1992, for example, he had backed Pat Buchanan's Republican presidential nomination) and a vehement critic of offshore production. In 1999 he had declared that, 'if someone wants to sell in America, they should come and manufacture in America' (cited in Nitschke, 1999: 1519). Milliken was accordingly opposed to NAFTA parity for the Caribbean on these grounds, and was able to draw upon close political and personal affiliations with key policy makers in both the Senate and the House in his attempt to ensure that the relevant legislation did not reach the statute book.

To reiterate briefly, then, the foregoing analysis has attempted to delineate the most significant social forces - both for and against NAFTA parity for the Caribbean - that have been engendered by the regionalization of the North American apparel commodity chain. In the specific terms of our stated objectives, this analysis can be said to have served two key purposes. First, in drawing attention to the particular social forces within the US that have coalesced around the issue of NAFTA parity, we have gone some way towards highlighting some of the more visible manifestations of the new political economy of US-Caribbean relations, at least in so far as it relates to our case study (i.e. apparel). Second, the foregoing analysis of the politics of NAFTA parity has served a more specific purpose in that it has alerted us to the various political wranglings that lay behind the passage of NAFTA parity legislation, which was finally enacted in May 2000 as the CBTPA. An examination of the specific entitlements offered to the Caribbean through the CBTPA constitutes the main task for the remaining section of this chapter.

The Caribbean Basin Trade Partnership Act (CBTPA)

Although the CBTPA was eventually approved by both the House and Senate by relatively healthy margins and was signed into law by President Clinton on 18 May 2000, the specific content of the bill actually reflected the numerous fissures within the NAFTA coalition. The legislative passage of the CBTPA can be briefly outlined as follows.[15] Even though evidence of a significant constituency of support in both the House and the Senate for parity treatment for the Caribbean had existed from as early as 1993, it was not until 1997 that a serious attempt was made to enact legislation. This came in the form of the relatively liberal Caribbean Basin Trade Enhancement Act, which was initially put before Congress by the Clinton administration as part of the 1997 Budget Reconciliation Act, but was later withdrawn due to fears of a Democratic revolt in Congress.[16]

Despite this setback, supporters within Congress continued to press for NAFTA parity for the Caribbean and by mid 1999 separate bills had been introduced to both the House of Representatives and the Senate. Herein lay the crux of the problem. Whereas the version introduced into the House was based upon a more or less literal interpretation of NAFTA parity (i.e. offering duty and tariff relief to Caribbean apparel exports approximate to that offered to Mexico by

NAFTA), the Senate version, which was also the version supported by the Clinton administration, stipulated more restrictive rules of origin and safeguards to prevent illegal transshipment. In the end the passage of the CBTPA was made possible after supporters of the bill within both houses agreed to attach it to a separate piece of legislation, the Africa Growth and Opportunity Act (AGOA), aimed at offering Africa similar production sharing incentives to those enjoyed by the Caribbean and Central America under the CBI. This move offered a greater chance of success, given that there was much more general support in Congress for a trade deal with Africa than there was either for CBI enhancement or for the extension of NAFTA. On the other hand, though, this move came with a price: the House version of the CBI bill had to defer to the much more restrictive rules of origin that were contained within the 'Africa bill'. In fact, the rules of origin generally matched those that the textile industry had been hoping for, stipulating that garments had to be made with US fabric (and, in some cases, sewn with US thread) in order to qualify for duty- and quota-free treatment. Moreover, the restrictive nature of the CBTPA language was compounded by the fact that, in areas which were generally more liberal, the wording was left deliberately vague in an attempt to appease those federal agencies - including the Department of Commerce and US Customs - which were opposed to the bill but were responsible for its implementation.[17]

Specifically, the CBTPA offered duty-free treatment to apparel assembled in the Caribbean Basin as follows:

- Apparel and textile luggage products made from fabrics wholly formed in the US from yarns wholly formed in the US and cut in the US or in a CBI eligible country if US thread is used

- Knit-to-shape apparel (excluding socks) and knit apparel cut and wholly formed in a CBI eligible country from fabrics formed in any CBI eligible country or the US of fabrics wholly formed in the US (approximate to 250 million square meters per year in 2000, increasing 16 per cent each year until September 2004)

- Post-assembly processing (e.g. dyeing, stone-washing, screen-printing, embroidery, etc.) of apparel made and cut in the CBI region from US fabrics wholly made from US yarns

- Brassieres cut and sewn in the CBI region and containing US fabric equal to or greater than 75 per cent of the aggregate customs value

- Apparel made from fibre, fabric or yarn that has been determined in accordance with NAFTA to be not supplied by US domestic industry in commercial quantities (i.e. 'short supply' goods)

Comparing these duty- and quota-free provisions with the textile and apparel-related aspects of the original NAFTA agreement, it is clear that the CBTPA fell short of offering genuine 'parity' to the Caribbean. A number of points support this observation. First, unlike the interpretation of yarn-forward contained within the original NAFTA treaty, the CBTPA did *not* allow for duty- and quota-free treatment for locally-sourced yarns and fabrics (apart from the knit fabric provision). Second, at the same time as the CBTPA permitted Caribbean garment exporters to use certain 'short supply' fabrics of non-US origin and still qualify for duty-free treatment, they are still effectively denied the Tariff Preference Levels (TPLs) which have enabled their Mexican counterparts to use fabric of any origin, provided it is cut and sewn in the NAFTA trade area (Welling, 2000). For example, under the original NAFTA agreement brassieres manufactured in the North American free trade area are entitled to qualify for duty- and quota-free treatment via TPLs without having to use any US, Canadian or Mexican fabric. In contrast, the CBTPA stipulates that brassieres manufactured in the Caribbean or Central America must contain US fabric at least equal to 75 per cent of the aggregate customs value of the item in order to qualify for the same entitlements (Welling, 2000: 17). A third aspect of the CBTPA which is at odds with the original NAFTA agreement relates to the provision allowing for tariff-free treatment for knit fabric made in the Caribbean from US yarns. Even though this provision - which in many ways constitutes the most liberal aspect of the CBTPA - allows for knit fabrics made in the Caribbean from US yarns to be given duty-free treatment, access to the US market is still restricted by import quotas (equivalent to 250 million square meters per year), which are being allocated on a 'first-come, first-served' basis. The imposition of import quotas on the knit fabric provision has led some of the smaller Caribbean states, such as Jamaica, to argue that the CBTPA not only places an artificial ceiling on their textile exports, but also that the 'first-come, first-served' principle will benefit disproportionately the larger Central America states, such as Honduras and El Salvador, which already possess textile-making facilities, at the expense of the insular Caribbean (James, 2000).

More worryingly, since the CBTPA was passed into law Congressional leaders have made significant attempts to claw back some of the most important provisions granted to the Caribbean and Central America through this programme. On 6 December 2001 the House of Representatives voted by a margin of one vote to approve the 'Bipartisan Trade Promotion Act' (TPA), more commonly known as 'fast track' trading authority. In approving this bill, which in theory grants the US president the authority to enter into trade negotiations without Congressional approval, House members representing the textile caucus stipulated that certain conditions would have to be met if they were to support the agreement. As specifically related to the Caribbean, this meant that fabrics dyed and finished in the region would not after all be eligible for duty-free entitlement under the terms of the CBTPA agreement (see Lamar, 2002). Originally, it was thought that the CBTPA would enable garment producers in the Caribbean Basin to dye, finish or otherwise transform US-made fabrics and still receive duty-free entitlements. In the view of the ATMI, however, a strict interpretation of CBTPA limits duty-free entitlements to the assembly of apparel *only*, and the legislation does not 'state or imply that the beneficiary countries will be permitted to engage in textile manufacturing or finishing operations,' other than for a limited exception for fabric knitted in the Caribbean.[18] It is also interesting to note that at the time that the House amendments were introduced many sources close to President George W. Bush, including the US Trade Representative (USTR), did not consider these amendments to be that serious, given that the 'dyeing and finishing' clause did not affect what they took to be the most important duty-free provisions of the CBTPA (Shiner, 2002).

Despite this, however, from the perspective of 'beneficiary' countries, the original understanding of the 'dyeing and finishing' aspects of the CBTPA had constituted one of the most innovative aspects of the NAFTA parity initiative. According to the USITC, typical dyeing and finishing procedures associated with the post-assembly phases of production often involve some of the most complex and skill-intensive aspects of the entire garment manufacturing process. In fact, the USITC estimates that dyeing and finishing account for anywhere between 35 per cent and 75 per cent of total production costs; and in some product lines the printing of designs alone can add as much as US$3 of value to every US$1 worth of fabric being processed (Rodriquez and Freund, 2002: 4). It is thus not entirely surprising that the domestically-orientated textiles industry would want to retain these tasks in the US or that CBTPA beneficiaries would wish to have duty-free entitlements extended to 'dyeing and finishing' in order to place them on a more equal footing with Mexico. In the end, though, it was the former view that prevailed in Congress, with both the House and the Senate ultimately deeming the more liberal interpretation of the 'dyeing and finishing' provision as not consistent with the main stipulation of the CBTPA that fabrics must 'wholly formed in the US from yarns wholly formed in the US' in order to qualify for duty- and quota-free treatment. President George W. Bush duly signed the 'Trade Promotion Authority Act', containing the appropriate amendments to the 'dyeing and finishing' aspects of the CBTPA, into the law on 6 August 2002.

This latter episode notwithstanding, it is still clear that, overall, the CBTPA gives considerably better market access for apparel assembled in the Caribbean Basin than was permitted under the 9802.00 regime, if for no other reason than by extending the duty-free provisions to the value added in the region. In addition to this, local apparel production in the Caribbean is unlikely to be hampered by the fact that the CBTPA requires stricter rules of origin than NAFTA, given that the overwhelming majority of Caribbean apparel is already made with US yarns and fabrics. Likewise, neither the exclusion of 'dyeing and finishing' from the duty-free entitlements of the CBTPA nor the quantitative limits place upon the knit fabric provisions are expected to have that much short-term effect since the Caribbean Basin garment sector was not eligible for these benefits in the first place. In the short term, then, the CBTPA should give a significant boost to garment production in the Caribbean, even though the initiative does not constitute 'parity' with Mexico in any meaningful sense (Bounds and James, 2000; Rodriquez, 2000).

However, the longer-term economic benefits of the CBTPA can be questioned on a number of grounds. As we have already shown, the most fundamental difference between NAFTA and 9802.00 in respect of fostering local industrial development rests not primarily with the issue of market access (although this is clearly of major importance), but with the scope for establishing backward and forward linkages between the EPZ factories and the domestic economy. In other words, while NAFTA's rules of origin are generally designed to encourage the use of North American fabrics, they also grant Mexico considerably more scope for establishing linkages with domestic suppliers than is allowed under the much more restrictive 9802.00 system. As a result - and notwithstanding the fact that the potential long-term benefits of NAFTA in respect of fostering integrated production and industrial upgrading in the Mexican apparel industry are yet to be seen - it is clear that NAFTA is aiding Mexico's move away from simple apparel assembly operations and towards the manufacture of apparel items with a higher local value added.

It is against this backdrop that the long-term economic benefits of the CBTPA need to be examined. Undoubtedly, the duty- and quota-free provisions of the CBTPA will serve to narrow the gap between the Caribbean Basin and Mexico in respect of preferential access to the US market. Then again, the CBTPA is unlikely to address the fundamental disparity between Mexico and the Caribbean Basin in terms of their respective roles in the emerging North American supply hierarchy, given that the initiative offers the region neither the scope nor the opportunity for creating the type of economic linkages that NAFTA has enabled Mexico to establish. On this basis, we can conclude that the CBTPA actually threatens to lock the Caribbean into a low value added form of apparel assembly isolated in a series of export processing enclaves. In fact, in the absence of a mechanism for moving beyond this format, it is unclear what long-term economic benefits 9802.00 apparel assembly offers the region, beyond strengthening the competitive position of US clothing firms.

Measured in the wider analytical sense, the process and outcome of the NAFTA parity campaign is revealing of the emerging political economy of US-Caribbean relations in a number of ways. On the one hand, as we have argued, the issue of NAFTA parity for the Caribbean was expressed not primarily through the conventional diplomatic channels, but rather via a nascent political constituency generated by the regionalization of the North American apparel commodity chain. Although disparate and, at times, incoherent, the political influence of these groups - which were doing no more than articulating their own narrowly-defined regional and sectoral interests - was sufficient to persuade a deeply divided and increasingly sceptical Congress to pass the first significant piece of US trade legislation for six years (Bussey, 2000). On the other hand, accounting for both the timing and character of the CBTPA requires us to take into consideration the numerous fissures that were evident within the NAFTA parity coalition. The most important issue in this respect was the division within the textile and apparel lobby, particularly in regard of yarn-forward. As we have seen, the regionalization of the North American apparel commodity chain has manifested itself politically, not only in the NAFTA parity coalition itself, but also in the fragmentation of the domestic textile and apparel industry complex as each of the major players - retailers and major buying groups, textile suppliers and apparel manufacturers - have sought to reposition themselves in the light of global and regional economic integration. In fact, extending this line of argument further, it is clear that the particular reconfigurations within the textile and apparel industry complex actually mirror the deeper cleavages within the US state/society complex between internationally-orientated and domestically-orientated groups. As a final point, it is worth concluding by saying that, irrespective of heightened levels of *de facto* regional economic integration, and notwithstanding the fact that the latest renewal of 'fast track' trading authority through the TPA gives President G.W. Bush considerable more scope for negotiating free trade agreements than was allowed to his predecessor after 1993, the cleavages running through contemporary US politics and society do not bode well for continued preferential treatment for the Caribbean, or even for the wider FTAA process as the Americas as a whole seek to grapple with the issue of hemispheric free trade.

Conclusion

To conclude, the central purpose of this final chapter has been to investigate some of the more visible and political aspects of US-Caribbean political economy in respect of the regionalization of the North American apparel commodity chain. Specifically, the chapter has sought to gauge the political consequences of *de facto* integration between the political economies of the US and the Caribbean by examining the events leading up to, and including, the enactment of the CBTPA. This act was designed to address the diversionary consequences of NAFTA in terms of apparel-related trade and investment in the Caribbean Basin. In so doing, the chapter has shown the degree to which the implementation and subsequent operation of NAFTA not only impacted upon the Caribbean countries themselves, but also upon an otherwise disparate set of US actors who had a subsequent collective interest in the establishment of a more equitable production sharing system for the Caribbean garment industry.

First, the issue of NAFTA parity was placed in a broader analytical context through an examination the new political economy of US trade policy making more generally. Drawing upon the work of Milner and Cox, this section of the chapter highlighted the ways in which global and regional economic integration had impacted upon the trade preferences of the most important interest groups within the US, but noted that this has not easily been translated into a coherent free trade agenda. More to the point, it was argued that the attendant contradictions associated with intra-firm/intra-industry trade have tended to exacerbate the fissures within the US state/society complex. Extending this line of argument to the specific case of the textile and apparel industry, it was then suggested that by the mid to late 1990s US textile trade policy increasingly came to serve two separate and irreconcilable constituencies.

Against this backdrop, we then went on to examine specifically the issue of NAFTA parity. We began by briefly setting out the background to the debate and then proceeded to identify the coalition of forces within the US which assumed a collective interest in securing a more equitable production sharing regime for the Caribbean Basin after the passage of NAFTA. In disaggregating this coalition in terms of the aims and objectives of the main protagonists, however, attention was drawn to the numerous inconsistencies and contradictions which existed within it. On this basis, the section concluded by saying that these inconsistencies and contradictions, in addition to the campaign mounted by those domestic social forces actually opposed to offshore sourcing, mainly accounted for the timing and character of the CBTPA as it was eventually enacted in May 2000.

Finally, this issue was dealt with in more detail by examining the specific entitlements offered to the Caribbean garment sector by the CBTPA. After briefly outlining the legislative passage of the CBTPA, we then went about describing the main duty- and quota-free entitlements of the bill and compared these with the apparel-related aspects of the original NAFTA agreement. At this point, it was noted that, even though the CBTPA does offer the region 'parity' with NAFTA in the sense of extending 9802.00 duty-free provisions to the local value added, it does little to address the fundamental disparity between Mexico and the Caribbean Basin in terms of their respective roles in the emerging North American supply hierarchy, given that it offers the region neither the scope nor the opportunity for creating the type of economic linkages that NAFTA has enabled Mexico to establish. Placing this in a wider analytical perspective, we can conclude that, while the politics of NAFTA parity was still broadly illustrative of the political consequences of closer *de facto* integration between the US and the Caribbean, divisions with the coalition, and US politics and society more generally, ultimately determined both the nature and character of the CBTPA as eventually passed.

Notes

1 The position of the US textile industry in respect of NAFTA is detailed in Maxfield and Shapiro (1998); and Lande (1991).

2 Elsewhere this has been referred to as 'Caribbean America'. See Heron and Payne (2002).

3 Personal interview with Douglas Bulcao, Deputy Executive Vice President, American Textile Manufacturers Institute (ATMI), Washington, DC, 15 September 2000.

4 Interestingly, though, not all sections of the US textile industry were in favour on this move. For vertically integrated textile firms, such as Fruit of the Loom, which at the time still manufactured 90 per cent of its underwear domestically, these calls were welcome. For other textile firms with substantial investments in overseas facilities throughout the Caribbean and Central America, moves to restrict 807 production were fiercely resisted. Regardless, in the end these calls were deemed to be illegal anyway, after Costa Rica brought and won a historic case before the World Trade Organization (WTO). On the WTO ruling, see 'US Underwear Quotas Found by the WTO to be Unfair to Costa Rica' (1996).

5 Personal interview with D. Bulcao.

6 *Ibid.*

7 Vinod Aggarwal (with Haggard, 1983) traces the subordinate position of the apparel industry within the overall commodity chain back to the original formation of the textile and apparel alliance in the early 1950s. According to Aggarwal, the original decision of the apparel industry to form an alliance with textiles for the purpose of persuading the US government to impose import quotas on low-wage apparel producing countries was not primarily motivated by economic considerations, but by the fear that the apparel industry would risk losing influence over US trade policy more generally if it did not support the position of the textile industry lobby. As it turned out, however, the interests of the apparel industry was neither served by supporting the textile industry nor trade protectionism, given that this led to an increased dependence on the domestic textile industry for the supply of inputs at higher prices and to the enactment of the MFA, which evidently failed to protect the apparel industry from low-wage competition.

8 Personal interview with Steve Lamar, Senior Vice President and Director of Government Relations, American Apparel Manufacturers Association (AAMA), Arlington, Virginia, 29 September 2000.

9 See 'Trade Development Act of 2000: A Florida Opportunity' (2001).

10 See, for example, Graham (1999).

11 The issue of fast-track trading authority itself has had a number of more specific consequences for the CBTPA, as we shall see.

12 This was most clearly expressed in President Clinton's opening speech to the WTO millennial meeting, held in Seattle in December 1999. For more details, see Jonquieres (1999).

13 This section is based on Levinson (1999).

14 See 'Garment Workers and Apparel Companies Unite to Blast Billion-Dollar Congressional Trade Giveaway' (1999).

15 This section is partly based on personal interviews conducted with: Meredith Broadbent, Professional Staff Member, Trade Subcommittee of the House Committee on Ways and Means, Washington, DC, 19 September 2000; and Timothy Keeler, Professional Staff Member, Senate Finance Committee, Washington, DC, 4 October 2000.

16 Others, however, attributed the failure of the 'Caribbean Basin Trade Enhancement Act' to unilateral opposition from the Chicago-based textile giant, Fruit of the Loom. See, for example, 'Fruit of the Lobbyist' (1997).

17 Personal interview with M. Broadbent.

18 Carlos Moore, Executive Vice President, American Textile Manufacturers Institute, letter to the US Customs Service, 4 December 2000, cited in Rodriquez and Freund (2002: 2).

Conclusion

Introduction

This book has sought to investigate the changing political economy of United States-Caribbean relations via a specific study drawn from the global apparel industry. At the same time, it has aimed also to develop and operationalize a theoretical framework capable of addressing these specific research issues in a manner relevant to those scholars working in the wider discipline of IPE. The theoretical framework advanced in Chapter One thus performed two important functions. First, it provided us with a general critical overview of the discipline of IPE as a whole. Second, and more importantly, it set out the more specific theoretical and conceptual terrain on which our case study was then undertaken. For the purpose of the second, more important task the chapter turned to Cox's method of 'historical structures' as an introduction to three key 'new' IPE debates - production, development and governance - which were elaborated upon subsequently. The aim of introducing these debates, then, was to raise a number of themes and issues salient to the case study but also of relevance to those working in the broader field. Accordingly, this concluding chapter returns to these debates and offers a number of critical reflections upon them in the light of the research findings outlined in previous chapters of the book.

Global Production and the New Spatial Division of Labour

In the process of discussing the Coxian notion of the internationalization of production, particular attention was paid to the 'cheap labour' arguments advanced by scholars such as Fröbel et al. (1981). To reiterate briefly, what these scholars claimed, in essence, was that the global sourcing strategies of Western TNCs has given rise to a new international division of labour characterized by a shift of manufacturing activity away from high-wage areas (e.g. the US and Western Europe) and towards low-wage areas (e.g. Asia and Latin America and the Caribbean). We are now in a position to reflect on these claims further. The first and most obvious point to make in relation to our case study is that, as a method of description, the new international division of labour does indeed capture important aspects of the North American apparel industry. The course of action described in Chapter Four, whereby US textile and apparel firms responded to increased competition from low-wage countries by establishing offshore production facilities in Mexico and the Caribbean Basin, would certainly seem to confirm aspects of the NIDL thesis. Indeed, extending this line of argument to the process of regionalization examined in Chapter Five, a number of researchers have gone as far as to argue that the North American apparel commodity chain actually constitutes a 'classic' case of the new international division of labour (Balkwell and Dickerson, 1994).

As a method of analysis, however, the NIDL thesis is less satisfactory. First, even though the comparatively 'footloose' nature of the global apparel industry would seem to lend itself to the NIDL 'cheap labour' hypothesis, it is evident from this case study that wages alone fail to account for the fact that most US offshore investment has gone to Mexico and the Caribbean Basin, rather than to lower-wage countries such as China. The case of Mexico illustrates this point further. Even though Mexico gained a considerable short-term cost advantage over the Caribbean Basin at the time of the 1994/5 peso devaluation, the majority of industry sources agreed that the most significant competitive aspect of its apparel industry was not its low labour costs, but rather the productive capacity of its export-orientated apparel sector. A second issue derived from our case study which points to the inadequacy of the NIDL thesis relates to the underlying political and security imperatives that impinge upon the locational decisions of TNCs. Most versions of the NIDL thesis operate on the basis of an economistic logic which presupposes that TNC investment strategies are determined solely by the rational calculations of corporate managers. As we have shown, however, the advent and subsequent growth of production sharing and offshore manufacturing in the Caribbean Basin has also served the independent political and security objectives of the US state as much as it has the competitive advantage of US apparel firms. There is thus a need to take into consideration a political and security dimension which is wholly absent from the NIDL thesis.

Applying this line of argument to the global commodity chains perspective, also introduced in Chapter One, it can be said that this study has also enabled us to discern both the strengths and weaknesses of this particular approach to global production. On the one hand, it is clear that the global commodity chains framework - and the concept of buyer-driven commodity chains more specifically - has made possible our delineation of the restructuring of the US apparel industry. In particular, the concept of buyer-driven chains has drawn attention to the importance of configurations of power *inside* particular industries. More to the point, this concept has also allowed us to appreciate the extent to which the restructuring of the US apparel industry not only corresponded to increased competition from low-wage countries, but also to an internally-driven process of restructuring whereby retailers and major buying chains came to dominate the industry. As with the NIDL thesis, however, a more general analysis of the *politics* of global production is more or less absent from the commodity chains framework. In other words, because this approach only offers what amounts to a 'firm-centric' account of global production, it does little to address the broader political and institutional context in which global and regional commodity chains are embedded. For this reason, this framework was unable to explain, for example, the political factors which underpin the differential roles of Mexico and the Caribbean Basin in the North American apparel commodity chain (Heron, 2002).

The Political Economy of Development

In Chapter One, an examination of the political economy of development literature was offered and particular attention was paid to the 'impasse' which is said to have characterized the discipline during the late 1970s and 1980s. The chapter then went on to assess critically various claims within the contemporary literature that have been put forward in order to address this impasse. Three of these are worth repeating. First, we reviewed the argument associated with David Booth *et al.* which suggested that the way out of this theoretical impasse was to be found in placing development research on a sounder empirical footing. Second, and relatedly, attention was drawn to insights gained from the research conducted within the field of comparative political economy, especially in relation to the rapid industrialization of the East Asians NICs. Third, we then concentrated on the argument initially put forward by Hettne, but subsequently taken by many others, that there was a need for development theory to take the issue of economic globalization much more seriously and to situate 'development theory' and 'new' IPE within a single analytical framework.

On the basis of the research findings detailed in the first section of this chapter, we are now in a position to reflect upon these claims. The first point to make is that, in respect of the recommendations of Booth *et al.*, this study has, clearly, attempted to understand the issue of development by placing it in a specific empirical context. In this manner, it has been able to discern a number of important aspects of Caribbean development of potential relevance to other developing areas. It has pointed to the dangers of establishing a long-term development strategy on the basis of non-reciprocal trade benefits (e.g. CBI, 9802.00) which can be withdrawn unilaterally at any point in time. It has also highlighted issues associated with the problem of collective action and the fallacy of composition, wherein the pursuit of industrial investment can lead to self-defeating policy competition. Yet, at the same time, the book has also shown that the pursuit of certain policy practices with regard to EPZ regimes can actually lead to positive-sum results. In this respect, the insights drawn from the comparative political economy of the Asian NICs are of some relevance. In Chapter Three, for instance, the examples of Taiwan and South Korea were used to illustrate how EPZ regimes can actually foster backward linkages and technology transfer. Moreover, even though some of these examples were shown to be of only partial relevance to the Caribbean, we were able to demonstrate that in other areas, e.g. the attitude of local customs authorities towards domestic sourcing, the NIC experience did offer a number of development lessons which could quite easily be put into practice (Willmore, 1995).

In regard to the third aspect of contemporary development theory outlined in Chapter One, it should be clear by now that this study has very much sought to place its study of Caribbean development inside a broader analysis of economic globalization and other related issues raised by 'new' IPE. It has done this in a number of ways. First, in a theoretical sense, the study has self-consciously placed its examination of Caribbean development within a broader conceptual framework built around the notion of political economy more generally. In so doing, it has shown the degree to which industrial development is shaped, not only, or even primarily, by narrow economic concerns, but by other aspects of political economy, such as power and security. Second, in a more substantive way, the book has tied its study of Caribbean development - or, more accurately, political economy - to the issue of economic globalization via its focus on the global apparel industry. In this way, it has shown how the globalization and regionalization of economic activity has created both constraints *and* opportunities for developing countries. On the one hand, it is clear that the regionalization of the North American apparel commodity chain has placed a number of constraints on the development options available to Caribbean states, not only in terms of the structural imperatives of this trade, but also in relation to the particular institutional mechanisms - specifically, the 9802.00 system - which underpin it. On the other hand, however, the book has also demonstrated that the participation of the northern Caribbean within the North American apparel commodity chains has offered these countries access to valuable industrial investment at a time when other developing areas have been struggling to attract foreign capital. Finally, it has also revealed the extent to which global and regional economic integration has generated a sizeable political constituency within the US acting 'for' the Caribbean. After all, it was only by considering the political consequences of *de facto* economic integration between the US and the northern Caribbean that we were able, for example, to account for the emergence of the NAFTA parity coalition and the passage of the CBTPA.

Governance, Regions and Regionalism

To recall, the main purpose served by introducing the notion of governance to our theoretical discussion was to better understand the complex, multi-layered character of 'new' regionalism' as manifest in US-Caribbean political economy. To be sure, 'new' regionalism itself has not, as yet, come to define US policy towards the Caribbean in the way that, say, NAFTA has done in relation to Mexico. Nevertheless, if we consider US policy towards the Americas as a whole in the post-hegemonic setting, it is clear that that 'new' regionalism has very much become the ordering principle of western Hemispheric economic affairs, even though the Caribbean has not been a top priority in this process. To put this another way, the new economic agenda, introduced in Chapter Two and investigated in subsequent chapters, has very much unfolded against the backdrop of the launching of the EAI, NAFTA and the FTAA and the Caribbean cannot be understood other than as an integral part of this process. Understood in this sense, our specific case study has shown the degree to which 'new' regionalism as a mode of governance is serving to reorder the political economy of North-South relations, certainly as seen in this specific empirical context.

In addition to this general contribution, the book can be said to offer a number of more specific insights in respect of the IPE literature dealing with 'new' regionalism. The first relates to the notion of governance. Even though, as we have argued, it is through highly institutionalized mechanisms such as NAFTA that regional integration in the Americas has found its clearest expression, this study has also drawn attention to other forms of regionalist governance. These are not normally associated with the term regionalism, but have nonetheless served to foster closer economic integration between the US and Latin America and Caribbean. The example of the CBI represents a case in point. While the CBI may be regarded in some senses as nothing more than a unilateral trade and aid package designed to assist the struggling economies of the Caribbean and Central America, it is important to note the extent to which in practice this initiative, by means of conditionality and particular rules of origins, fostered a form of regional integration, albeit one that was highly skewed. The same could be said of the 9802.00 production sharing system. While this tariff regime was clearly not designed for the sole purpose of fostering regional economic integration, it has nonetheless acted to integrate the political economies of the US, Mexico and the Caribbean Basin. Of course, this is not to suggest that either the CBI or the 9802.00 should be regarded as forms of regionalism in the same way as NAFTA or the FTAA. Nevertheless, if we are to understand regionalism as a mode of governance, then clearly we also need to take account of all the many and varied institutional mechanisms that serve to foster closer economic integration between participating countries.

A second set of related issues centres on the specific relationship between regionalism and regionalization. In Chapter One, particular attention was paid to the notion of regionalism as a state-sponsored project designed to foster closer political and economic ties between contiguous territories. In the subsequent analysis, however, attention was drawn increasingly towards the idea of regional integration - at least in terms of the case examined here - as a *de facto* process of regionalization. Yet, while it may be tempting to regard these twin processes as dichotomous, what this study has shown is that regionalization as a process of *de facto* integration can also be a logical consequence of various region-building schemes advanced by political elites. Placed in wider theoretical terms, it has shown in effect that, while it still makes sense to draw an analytical distinction between regionalism and regionalization, these twin processes should by no means be considered as mutually exclusive and that there is definitely a need within IPE to pay more attention to the reciprocal relationship between the two.

The Future Research Agenda

The final section of this chapter offers briefly a number of avenues for further research. The intention here is not so much to raise every issue dealt with in the book, but rather to offer a number of examples of some of the research possibilities that the further deployment of the theoretical framework developed in this study has to offer. The following suggestions should therefore be considered as illustrative rather than exhaustive.

The 'New' Political Economy of United States-Caribbean Relations

This study has developed a research agenda appropriate for understanding the changing nature of US-Caribbean political economy. In the process, it has deployed the concept of 'new political economy' - understood as both a method of analysis and a term of description - and has examined this through an industry-specific case study drawn from the global apparel industry. The merits of the new political economy framework in respect of this case study have already been made clear and have been detailed in this summary chapter. What remains to be demonstrated, however, is the degree to which the new political economy framework can be applied successfully to other areas of US-Caribbean relations. Certainly, there is no shortage of empirical case studies from which to choose. One could, for example, deploy the new political economy framework in respect of those northern Caribbean countries - Puerto Rico and Cuba - which have been deliberatively omitted from this study. How have structural changes within the global political economy affected relations between the US and these two countries?

Alternatively, one could use the new political economy framework to look at other aspects of US-Caribbean relations highlighted by different case studies. This could be done in respect of other economic sectors, such offshore industries like services, or in respect of other issues, such as migration and narcotics. Certainly, the case of narcotics would seem ripe for investigation using the new political economy framework. Like the apparel case examined here, the US-Caribbean narcotics industry is very much organized around a 'commodity chain', which entails an analogous transnational network of production, marketing and distribution (Wilson and Zambrano, 1994). Whatever aspect of US-Caribbean political economy is highlighted, it seems plausible to suggest that the new political economy framework can help to delineate these issues further. Again, this can only be done by the further application of this framework to empirical situations.

The North American Apparel Commodity Chain

Returning to the specific case examined here, while this study has addressed fully a number of important issues in respect of the North American apparel commodity chain, it has also raised a number of questions which require further investigation. Three such issues are worth elaborating. The first relates to the full implementation of the CBTPA. Although, as we discovered in Chapter Six, the precise detail of this initiative was finally resolved in August 2002, it remains to be seen what - if any - the long-term consequences of the CBTPA will be. There is thus a need for the CBTPA to be considered further, especially in addressing the disparity between Mexico and the Caribbean Basin with respect to US apparel-related trade, investment and production. This is clearly an issue that requires more investigation.

A second unresolved issue centres on the likely consequences of the ending of the MFA quota system, which is scheduled for January 2005. As we have already made clear, this eventuality is far from assured. Nevertheless, it goes without saying that the further liberalization of the textile and apparel trade will generate additional competitive pressures for US clothing firms in the form of low-wage competition. Subsequent research therefore needs to address the likely consequences of the ending of the MFA - both in terms of its effects on US industry and its costs for offshore manufacturing in the Caribbean Basin. For example, how will domestic clothing firms respond to further competition from cheap imports without the support of MFA quota protection? Will offshore garment production remain viable in the Caribbean in the light of lower-wage competition from China? To what extent will the US federal government seek to promote further production sharing in Mexico and the Caribbean Basin with the passage of additional 9802.00 measures?

A third, and related, set of issues that would benefit from further research concerns internal competition within the North American apparel commodity chain. Specifically, are the EPZ platforms of Central America likely to assume an ever-increasing share of the 9802.00 apparel trade because of the particular advantages that these countries hold over the insular Caribbean? Is this trend likely to lead to even more zero-sum policy competition and the pursuit of what Palan and Abbott (1996) have lately referred to as strategies of 'downward mobility'? Alternatively, what are the possibilities of other Caribbean countries replicating the Costa Rican experience, which has been able to offset the loss of 9802.00 investment by upgrading into more integrated forms of garment production and attracting non-US sources of foreign direct investment? In the light of the Costa Rican experience, future comparative research might shed light on the variables that have enabled Costa Rica to upgrade successfully, even though it has faced more or less the same structural and institutional obstacles as other Caribbean Basin countries.

The Comparative Research Agenda

Finally, a successful route out of the 9802.00 enclave model might be uncovered by extending comparative analysis to another analogous regions such as Asia. As we have shown already, the Asian NICs do hold out a number of lessons in terms of how - in certain circumstances - EPZs can actually aid the industrialization process by fostering industrial upgrading and technology transfer. In the same manner, extending comparative analysis to include other countries where EPZs have shown positive-sum results (e.g. Mauritius) might provide further lessons for the Caribbean in respect of industrialization and economic development (for one such attempt, see Roberts, 1992). By the same token, this line of comparative analysis might be extended to a fuller investigation of the relationship between EPZs and production sharing regimes and global and regional production networks more generally. Already, a burgeoning literature is beginning to testify to the fact that approximately the same type of emergent regional political economy investigated in this study is also unfolding in the other core regions of Europe and Asia (cf. Breslin and Hook, 2002a; Breslin, 2000; and Zysman and Schwartz, 1998). Comparative research might therefore enable us to gauge the wider significance of these production networks, both in terms of the developmental consequences for participating countries and the future direction of the global political economy.

Conclusion

To sum up, then, the above suggestions offer of a number of illustrative ways in which the new political economy framework and the substantive issues that this book has raised may be delineated further. In the meantime, however, it has shown that this framework can deliver tangible insights when applied to particular regions. In our specific case, it has shed light on the changing nature of US-Caribbean political economy against the backdrop of the ending of the Cold War and the onset of globalization and regionalization within the wider world order. Analysed in terms of the specific case of apparel, it has shown how these structural changes have created both opportunities and constraints for states and in the process acted to blur the distinction between North and South. As such, these insights have helped to define important aspects of political economy - power, security and economic development - within the context of the newly emerging global order. It now remains for other researchers to establish whether these insights can be verified by further case study and comparative analysis.

Bibliography

Aggarwal, V. K. (1983), 'The Unravelling of the Multi-Fibre Arrangement, 1981: An Examination of International Regime Change', *International Organization*, Vol. 37, No. 4, pp. 617-45.

Aggarwal, V. K. (1985), *Liberal Protectionism: The International Politics of Organised Textile Trade* (Berkeley, CA: University of California Press).

Aggarwal, V. K., with Haggard, S. (1983), 'The Politics of Protection in the US Textile and Apparel Industries', in J. Zysman and L. Tyson, eds. *American Industry in International Competition* (London: Cornell University Press), pp. 249-313.

American Apparel Manufacturers Association (AAMA) (1999), *Focus: An Economic Profile of the Apparel Industry* (Arlington, VA: AAMA).

American Textile Manufacturers Institute (ATMI) (1999), *Analysis of the Effects of Yarn Forward/CBI Enhancement on US Textile Production and Employment* (Washington, DC: ATMI).

Amin, A., Palan, R. and Taylor, P. (1994), 'Editorial: Forum for Heterodox International Political Economy', *Review of International Political Economy*, 1, 1 (1994), pp. 1-11.

Amoore, L., Dodgson, R., Gills, B. K., Langley, L., Marshall, D. and Watson, I. (1997), 'Overturning Globalisation: Resisting the Teleological, Reclaiming the "Political"', *New Political Economy*, Vol. 2, No. 1, pp. 179-95.

Amsden, A. (1989), *Asia's Next Giant: South Korea and Late Industrialisation* (Oxford: Oxford University Press).

Anderson, J. and Goodman, J. (1995), 'Regions, States, and the European Union: Modernist Reaction or Postmodern Adaptation?', *Review of International Political Economy*, Vol. 2, No. 4, pp. 600-31.

Anduze, M. (1990), 'The CBI and the U.S. Hegemony: Something Old or Something New?', *Caribbean Affairs*, Vol. 3, No. 4, pp. 182-201.

Appelbaum, R. P. and Gereffi, G. (1994), 'Power and Profits in the Apparel Commodity Chain', in E. Bonacich, L. Cheng, N. Chinchilla, N. Hamilton and P. Ong, eds. *Global Production: The Apparel Industry in the Pacific Rim* (Philadelphia, PA: Temple University Press), pp. 42-62.

Bair, J. and Gereffi, G. (2001), 'Local Clusters in Global Chains: The Causes and Consequences of Export Dynamism in Torreón's Blue Jeans Industry', *World Development*, Vol. 29, No. 11, pp. 1885-1903.

Baldwin, D. (1993), 'Neoliberalism, Neorealism, and World Politics', in D. Baldwin, ed. *Neorealism and Neoliberalism: The Contemporary Debate* (New York, NY: Columbia University Press), pp. 3-25.

Balkwell, C. and Dickerson, K. G. (1994), 'Apparel Production in the Caribbean: a Classic Case of the New International Division of Labour', *Clothing and Textiles Research Journal*, Vol. 12, No. 3, pp. 6-15.

Beckford, G. (1972), *Persistent Poverty: Underdevelopment in Plantation Economies of the Third World* (London: Oxford University Press).

Bernal, R. L., Winsom, L. J. and Lamar, S. E. (2000), 'Debt, Drugs and Structural Adjustment in the Caribbean', in I. L. Griffith, ed. *The Political Economy of Drugs in the Caribbean* (London: Macmillan), pp. 58-80.

Bernard, M. (1996), 'States, Social Forces, and Regions in Historical Time: Towards a Critical Political Economy of Eastern Asia', *Third World Quarterly*, Vol. 17, No. 4, pp. 649-65.

Bernard, M. and Ravenhill, J. (1995), 'Beyond Product Cycles and Flying Geese: Regionalization, Hierarchy, and the Industrialization of East Asia', *World Politics*, Vol. 47, No. 2, pp. 171-209.

Best, L. (1971), 'Size and Survival', in N. Girvan and O. Jefferson, eds. *Readings in the Political Economy of the Caribbean* (Kingston, Jamaica: Institute for Social and Economic Research, University of the West Indies), pp. 29-34.

Best, L. and Levitt, K. (1969), 'Export Propelled Growth and Industrialization in the Caribbean', Center for Developing Area Studies, McGill University, Montreal.

Bonacich, E. and Waller, D. V. (1994), 'Mapping a Global Industry: Apparel Production in the Pacific Rim Triangle', in E. Bonacich, L. Cheng, N. Chinchilla, N. Hamilton and P. Ong, eds. *Global Production: The Apparel Industry in the Pacific Rim* (Philadelphia, PA: Temple University Press), pp. 21-41.

Booth, D. (1985), 'Marxism and Development Sociology: Interpreting the Impasse', *World Development*, Vol. 13, No. 7, pp. 761-87.

Bounds, A. and James, C. (2000), 'Caribbean Textile Sector Hopeful for Future', *Financial Times,* 15 June.

Bradsher, K. (1992), 'Congress Set to Rein in Foreign Aid Agency', *New York Times*, 4 October.

Breslin, S. (2000), 'Decentralisation, Globalisation and China's Partial Re-engagement with the Global Economy', *New Political Economy*, Vol. 5, No. 2, pp. 205-26.

Breslin, S. and Higgott, R. (2000), 'Studying Regions: Learning From the Old, Constructing the New', *New Political Economy*, Vol. 5, No. 3.

Breslin, S. and Hook, G. (2002), 'Microregionalism and World Order: Concepts, Approaches, and Implications', in S. Breslin and G. Hook, eds. *Microregionalism and World Order* (London: Palgrave), pp. 1-22.

Breslin, S. and Hook G. (2002a), eds. *Microregionalism and World Order* (London: Palgrave).

Briggs, B. and Kernaghan, C. (1994), 'The US Economic Agenda: A Sweatshop Model of Development', *NACLA: Report of the Americas*, Vol. 48, No. 4, pp. 37-40.

Buitelaar, R. M., Padilla R. and Urrutia, R. (1999), 'The In-Bond Assembly Industry and Technical Change', *Cepal Review*, Vol. 67, pp. 137-56.

Buitelaar, R. M. and Pérez, R. D. (2000) 'Maquila, Economic Reform and Corporate Strategies', *World Development*, Vol. 28, No. 9, pp. 1633-34.

Bull, H. (1977), *The Anarchical Society: A Study of Order in World Politics* (London: Macmillan).

Burnham, P. (1991), 'Neo-Gramscian Hegemony and International Order', *Capital and Class*, Vol. 45, pp. 73-93.

Burnham, P. (1999), 'The Politics of Economic Management in the 1990s', *New Political Economy*, Vol. 4, No. 1, pp. 37-54.

Burns, G. (1995), 'Free Trade Zones: Global Overview and Future Prospects', *Industry, Trade and Technology Review*, September, pp. 35-47.

Bussey, J. (1997), 'New Orleans Plans Battle for Apparel Trade', *Miami Herald*, 13 January.

Bussey, J. (2000), 'Clinton Signs Africa-Caribbean Trade Bill Into Law', *Miami Herald*, 19 May.

Caporaso, J. A. (1978), 'Dependence, Dependency and Power in the Global System: A Structural and Behavioural Analysis', *International Organization*, Vol. 32, No. 1, pp. 2-43.

Caporaso J. A. and Levine, D. P. (1996), *Theories of Political Economy* (Cambridge: Cambridge University Press).

Cline, W. R. (1990), *The Future of World Trade in Textiles and Apparel*, revised edition (Washington, DC: Institute for International Economics).

Cox, R. W. (1987), *Production, Power, and World Order* (New York, NY: Columbia University Press).

Cox, R. W. (1989), 'Production, the State, and Changes in World Order', in E. O. Czempiel and J. N. Rosenau, eds. *Global Changes and Theoretical Challenges* (Lexington, MA: DC Heath), pp. 37-50.

Cox, R. W. (1996), 'Social Forces, States, and World Orders: Beyond International Relations Theory', in R. W. Cox, with T. J. Sinclair, *Approaches to World Order* (Cambridge: Cambridge University Press), pp. 85-123.

Cox, R. W. (1996a), 'Gramsci, Hegemony, and International Relations: An Essay in Method', R. W. Cox, with T. J. Sinclair, *Approaches to World Order* (Cambridge: Cambridge University Press), pp. 124-143.

Crane, G. T. and Amawi, A. (1991), 'Introduction: Theories of International Political Economy', in G. T. Crane and A. Amawi, eds. *The Theoretical Evolution of International Political Economy* (Oxford: Oxford University Press), pp. 3-33.

Cumings, B. (1999), 'Still the American Century', *Review of International Studies*, Vol. 25, No. 5, pp. 271-99.

Deere, C. D. (1990), *In the Shadows of the Sun: Caribbean Development Alternatives and U.S. Policy*, (Boulder, CO: Westview Press).

Deere, C. and Melendez, E. (1992), 'When Export Growth Isn't Enough: US Trade Policy and Caribbean Basin Economic Recovery', *Caribbean Affairs*, Vol. 5, No. 1, pp. 61-70.

Demas, W. G. (1965), *The Economics of Development in Small Countries with Special Reference to the Caribbean* (Montreal: McGill University Press).

Destler, I. M. (1995), *American Trade Politics*, third edition (Washington, DC: Institute for International Economics).

Dicken, P. (1998), *Global Shift: Transforming the World Economy* (London: Sage).

Dickerson, K. G. (1999), *Textiles and Apparel in the Global Economy*, third edition (Upper Saddle River, NJ: Prentice Hall).

Dietz, J. L. (1986), *Economic History of Puerto Rico* (Princeton, NJ: Princeton University Press).

Domínquez, J. I. (1995), 'The Caribbean in a New International Context: Are Freedom and Peace a Threat to its Prosperity?', in A. T. Bryan, ed. *The Caribbean: New Dynamics in Trade and Political Economy* (London: Transaction Publishers), pp. 1-23.

Dupuy, A. (1989), *Haiti in the World Economy: Class, Race, and Underdevelopment Since 1700* (Boulder, CO: Westview Press).

Dupuy, A. (1997), *Haiti in the New World Order* (Boulder, CO: Westview Press).

Elson, D. and Pearson, R. (1981), 'Nimble Fingers Make Cheap Workers: An Analysis of Women's Employment in Third World Export Manufacturing', *Feminist Review*, Vol. 7, pp. 87-107.

Fernández-Kelly, M. P. (1983), *For We Are Sold, I and My People: Women and Industry on Mexico's Northern Frontier* (Albany, NY: State University of New York Press).

Fields, G. (1997), 'Draining Away in Dade', *Miami Herald*, 11 August.

Finnie, T. A. (1992), *Textiles and Apparel in the USA: Restructuring in the 1990s* (London: Economist Intelligence Unit).

Franklin, S. (2000), 'Farley's Fruit: A Firm in Ruins', *Chicago Tribune*, 9 January.

Fröbel, F., Heinrichs, J. and Kreye, O. (1981), *The New International Division of Labour* (Cambridge: Cambridge University Press).

'Fruit of the Lobbyist' (1997), *Wall Street Journal Europe*, 30 July.

Galtung, J. (1971), 'A Structural Theory of Imperialism', *Journal of Peace Research*, Vol. 13, No. 2, pp. 81-117.

Gamble, A. (1995), 'New Political Economy', *Political Studies*, Vol. 43, No. 3, pp. 516-30.

Gamble, A., Payne, A. J., Hoogvelt, A., Dietrich, M. and Kenny, M. (1996), 'Editorial: New Political Economy', *New Political Economy*, Vol. 1, No. 1, pp. 5-11.

Gamble, A. and Payne, A. J. (1996), 'Conclusion: The New Regionalism', in A. Gamble and A. J. Payne (eds.) *Regionalism and World Order* (London: Macmillan), pp. 247-64.

'Garment Workers and Apparel Companies Unite to Blast Billion-Dollar Congressional Trade Giveaway' (1999), *PR Newswire*, 22 September.

Gereffi, G. (1994), 'The Organisation of Buyer-Driven Commodity Chains: How US Retailers Shape Overseas Production Networks', in G. Gereffi and M. Korzeniewicz, eds. *Commodity Chains and Global Capitalism* (London: Praeger), pp. 95-122.

Gereffi, G. (1995), 'Global Production Systems and Third World Development', in B. Stallings, ed. *Global Change: Regional Response: The New International Context of Development* Cambridge: Cambridge University Press), pp. 100-42.

Gereffi, G. (1996), 'Mexico's "Old" and "New" Maquiladora Industries: Contrasting Approaches to North American Integration', in G. Otero, ed. *Neo-liberalism Revisited: Economic Restructuring and Mexico's Political Future* (Boulder, CO: Westview Press), pp. 85-105.

Gereffi, G. 'Global Shifts, Regional Response: Can North America meet the Full-Package Option?', *Bobbin*, November 1997, pp. 16-31.

Gereffi, G. (1999), 'International Trade and Industrial Upgrading in the Apparel Commodity Chain', *Journal of International Economics*, Vol. 48, pp. 37-70.

Gereffi, G. (2000a), 'The Transformation of the North American Apparel Industry: Is NAFTA a Curse or a Blessing?', *Serie Desarrollo Productivo*, No. 84 (Santiago, Chile: ECLAC).

Gereffi, G. (2000a), 'The Mexico-US Connection: Economic Dualism and Transnational Networks', in R. Tardanico & M. B. Rosenberg, eds. *Poverty or Development: Global Restructuring and Regional Transformation in the US South and the Mexican South* (New York: Routledge), pp. 59-89.

Gereffi, G. and Bair, J. 'US Companies Eye NAFTA's Prize', *Bobbin*, 26 March 1998, pp. 26-35.

Gereffi, G. Garcia-Johnson, R. and Sasser, E. (2001), 'The NGO-Industrial Complex', *Foreign Policy*, Vol. 56, pp. 56-65.

Gereffi, G., Korzeniewicz, M. and Korzeniewicz, R. P. (1994), 'Introduction: Global Commodity Chains', in G. Gereffi and M Korzeniewicz, eds. *Commodity Chains and Global Capitalism* (London: Praeger), pp. 1-14.

Germain, R. D. and Kenny, M. (1998), 'Engaging Gramsci: International Relations Theory and the New Gramscians', *Review of International Studies*, Vol. 24, No. 1, pp. 3-21.

Gill, S. (1993), ed. *Gramsci, Historical Materialism, and International Relations* (Cambridge: Cambridge University Press).

Gill, S. (1995), 'Globalisation, Market Civilisation and Disciplinary Neo-liberalism', *Millennium: Journal of International Studies,* Vol. 24, No. 3, pp. 399-423.

Gill, S. and Mittelman, J. H. (1997), eds. *Innovation and Transformation in International Studies* (Cambridge: Cambridge University Press).

Gilpin, R. (1975), *US Power and the Multinational Corporation: The Political Economy of US Foreign Direct Investment* (Princeton, NJ: Princeton University Press).

Gilpin, R. (1987), *The Political Economy of International Relations* (Princeton, NJ: Princeton University Press).

Girvan, N. (1971), *Foreign Capital and Economic Underdevelopment in Jamaica* (Kingston, Jamaica: Institute for Social and Economic Research, University of the West Indies).

Girvan, N. and Jefferson, O. (1971), eds. *Readings in the Political Economy of the Caribbean* (Kingston, Jamaica: Institute for Social and Economic Research, University of the West Indies).

Glasmeier, A., Thompson, J. W., and Kays, A. (1993), 'The Geography of Trade Policy: Trade Regimes and Location Decisions in the Textile and Apparel Complex', *Transactions: Institute of British Geographers*, Vol. 18, pp. 19-35.

Gordon, D. M. (1989), 'The Global Economy; New Edifice or Crumbling Foundations?', *New Left Review*, Vol. 186, pp. 24-64.

Graham, B. *Testimony before the Subcommittee on Trade of the House Committee on Ways and Means*, 23 March 1999.

Gramsci, A. (1971), *Selections from Prison Notebooks*, eds. and trans. Q. Hoare and Nowell-Smith (London: Lawrence and Wishart).

Green, G. and Griffith, M. (2002), 'Globalization and its Discontents', *International Affairs*, Vol. 78, No. 1, pp. 49-68.

Griffith, W. H. (1987), 'Can CARICOM Countries Replicate the Singapore Experience?', *Journal of Development Studies*, Vol. 24, No. 1, pp. 60-82.

Griffith, W. H. (1990), 'CARICOM Countries and the Caribbean Basin Initiative', *Latin American Perspectives*, Vol. 17, No. 1, pp. 33-54.

Grosfoguel, R. (1995), 'Global Logics in the Caribbean City System: The Case of Miami', in P. J. Taylor and P. L. Knox, eds. *World Cities in a World System* (Cambridge: Cambridge University Press), pp. 156-70.

Grugel, J. (1995), *Politics and Development in the Caribbean Basin: Central America and the Caribbean in the New World Order* (London: Macmillan).

Grugel, J. and Hout, W. (1998), eds. *Regionalism Across the North South Divide* (London: Macmillan).

Grunwald, J. and Flamm, K. (1985), *The Global Factory: Foreign Assembly in International Trade* (Washington, DC: The Brookings Institution).

Guzzini, S. (1998), *Realism in International Relations and International Political Economy* (London: Routledge).

Haas, E. B. (1964), *Beyond the Nation State: Functionalism and International Organisation* (Stanford, CA: Stanford University Press).

Haggard, S. (1990), *Pathways from the Periphery: The Politics of Growth in Newly Industrializing Countries* (London: Cornell University Press).

Haggard, S. (2000), 'The Politics of the Asian Financial Crisis', *Journal of Democracy*, Vol. 11, No. 2, pp. 130-44.

Haggard, S. and Simmons, B. (1987), 'Theories of International Regimes', *International Organization*, Vol. 41, No. 3, pp. 491-517.

Hamilton, C. (1986), *Capitalist Industrialisation in Korea* (Boulder, CO: Westview).

Harvey, D. (1989), *The Condition of Postmodernity* (Oxford: Blackwell).

Heine, J. (1990), ed. *A Revolution Aborted: The Lessons of Grenada* (Pittsburgh, PA: University of Pittsburgh Press).

Heine, J. and García-Passalacqua, J. M. (1993), 'Political Economy and Foreign Policy in Puerto Rico', in A. J. Payne and P. K. Sutton, eds. *Modern Caribbean Politics* (London: Johns Hopkins University Press), pp. 198-211.

Held, D. and McGrew, A., Goldblatt, D. and Perraton, J. (1998), *Global Transformations: Politics, Economic, and Culture* (Cambridge: Polity Press).

Helleiner, G. K. (1977), 'Transnational Enterprises and the New Political Economy of US Trade Policy', *Oxford Economic Papers*, Vol. 29, No. 1, pp. 102-116.

Hemstad, A. R. (1991), 'Bittersweet: U.S. Sugar Import Quotas and the Caribbean Basin', in S. B. Macdonald and G. A. Fauriol, eds. *The Politics of the Caribbean Basin Sugar Trade* (London: Praeger), pp. 13-31.

Henderson, J. (1989), *The Globalisation of High Technology Production: Society, Space and Semiconductors in the Restructuring of the Modern World* (London: Routledge).

Heron, T. (2002), 'The US-Caribbean Apparel Connection and the Politics of "NAFTA Parity"', *Third World Quarterly*, Vol. 23, No. 3, pp. 753-67.

Heron, T. and Payne, T. (2002), 'Microregionalisation Across Caribbean America', in S. Breslin and G. Hook, eds. *Microregionalism and World Order* (London: Palgrave), pp. 42-65.

Hettne, B. (1995), *Development Theory and the Three Worlds*, second edition (Harlow: Longman).

Hettne, B. and Soderbaum, F. (1998), 'Towards the New Regionalism Theory', paper presented at the British International Studies Association Conference, University of Sussex, Brighton, 15 December.

Higgott, R. (1995), 'Economic Cooperation in the Asia Pacific: A Theoretical Comparison with the European Union', *Journal of European Public Policy*, Vol. 2, No. 2, pp. 361-83.

Higgott, R. (1999), 'Economics, Politics, and (International) Political Economy: The Need for a Balanced Diet in an Era of Globalisation', *New Political Economy*, Vol. 4, No. 1, pp. 23-36.

Hill, R. C. (1989), 'Comparing Transnational Production Systems: The Automobile Industry in the U.S.A. and Japan', *International Journal of Urban and Regional Research*, Vol. 13, No. 3, pp. 462-80.

Hirst, P. and Thompson, G. (1996), *Globalization in Question: The International Economy and the Possibilities of Governance* (Cambridge: Polity Press).

Hoekman, B. and Kostecki, M. (2001), The *Political Economy of the World Trading System: The WTO and Beyond*, second edition (Oxford: Oxford University Press).

Hoffman, K. (1985), 'Clothing, Chips and Competitive Advantage: The Impact of Microelectronics on Trade and Production in the Garment Industry', *World Development*, Vol. 13, No. 3, pp. 371-92.

Hoogvelt, A. (1997), *Globalisation and the Postcolonial World: The New Political Economy of Development* (London: Macmillan).

Hopkins, T. K. and Wallerstein, I. (1986), 'Commodity Chains in the World Economy Prior to 1800', *Review*, Vol. 10, No. 1, pp. 157-70.

Hout, W. (1988), 'Theories of International Relations and the New Regionalism', in J. Grugel and W. Hout, eds. *Regionalism Across the North South Divide* (London: Macmillan), pp. 14-28.

Hufbauer, G. C. and Scott, J. J. (1993), *NAFTA: An Early Assessment* (Washington, DC: Institute for International Economics).

Hurrell, A. (1993), 'Explaining the Resurgence of Regionalism in World Politics', *Review of International Studies*, Vol. 21, No. 4, pp. 331-58.

Jacobs, B. A. (1997), 'US Moves to Control 807 Trade', *Bobbin*, June, pp. 12-17.

Jacobs, B. A. (1998), 'Before and After: Sourcing Trends in the Post-MFA World', *Bobbin*, September, pp. 102-105.

Jacobs, B. A. (1999), 'Mexico Promises to Remain Number 1', *Bobbin*, March, pp. 21-5.

'Jamaica Suffers from Competition with Mexico', http://www.emergingtextiles.com/cg.../more.cgi/garments06400print.html, retrieved 22 September 2000.

James, C. 'Caribbean Appeals on US Trade', *Financial Times*, 2 December 2000.

Jameson, F. (1984), 'Postmodernism, or the Cultural Logic of Late Capitalism', *New Left Review*, Vol. 146, pp. 53-92.

Jefferson, O. (1972), *The Post-war Economic Development of Jamaica* (Kingston, Jamaica: Institute for Social and Economic Research, University of the West Indies).

Jenkins, R. (1984), 'Divisions Over the International Division of Labour', *Capital and Class*, Vol. 22, pp. 28-57.

Jervis, R. (1988), 'Realism, Game Theory, and Cooperation', *World Politics*, Vol. 40, No. 3, pp. 317-49.

Jones, J. (1995), 'Forces Behind Restructuring in US Apparel Retailing and its Effects on the US Apparel Industry', *Industry, Trade and Technology Review*, March, pp. 23-27.

Jonquieres De, G. (1999), 'Clinton's Demands Threaten Turmoil at the WTO Summit', *Financial Times*, 2 December.

Kaplinsky, R. (1993), 'Export Processing Zones in the Dominican Republic: Transforming Manufactures into Commodities', *World Development*, Vol. 21, No. 11, pp. 1851-65.

Kaplinsky, R. (1995), 'A Reply to Willmore', *World Development*, Vol. 23, No. 3, pp. 537-40.

Kaplinsky, R. (2001), 'Is Globalization all its Cracked Up To Be?', *Review of International Political Economy*, Vol. 8, No. 1, pp. 45-65.

Katzenstein, P. J. (1978), ed. *Between Power and Plenty: Foreign Economic Policies of Advanced Industrial States* (Madison, MD: University of Wisconsin Press).

Katzenstein, P. J. Keohane, R. O. and Krasner, S. D. (1998), 'International Organization and the Study of World Politics', *International Organization*, Vol. 52, No. 4, pp. 645-85.

Kaufman, L. and Gonzales, D. (2001), 'Labour Standards Clash with Global Reality', *New York Times*, 24 April.

Kaufman, M. (1985), *Jamaica Under Manley: Dilemmas of Socialism and Democracy* (London: Zed Books).

Kennedy, P. (1988), *The Rise and Fall of the Great Powers* (London: Unwin Hyman).

Keohane, R. O. (1980), 'The Theory of Hegemonic Stability and Changes in International Economic Regimes, 1967-1977', in R. Holsti, R. M. Siverson, and A. L. George, eds. *Change in the International System* (Boulder, CO: Westview Press), pp. 131-62.

Keohane, R. O. (1984), *After Hegemony: Co-operation and Discord in World Political Economy* (Princeton, NJ: Princeton University Press).

Keohane, R. O. (1986), 'Theory of World Politics: Structural Realism and Beyond', in R. O. Keohane, ed. *Neorealism and its Critics* (New York, NY: Columbia University Press), pp. 158-203.

Keohane, R. O. (1988), 'International Institutions: Two Approaches', *International Studies Quarterly*, Vol. 32, No. 4, pp. 379-96.

Keohane, R. O. and Nye, J. S. (1971), 'Transnational Relations and World Politics: An Introduction', *International Organization*, Vol. 25, No. 3, pp. 329-49.

Keohane, R. O. and Nye, J. S. (1977), *Power and Interdependence: World Politics in Transition* (Boston, MA: Little, Brown).

Keohane, R. O. and Nye, J. S. (1987), 'Power and Interdependence Revisited', *International Organization*, Vol. 41, No. 4, pp. 725-53.

Kindleberger, C. P. (1973), *The World in Depression, 1929-39* (Berkeley, CA: University of California Press).

Klak, T. 'A Framework for the Studying Caribbean Industrial Policy', *Economic Geography*, Vol. 71, No. 2, pp. 297-317.

Kornis, M. 'Is NAFTA affecting US Imports from the Caribbean Basin?', *International Economic Review*, September 1997, pp. 1-8.

Krasner, S. D. (1976), 'State Power and the Structure of International Trade', *World Politics*, Vol. 28, No. 3, pp. 317-47.

Krasner, S. D. (1982), 'Structural Causes and Regime Consequences: Regimes as Intervening Variables', *International Organization*, Vol. 36, No. 2, pp. 185-205.

Krasner, S. D. 'International Political Economy: Abiding Discord', *Review of International Political Economy*, 1, 1 (1994), 13-19.

Kratochwil, F. and Ruggie, J. G. (1986), 'International Organization: A State of the Art on the Art of the State', *International Organization*, Vol. 40, No. 4, pp. 753-775.

Lamar, S. 'Problems and Politics on the TPA', *Bobbin*, March 2002.

Lande, S. (1991), 'Textiles: US Perspective', in S. Weintraub, ed. *US-Mexican Industrial Integration: The Road to Free Trade* (Boulder, CO: Westview Press), pp. 221-45.

Leaver, R. (1994), 'International Political Economy and the Changing World Order: Evolution or Involution?', in R. Stubbs and G. R. D. Underhill, eds. *Political Economy and the Changing Global Order* (London: Macmillan), pp. 130-41.

LeoGrande, W. M. (1990), 'From Bush to Reagan: The Transition in US Policy Towards Central America', *Journal of Latin American Studies*, Vol. 22, pp. 595-621.

Levinson, M. (1999), *Testimony Before the Subcommittee on Trade of the House Committee on Ways and Means*, 23 March.

Lewis, W. A. (1949), 'Industrial Development in Puerto Rico', *Caribbean Economic Review*, Vol. 1, pp. 153-76.

Lewis, W. A. (1950), 'The Industrialisation of the British West Indies', *Caribbean Economic Review*, Vol. 2, pp. 1-61.

Leys, C. (1996), 'The Crisis in "Development Theory"', *New Political Economy*, Vol. 1, No. 1, pp. 41-58.

Ling, L. H. M. (1996), 'Hegemony and the Internationalisation of the State: A Post-Colonial Analysis of China's Integration into Asian Corporatism', *Review of International Political Economy*, Vol. 3, No. 1, pp. 1-26.

Little, R. (1996), 'The Growing Relevance of Pluralism', in K. Booth, S. Smith, and M. Zalewski, eds. *International Theory: Positivism and Beyond* (Cambridge: Cambridge University Press), pp. 108-27.

Lowenthal, A. F. (1972), *The Dominican Intervention* (Cambridge, MA: Cambridge University Press).

Lowenthal, A. F. and Burgess, K. (1993), eds. *The California-Mexican Connection* (Stanford, CA: Stanford University Press).

Lundahl, M. (1992), *Politics or Markets? Essays on Haitian Underdevelopment* (London: Routledge).

MacAfee, C. (1991), *Storm Signals: Structural Adjustment and Development Alternatives in the Caribbean* (London: Zed Books).

Maingot, A. P. (1988), 'The State of Florida and the Caribbean', in J. Heine and L. F. Manigat, eds. *The Caribbean and World Politics: Cross Currents and Cleavages* (New York, NY: Holmes and Meier), pp. 324-343.

Maingot, A. P. (1993), 'The Offshore Caribbean', in A. J. Payne and P. K. Sutton, eds. *Modern Caribbean Politics* (London: The Johns Hopkins University Press), pp. 259-76.

Mansbach, R. and Vasquez, J. (1981), *In Search of Theory: A New Paradigm for Global Politics* (New York, NY: Columbia University Press).

Matthews, D. (1994), 'The Impact of Export Processing Zones on the Dominican Republic Economy', unpublished PhD thesis, University of Sussex, Brighton.

Maxfield, S. and Shapiro, A. (1998), 'Assessing the NAFTA Negotiations', in C. Wise, ed. *The Post-NAFTA Political Economy: Mexico and the Western Hemisphere* (University Park, PA: The Pennsylvania State University Press), pp. 82-118.

Millman, J. (2000), 'Mexico Weaves More Ties', *Wall Street Journal*, 21 August.

Milner, H. V. (1988), *Resisting Protectionism: Global Industries and the Politics of International Trade* (Princeton, NJ: Princeton University Press).

Mittelman, J. H. (1997), 'Restructuring the Global Division of Labour: Old Theories and New Realities', in S. Gill, ed. *Globalisation, Democratisation, and Multilateralism* (London: Macmillan), pp. 77-103.

Mody, A. and Wheeler, D. (1987), 'Towards a Vanishing Middle: Competition in the World Garment Industry', *World Development*, Vol. 15, No. 10, pp. 1269-84.

Mortimore, M. (1999), 'Apparel-Based Industrialisation in the Caribbean Basin: A Threadbare Garment?', *Cepal Review,* Vol. 67, pp. 119-36.

Mortimore, M. and Peres, W. (1998), 'Policy Competition for Foreign Direct Investment in the Caribbean Basin: Costa Rica, the Dominican Republic and Jamaica', *Serie Desarrollo Productivo*, No. 49 (Santiago, Chile: ECLAC).

Mortimore, M. and Zamora, R. (1999), 'The International Competitiveness of the Costa Rican Clothing Industry', *Serie Desarrollo Productivo*, No. 46 (Santiago, Chile: ECLAC).

Murphy, C. and Tooze, R. (1991), eds. *The New International Political Economy* (Boulder, CO: Rienner).

Murphy, C. N. and Tooze, R (1999a). 'Getting Beyond the "Common Sense" of the IPE Orthodoxy', in C. N. Murphy and R. Tooze, eds. *The New International Political Economy* (Boulder, CO: Rienner), pp. 11-32.

Newfarmer, R. S. (1985), 'Economic Policy Toward the Caribbean Basin: The Balance Sheet', *Journal of Inter-American Studies and World Affairs*, Vol. 27, No. 1, pp. 63-98.

Nitschke, L. (1999), 'Textile Industry Torn over Survival Strategy', *Congressional Quarterly Weekly*, 26 June.

Nye, J. S. (1990), *Bound to Lead: The Changing Nature of American Power* (New York, NY: Basic Books).

O'Brien, P. (1975), 'A Critique of Latin American Theories of Dependency', in I. Oxaal, T. Barnett and D. Booth, eds. *Beyond the Sociology of Development: Economy and Society in Latin America and Africa* (London: Routledge and Kegan Paul), pp. 7-49.

Ohmae, K. (1995), *The End of the Nation State* (New York, NY: Free Press).

Oxaal, I. (1975), 'The Dependency Economist as Grassroots Politician in the Caribbean', I. Oxaal, T. Barnett and D. Booth, eds. *Beyond the Sociology of Development: Economy and Society in Latin America and Africa* (London: Routledge and Kegan Paul), pp. 28-49.

Palma, G. (1978), 'Dependency: A Formal Theory of Underdevelopment or a Methodology for the Analysis of Concrete Situations?', *World Development*, Vol. 6, No. 7, pp. 881-924.

Panitch, L. (1994), 'Globalisation and the State', in R. Milliband and L. Panitch, eds. *The Socialist Register: Between Globalism and Nationalism* (London: Merlin Press), pp. 60-93.

Pantojas-García, E. (1985), 'The U. S. Caribbean Basin Initiative and the Puerto Rican Experience', *Latin American Perspectives*, Vol. 12, No. 4, pp. 105-28.

Pantojas García, E. (1991), 'Restoring Hegemony: the Complementarity Among the Security, Economic and Political Components of US Policy in the Caribbean Basin during the 1980s', in J. Rodriguez Beruff, J. Figueroa and J. E. Green, eds. *Conflict, Peace, and Development in the Caribbean* (London: Macmillan), pp. 22-61.

Pantojas-García, E. (2001), 'Trade Liberalization and Peripheral PostIndustrialization in the Caribbean', *Latin American Politics and Society*, Vol. 43, No. 1, pp. 57-77.

Parsons, C. A. (1988), 'The Domestic Employment Consequences of Managed International Competition in Apparel', in L. Tyson, W. T. Dickens and J. Zysman, eds. *The Dynamics of Trade and Employment* (Cambridge, MA: Harper Row), pp. 113-54.

Pastor, R. A. (1992), *Whirlpool: US Foreign Policy Toward Latin America and the Caribbean* (Princeton, NJ: Princeton University Press).

Payne, A. J. (1988), *Politics in Jamaica* (London: Christopher Hurst).

Payne, A. J. (1994), 'US Hegemony and the Reconfiguration of the Caribbean', *Review of International Studies*, Vol. 20, No. 2, pp. 149-68.

Payne, A. J. (1996), 'The United States and its Enterprise for the Americas', in A. Gamble and A. J. Payne, eds. *Regionalism and World Order* (London: Macmillan), pp. 93-129.

Payne, A. J. (1998), 'The New Political Economy of Area Studies', *Millennium: Journal of International Studies*, Vol. 27, No. 2, pp. 253-73.

Payne, A. J. (1998a), 'The New Politics of Caribbean America', *Third World Quarterly*, Vol. 19, No. 2, pp. 205-19.

Payne, A. J. (1998b), 'The Association of Caribbean States', in I. Kearns and G. Hook, eds. *Subregionalism and World Order* (London: Macmillan), pp. 117-137.

Payne, A. J. (1999), 'Globalization and Modes of Regionalist Governance', in J. Pierre, ed. *Debating Governance* (Oxford: Oxford University Press), pp. 201-18.

Payne, A. J. and Gamble, A. (1996), 'The Political Economy of Regionalism and World Order', in A. Gamble and A. J. Payne, eds. *Regionalism and World Order* (London: Macmillan), pp. 1-20.

Payne, A. J. and Sutton, P. K. (1992) 'The Commonwealth Caribbean in the New World Order: Between Europe and North America?', *Journal of Inter-American Studies and World Affairs*, Vol. 34, No. 4, pp. 39-75.

Payne, A. J. and Sutton, P. K. (1993) 'Introduction: The Contours of Modern Caribbean Politics', in A. J. Payne and P. K. Sutton, eds. *Modern Caribbean Politics* (London: Johns Hopkins University Press), pp. 1-27.

Payne, A. J. and Sutton, P. K. (2001), *Charting Caribbean Development* (London: Macmillan).

Piore, M. J. and Sabel, C. F. (1984), *The Second Industrial Divide: Possibilities for Prosperity* (New York, NY: Basic Books).

Porter, M. E. (1990), *The Competitive Advantage of Nations* (New York, NY: Free Press).

Powell, R. (1994), 'Anarchy and International Relations Theory: The Neorealist-Neoliberal Debate', *International Organization*, Vol. 48, No. 2, pp. 313-44.

Rabon, L. C. (2000), 'Full Package: Central America's Last Stand', *Bobbin*, April 2000.

Radice, H. (2000), 'Responses to Globalisation: A Critique of Progressive Nationalism', *New Political Economy*, Vol. 5, No. 1, pp. 5-19.

Rhodes, R. A. W. (1996), 'The New Governance: Governing Without Government', *Political Studies*, Vol. 44, No. 4, pp. 652-67.

Risse-Kappen, T. (1995), 'Bringing Transnational Relations Back In: Introduction', in T. Risse-Kappen, ed. *Bringing Transnational Relations Back In* (Cambridge: Cambridge University Press), pp. 3-33.

Risse-Kappen, T. (1996), 'Exploring the Nature of the Beast: International Relations Theory and Comparative Policy Analysis Meet the European Union', *Journal of Common Market Studies*, Vol. 34, pp. 53-80.

Robinson, W. I. (2001), 'Transnational Processes, Development Studies and Changing Social Hierarchies in the World System: A Central American Case Study', *Third World Quarterly*, Vol. 22, No. 4, pp. 529-63.

Rodriquez, L. (2000), 'New Legislation Places CBERA on a More Equal Competitive Basin with Mexico', *Industry, Trade and Technology Review*, July, pp. 19-32.

Rodriquez, L. and Freund, K. (2002), 'Dyeing and Finishing of Apparel Fabrics', *Industry, Trade and Technology Review*, March, pp. 1-5.

Rohter, L. (1997), 'The Impact of NAFTA Pounds the Economies of the Caribbean', *New York Times*, 30 January.

Rosenau, J. (1997), *Along the Domestic-Foreign Frontier: Exploring Governance in a Turbulent World* (Cambridge: Cambridge University Press).

Rosenberg, M. B. 'Florida's Foreign Policy', *Florida Trend*, February 1996.

Rosenberg, M. B. and Hiskey, J. T. (1994), 'Changing Trading Patterns of the Caribbean Basin', *Annals of the American Academy of Political and Social Science*, Vol. 533, pp. 100-11.

Rothstein, R. (1989), *Keeping Jobs in Fashion: Alternatives to the Euthanasia of the US Apparel Industry* (Washington, DC: Economic Policy Institute).

Ruggie, J. G. (1982), 'International Regimes, Transactions, and Change: Embedded Liberalism in the Postwar Economic Order', *International Organization*, Vol. 36, No. 2, pp. 379-415.

Ruggie, J. G. (1986), 'Continuity and Transformation in the World Polity: Towards a Neorealist Synthesis', in R. O. Keohane, ed. *Neorealism and its Critics* (New York, NY: Columbia University Press), pp. 131-57.

Ruggie, J. G. (1998), 'Introduction: What Makes the World Hang Together? Neo-utilitarianism and the Social Constructivist Challenge', in J. G. Ruggie, *Constructing a World Polity* (London: Routledge), pp. 1-39.

Ruggie, J. G. (1998), 'Territoriality at the Millennium's End', in J. G. Ruggie, *Constructing a World Polity* (London: Routledge), pp. 172-97.

Russett, B. (1985), 'The Mysterious Case of Vanishing Hegemony, or is Mark Twain Really Dead?', *International Organization*, Vol. 39, No. 2, pp. 207-32.

Safa, H. I. (1994), 'Export Manufacturing, State Policy, and Women Workers in the Dominican Republic', in E. Bonacich, L. Cheng, N. Chinchilla, N. Hamilton and P. Ong, eds. *Global Production: The Apparel Industry in the Pacific Rim* (Philadelphia, PA: Temple University Press), pp. 247-67.

Safa, H. I. (1995), *The Myth of the Male Breadwinner: Women and Industrialization in the Caribbean* (Boulder, CO: Westview Press).

Schoepfle, G. K. (1997), 'US-Caribbean Trade Relations over the Last Decade: From CBI to ACS', in R. W. Palmer, ed. *The Repositioning of US-Caribbean Relations in the New World Order* (London: Praeger), pp. 101-50.

Schoepfle, G. K. and Pérez-López, J. F. (1989), 'Export Assembly Operations in Mexico and the Caribbean', *Journal of InterAmerican Studies and World Affairs*, Vol. 31, No. 4, pp. 131-61.

Schoepfle, G. K. and Pérez-López, J. F. (1992), 'Export Assembly Operations in the Caribbean', in I. Tirado de Alonso, ed. *Trade Issues in the Caribbean* (Philadelphia, PA: Gordon and Breach), pp. 125-58.

Schuurman, F. J. (1993), eds. *Beyond the Impasse: New Directions in Development Theory* (London: Zed Books).

Serbin, A. (1994), 'Towards an Association of Caribbean States: Raising Some Awkward Questions', *Journal of Inter-American Studies and World Affairs*, Vol. 36, No. 4, pp. 61-90.

Shepherd, M. (1994), 'U. S. Domestic Interests and the Latin American Debt Crisis', in R. Stubbs and G. R. D. Underhill, eds. *Political Economy and the Changing Global Order* (London: Macmillan), pp. 302-312.

Shiner, J. (2002), 'America's Key to Free Trade and Global Leadership', *Financial Times*, 25 January.

Segal, A. (1994), 'Caribbean Trade Options: Playing the North American, European and Latin American Cards', in L. A. Swatuk and T. Shaw, eds. *The South at the End of the Twentieth Century* (London: Macmillan), pp. 188-209.

Sklair, L. (1988), *Assembling for Development: The Maquila Industry in Mexico and the United States* (London: Unwin Hyman).

Snidal, D. 'The Limits of Hegemonic Stability Theory', *International Organization*, Vol. 39, No. 4, pp. 579-614.

Steele, P. (1988), *The Caribbean Clothing Industry: The US and Far East Connections* (London: Economist Intelligence Unit).

Stephens, E. H. and Stephens, J. D. (1986), *Democratic Socialism in Jamaica: The Political Movement and Social Transformation in Dependent Capitalism* (London: Macmillan).

Stokes, B. (2000), 'Still Cut From a Different Cloth?', *National Journal*, 22 April.

Strange, S. (1982), 'Cave! Hic Dragones: A Critique of Regime Analysis, *International Organization*, Vol. 36, No. 2, pp. 479-496.

Strange, S. (1985), 'Protectionism in World Politics', *International Organization*, Vol. 39, No. 3, pp. 233-59.

Strange, S. (1987), 'The Persistent Myth of Lost Hegemony', *International Organization*, Vol. 41, No. 4, pp. 551-74.

Sutton, P. K. (1988), 'The Caribbean as a Focus for Strategic and Resource Rivalry', in P. Calvert, ed. *The Central American Security System: North-South or East-West?* (Cambridge: Cambridge University Press), pp. 18-44.

Sutton, P. K. (1993), 'The Banana Regime of the European Union, the Caribbean, and Latin America', *Journal of Inter-American Studies and World Affairs*, Vol. 39, No. 2, pp. 5-36.

Taplin, I. M. (1994), 'Strategic Reorientations of US Apparel Firms', in G. Gereffi and M. Korzeniewicz, eds. *Commodity Chains and Global Capitalism* (London: Praeger), pp. 205-22.

'The Caribbean's Tarnished Jewel' (1999), *The Economist*, 2 October.

Thomas, C. Y. (1984), 'Guyana: The Rise and Fall of "Co-operative Socialism"', in A. J. Payne and P. K. Sutton, eds. *Dependency Under Challenge: The Political Economy of the Commonwealth Caribbean* (Manchester: Manchester University Press, pp. 77-104.

Thomas, C. Y. (1987), *The Poor and the Powerless* (New York, NY: Monthly Review Press).

'Trade Development Act of 2000: A Florida Opportunity' (2000), http://www.Americasnet.net/eng/index.htm, retrieved 8 June.

Underhill, G. R. D. (1990), 'Industrial Crisis and International Regimes: France, the EEC and International Trade in Textiles', 1974-84, *Millennium: Journal of International Studies*, Vol. 19, No. 2, pp. 185-206.

United Nations Economic Commission for Latin America and the Caribbean (ECLAC) (2000), *Foreign Investment in Latin America and the Caribbean: 1999 Report* (Santiago, Chile: ECLAC).

United States International Trade Commission (USITC) (1990), *Report on the Impact of the Caribbean Basin Economic Recovery Act, Sixth Report* (Washington, DC: USITC).

United States International Trade Commission (USITC) (1997), *Production Sharing: The Use of US Materials in Foreign Assembly Operations, 1992-1995*, (Washington, D.C.: USITC).

United States International Trade Commission (USITC) (1998), *Report on the Impact of the Caribbean Basin Economic Recovery Act, Fourteenth Report* (Washington, DC: USITC).

United States International Trade Commission (USITC) (1999), *Production Sharing: The Use of US Materials in Foreign Assembly Operations, 1995-1998*, (Washington, D.C.: USITC).

United States International Trade Commission (USITC) (1999a), *Industry and Trade Summary: Apparel* (Washington, DC: USITC).

United States Office of Textiles and Apparel (OTEXA) (2001), 'Textiles and Apparel in the North American Free Trade Agreement (NAFTA)', http://www.otexa.ita.doc.gov/nafta/apparel.htm, retrieved 14 September.

United States Office of Textiles and Apparel (OTEXA) (2001a), 'Special Access Program', http://www.otexa.ita.doc.gov/ita370pf.htm, retrieved 24 September.

'US Underwear Quotas Found by the WTO to be Unfair to Costa Rica' (1996), *Wall Street Journal Europe*, 12 November.

Wade, R. (1990), *Governing the Market: Economic Theory and the Role of Government in East Asian Industrialisation* (Princeton, NJ: Princeton University Press).

Waltz, K. N. (1979), *Theory of International Politics* (Reading, MA: Addison-Wesley).

Waltz, K. N. (1986), 'Reflections on *Theory of International Politics*: A Response to My Critics', in R. O. Keohane, ed. *Neorealism and its Critics* (New York, NY: Columbia University Press, 1986), pp. 322-45.

Watson, W. A. (1982), 'The Caribbean Basin Initiative: Consolidating American Hegemony', *TransAfrica Forum*, Vol. 1, pp. 59-71.

Weintraub, S. (1990), 'The North American Free Trade Debate', *Washington Quarterly*, Vol. 13, pp. 119-30.

Weiss, L. (1997), 'Globalisation and the Myth of the Powerless State', *New Left Review*, Vol. 225, pp. 3-27.

Welling, H. (2000), 'Caribbean Boon: Lurching after NAFTA', *Apparel Industry Magazine*, August, pp. 14-18.

White, G. (1987), *Developmental States in East Asia* (New York, NY: St. Martin's Press).

Whitworth, S. (1994), 'Theory as Exclusion: Gender and International Political Economy', in R. Stubbs and G. R. D. Underhill, eds. *Political Economy and the Changing Global Order* (London: Macmillan), pp. 116-29.

Willette, A. and Overstreet, J. (1994), 'US Investors are Hesitant about Haiti', *USA Today*, 20 September.

Williams, F. (1996), 'Fruit of Textiles Pact Fail to Ripen', *Financial Times*, 10 January.

Williamson, J. (1990), 'What Washington Means by Policy Reform', in J. Williamson, ed. *Latin American Adjustment: How Much Has Happened?* (Washington, DC: Institute for International Economics, pp. 5-38.

Willmore, L. (1994), 'Export Processing in the Caribbean: The Jamaican Experience', *Cepal Review*, Vol. 52, pp. 91-104.

Willmore, L. (1995), 'Export Processing Zones in the Dominican Republic: A Comment on Kaplinsky', *World Development*, Vol. 23, No. 3, pp. 529-35.

Wilson, P. A. (1992), *Exports and Local Developments: Mexico's New Maquiladoras* (Austin, TX: University of Texas Press).

World Bank (1993), *The East Asian Miracle: Economic Growth and Public Policy* (Oxford: World Bank and Oxford University Press).

Zysman, J. (1996), 'The Myth of the "Global" Economy: Enduring National Foundations and Emerging Regional Realities', *New Political Economy*, Vol. 1, No. 1, pp. 157-84.

Zysman, J. and Schwartz, A. (1998), 'Reunifying Europe in an Emerging World Economy: Economic Heterogeneity, New Industrial Options and Policy Choices', *Journal of Common Market Studies*, Vol. 36, No. 3, pp. 405-29.

Personal Interviews

Laura Rodriquez, Trade Analyst, United States International Trade Commission, Washington, DC, 14 September 2000.

Douglas Bulcao, Deputy Executive Vice President, America Textile Manufacturers Institute (ATMI), Washington, DC, 15 September 2000.

Meredith Broadbent, Permanent Staff Member, Trade Subcommittee of the House Committee on Ways and Means, Washington, DC, 19 September 2000.

Chris Wilson, Director for Central America and Caribbean Affairs, Office of United States Trade Representative (USTR), Washington, DC, 27 September 2000 (telephone interview).

Steve Lamar, Senior Vice President and Director of Government Relations, American Apparel Manufacturers Association (AAMA)/American Apparel and Footwear Association (AAFA), Arlington, Virginia, 29 September 2000.

Laura Jones, Executive Director, United States Association of Importers of Textiles and Apparel, New York, 5 October 2000 (telephone interview).

Ambassador Richard Bernal, Embassy of Jamaica, Washington, DC, 5 and 7 October 2000.

Timothy Keeler, Permanent Staff Member, Senate Finance Committee, Washington, DC, 4 October 2000.

John Struble, Economic Officer, United States Embassy of Jamaica, Kingston, Jamaica, 7 November 2000.

Peter King, Director, Caribbean Textile and Apparel Institute, Kingston, Jamaica, 7-9 November 2000.

Index